He was born in Lucca, Tuscany at the beginning of WWII in 1940. Studied agriculture and hotel management before his army service in Italy. Came to England in 1964, worked in Claridges for a couple of years, then as and actor and model. In the early 70's he started to sculpt and became a bespoke gold and silversmith making jewellery. He retired in 2016 and now lives in South West London.

Leonardo Pieroni

A BOY FULL OF EMPTINESS

AUSTIN MACAULEY PUBLISHERS™
LONDON · CAMBRIDGE · NEW YORK · SHARJAH

Copyright © Leonardo Pieroni 2022

The right of Leonardo Pieroni to be identified as author of this work has been asserted by the author in accordance with sections 77 and 78 of the Copyright, Designs and Patents Act 1988.

All rights reserved. No part of this publication may be reproduced, stored in a retrieval system, or transmitted in any form or by any means, electronic, mechanical, photocopying, recording, or otherwise, without the prior permission of the publishers.

Any person who commits any unauthorised act in relation to this publication may be liable to criminal prosecution and civil claims for damages.

The story, the experiences, and the words are the author's alone.

A CIP catalogue record for this title is available from the British Library.

ISBN 9781398450592 (Paperback)
ISBN 9781398450608 (ePub e-book)

www.austinmacauley.com

First Published 2022
Austin Macauley Publishers Ltd®
1 Canada Square
Canary Wharf
London
E14 5AA

To my friend and assistant, Lark Harrison. For her invaluable help and support and my friend and author, Justin Wintle, for his encouragement and advice.

I came to know Leo Peroni when we had studios close to each other in Richmond. He made exquisite jewellery. Leo is very tall, handsome, quietly charismatic, his voice melodious and his manner soothing. When I first read these stories of his childhood I found it hard to link the mischievous and sometimes vulnerable little boy he described with the powerful man he had become. That boy saw his provincial Italian childhood through the eyes of a poetically gifted fantasist struggling to become real. Leo tells the stories of his life as though he is living it all over again; it an extraordinary gift. Every scene comes to life: every fragrance, every bad smell, every delicious morsel of food or stinging slap becomes real.

Then the boy becomes something of man, and the thrill of sexual and romantic chance and exploration reveals that – yes – in the hills of his boyhood the women were very, very special. When he asks his friend Christiano what it is like to be in love, the reply is so simple and pure that it seems beyond elaboration – the best description of infatuated love that I have ever heard. This girl is always in my thoughts. Soon Leo is a sexual being, and the beautiful and handsome young man had grown enough to entice many real women. Again, Leo brings these affairs to life in such a way that we long to have enjoyed the same experiences. Perhaps some of us did, or will….. but we may never describe them so perfectly and heartily.

When I first read these stories they sparked colourful images, like a movie, and I was reminded of Cinema Paradiso. But Leo's stories come from the mind of an artist and a dreamer, and – if you read this book – you will enjoy a movie in your mind that carries you into an Italy that we may sadly never know again.

Pete Townshend

Early Memories

Writing about one's life has a strange effect on memories; they seem to change imperceptibly with every re-writing, with every embellishment you apply, so that you end up with the basic memory but changed details. When you think of the story again, you remember the embellished version, the original slowly paling, sinking into the subconscious, forgotten.

Through the years, often before falling asleep, I have tried to recall my first memories. In that dreamy state, I have mixed memories and fantasies, magic lanterns, stuffed tigers, Mussolini and bombs, pikes, fireflies and dancing bears, making the task even more elusive.

There are memories, however confused, which seem to emerge from the past more often, like the warm feeling of a summer's afternoon, in bed after lunch, with sounds and slivers of light coming through the shutters and reflecting ghostly shapes of passers-by on my walls, as in a magic lantern show. When Mother came in to wake me, I would try to describe to her what I had seen, the distorted figures dancing upside down on the walls and ceiling. By the time she opened the door, the figures disappeared with the light and I believed the images only appeared when I was alone in the dark. This happened I discovered in 1943 on a holiday in Viareggio, a seaside town near Lucca. I have a photo of that time showing a stocky little boy with blond curls wearing what looks like a wrestler's outfit and staring hard at the camera from a sandy beach.

My Uncle 'Nanni' kept a stuffed tiger's head called 'Gargantua' on top of a tall wardrobe in a dark corridor. The shining staring yellow eyes, the sharp fangs, white against the sanguine tongue, made me stiff with fear. The grown-ups made growling noises when I passed the wardrobe – they laughed, and they did not show me that the head was not connected to a large striped body living inside the wardrobe. I got used to its silent stares and came to think of it as not so dangerous.

One day, I ventured into the dark corridor carrying a long cane in one hand, feeling the gritty texture of the wall with the other for reassurance. I used the cane and managed to push the beast off the top of the wardrobe and sent it crashing to the floor. It was only a head, cut off at the neck! It made a noise like an egg breaking. The striped hide split, revealing its plaster innards, one massive fang loose on the red tile floor, the yellow eyes still staring, the now crooked mouth twisted in a smile. I felt sorry for the poor beast, but I never admitted pushing it off the wardrobe.

One windy day in spring, Mussolini passed through Lucca. I had been dressed as a Balilla, the Italian equivalent of a Hitler youth, and I carried a toy rifle. I sat on Uncle Nanni's shoulders. "Duce, Duce, Duce," shouted the crowd around us. The stout man in a black shirt, standing in the open car surrounded by guards balancing on the footholds, had a wide frowning face, a bald head and waved stiffly at the hailing crowd.

Uncle Nanni took me for a ride in his new buggy. I liked sitting on the soft leather seat of the open buggy, smelling the strong smell of the horse, the wind on my face. Uncle let me hold the reins. I stood between his legs; his hairy brown arms had veins sticking out like the ones on the legs of the horse. I looked at my thin white arms, and we laughed.

We passed a bar outside Lucca and some of Uncle's friends came to greet him. He was a horse dealer and his friends had dark whiskered faces, flashing teeth and wore handkerchiefs around their necks, like gypsies. Uncle stood proudly, while his friends admired his new buggy and spirited horse, bending, touching, slapping and slowly, lovingly pressing dark hands with gold rings over the horse's flanks. They smelled of horses, tobacco and grappa, and they squeezed me too hard.

Later, on a wide dusty road in the sunshine, an enormous stag beetle landed on the horse's head. There was a sudden stop, the horse reared, neighing and shaking its head. Uncle calmed him down with soft clicking sounds. I saw the horse turning its head, showing the whites of its eyes rolling in the shade of the blinkers, trying to see the beetle slowly moving on its sweaty mane.

Uncle pulled a long strand of hair from the horse's tail and tied it to the beetle so that it would not fly off. I held the long hair and looked at the sharp black hooks on the beetle's legs, the menacing antlers slowly closing, its shiny black back reflecting the sky. We stopped at another bar in the village, and while Uncle talked to more friends I placed my sticky drink on the dusty floor and untied the beetle. Sensing its freedom, he reared on the back legs and gently opened its curved black wing covers, revealing pale diaphanous vibrating wings. With a sudden buzz, the great beetle flew in an upright position, almost hitting the horse again. It took to the sky and the trees in the distance.

Once, I woke up with the sound of agitated voices. Granny Armanda was talking to Uncle Nanni in the kitchen. Straining at the rope which tied her neck to the sewing machine, was a young fox! Uncle came smiling into the room, followed by Granny who was still grumbling. He tried to take me close to the fox, but the animal pulled, choking on the rope, panting her red tongue out. The fox sat on a dirty sack, her strong smell filling the room.

While Uncle drank his coffee I sat closer to the fox taking in her wonderful colour and shape, the delicate face, wild eyes and white teeth. She calmed down and started to lick her soiled tail, still staring at me. I never knew what happened to that fox – she disappeared as swiftly as she had arrived.

I don't remember who showed me how to build a kite. I loved the noise the cane made as it was split by the kitchen knife into long thin strips. I made a cross with two strips tied in the centre; passed a thin string around a groove at the end of each strip of cane and folded coloured transparent paper, glued with flour glue, around the string. The tail was made of strips of paper tied around the string in a chain. I remember waiting for the glue to dry, the kite on the floor in the sun, alive with every breath of air. Then running, the dry summer grass slippery under my sandals, the kite on a long string flying behind me, pulling and vibrating in the wind, straining to be free.

My father, Ugo and my mother, Giulia, got married in 1937. My maternal granny, Armanda, rented rooms and my father lodged there during his studies to be a schoolteacher. They became romantically involved, but Granny resented my father having come from the mountains. 'Montanaro', she would call him. They got married nevertheless and rented a small flat near the Mura in Piazza Santa Maria. Mother had two miscarriages before me, and I was born in March 1940. Granny Armanda had three children, Giulia my mother, Nanni her horse dealer son, and Bice my unmarried auntie who owned our apartment. We all lived in the large attic apartment in Via Fillungo in Lucca. At the outbreak of war, when Father volunteered, Mother moved back to the apartment to be with her family.

In that summer of 1944, the bombing started. The sirens would sound their sad sound, and we would all run downstairs to the communal cellar, impatient frightened people, with worried faces pushing towards the door of the cellar.

Inside almost in darkness, I found Luana, my friend from next door. She had wrapped her cat in a shawl like a doll, only its head showing, mewing incessantly. As we sat together on the cool floor, the sirens stopped one by one, only the mewing of the cat loud in the airless space. "Get that cat out of here!" said a man's voice, a shadow moving towards Luana, grabbing at the shawl. Luana turned and I stood and tried to push the man away. I got slapped in the face, hard; I felt blood running warm from my nose into my mouth. The cat had stopped mewing. I sat with my head between my knees. Someone near me lit a candle. The smell of sulphur and blood made me feel sick. I could see the drops of blood falling dark on the pale brick floor, a film of dust settled on each convex spot. People whispered like in a church, the noise of the bombs now falling in the distance, muffled, regular, like the sound of the blood beating in my ears.

When I was five, I caught diphtheria and was taken to the hospital by Mother, pushing a bike in the noon sunshine, with me sitting on the saddle hearing the noise of the crickets in the fields outside the walls of Lucca. I was kept in the hospital in the infectious diseases ward. I made friends with a large bald policeman, another patient. He gave me dried figs and almonds to eat and reassured me during the air raids, reading me poems from Dante's comedy. Before turning a page, he would stick his whole finger in his mouth and stare at me in a strangely frightening way, then flicked the paper delicately with the point of the wet finger. From the windows, I saw carts arriving with injured people on mattresses stained with blood.

I saw Mother once. "Did they cut your nails? Are you eating? I am not allowed to visit you!" she shouted at me, standing in the sunshine, the wind in her red dress, her hands high on the wire fence.

Somehow, I was saved by a vaccine brought in by the liberating American army. I came out of hospital during a thunderstorm and Mother covered me with her raincoat. Everything smelled new and clean, even the bombed buildings we saw on the way home. On entering the walls of Lucca, it stopped raining and in the bright sunlight, my mother noticed the lice in my hair. When we arrived home, Via Fillungo was full of people. The American army was going to march through the town. Upstairs, I stood at the corridor window, blinking in the sunshine, my head on my arms, skinny and pale with Mother killing the lice in my hair with cotton wool and petrol. Below, the first soldiers started the parade. Later, a tall black soldier with a big white smile winked at me and gave me a stick of chewing gum.

I was given a shining scooter, all made of wood. It smelled of fresh paint and was red and green; the handles and the wheels were left unpainted and a strip of metal was nailed around the wheels to stop them wearing. I liked the feeling of the new wooden handles that soon became smooth and dark – they left a smell of pitch on my hands.

Our house had been damaged by the bombing, and we moved to Lammari, a place in the countryside near Lucca. We left by cart from Lucca, and when it started to rain, Uncle Nanni covered me with a sack. I could not see but I remember the smells, the horse, the rain on the sack and the bag with the salami. When we got to the house, a large dog came suddenly very close. I was afraid, but he was more interested in the bag than me. The house was old and full of new faces. A steaming bowl of bread and milk was put in front of me on a marble table. I ate, looking closely at the blue figures on the bowl. They seemed to move in the dim firelight. Later, I showed everyone how to be a 'radio' by going under a chair and broadcasting news of the war. The large dog came back, and we started to play. He had many scabs on his body, and Mother told me off for hugging him.

In the morning, Uncle Nanni showed me around the farm: a stone well covered with moss; the rusty chain with the copper pail; the dark cave-like cellar where the wine was kept in large barrels, and the rabbits in a pen inside the stable. A few children had gathered around the yard, and they were eyeing me with hands behind their backs, sniffling and drawing in the dust with bare toes. When Uncle Nanni opened the door of the stable, they all surged forward. There, almost in the darkness, was a shiny red motorbike. Uncle lifted me on to the back seat, released the fork and kicked the starter. Noise and fumes filled the stable and the children stood back, covering their ears, eyes glinting. We rode through the yard, chickens running wildly. On the open road, the noise changed and the speed made me grasp Uncle's shirt. The road and the dusty hedges, white in the sunshine, made me close my eyes. At the church, we turned back. The children accepted me after that.

I was still weak from the attack of diphtheria, and in the afternoon, I was sent to bed. One afternoon, I made my way down the creaky wooden steps, past Mother asleep in a chair, my sister at her breast. The yard was full of light and the continuous noise of the crickets. The stones burned my bare feet. I lowered a copper pail with its rusty chain in the cool depth of the well lifted it out and drank in long gulps.

The door of the stable was ajar and two barefooted girls were looking at the bike, passing light fingers over the chrome pipes and chatting all the while. When I entered, they smiled. I had hoped to startle them but their smiles disarmed me. I decided to be bold. "Would you like to come for a ride?" I asked.

"You cannot drive it," one of the girls said, the other was already jumping with excitement.

I paused and then said, "No, but you can climb on the back seat, and I will make a noise like the bike. It will be the same." After looking at each other, they agreed, and with my help, they climbed astride the back seat, waiting.

"If you want me to drive you, first you will have to play mummies and daddies with me," I said. They looked alarmed but then started to giggle. I was surprised at my boldness and excited at the same time. I helped them down from the bike, and we played in the straw. In the darkness, we wrestled and hugged for a long time, until our throats were full of dust.

Later, on the bike, I got drowsy with the noise and the vibration of my lips. I felt happy and proud, the hand of one girl circling my chest. We 'rode' on the white road, past the church and further on the tarmac road by the river, over the bridge on the avenue of horse chestnuts leading to the walls of Lucca.

I loved the change of colour of wood getting older, like the smooth wood of the machinegun butt that Father left in the corner of the bedroom when he came home on leave for the birth of my sister. My father was absent from my life in those early memories. I was told that when I was born on the marble kitchen table in Lucca, at eight o'clock in the evening, he was out with the local amateur dramatic society in a play. He was sent for and because he was a good runner, he had to go and get the oxygen. I was born with the help of forceps. I still have the scar on my forehead. I did not cry and only repeated immersions in hot and cold water made me take my first breath. The doctor told my mother of the possible danger of brain damage, and she told me that she lived in fear until she realised that there was nothing wrong with my brain that a good slap could not cure.

My father volunteered shortly after my birth and was sent as an artillery officer to the Palmaria Island, off the coast of Sardinia – I have a photo of him standing in a neat uniform, flashing his teeth, near a group of high officers inspecting his coastal artillery post. I remember almost nothing about him apart from his uniform, rough on my face and his pistol, cold and heavy on the bedside table. I heard from an uncle that after the Fascists came to power in the late thirties, Mussolini relied on the Militzia to keep power. My father had been part of the Militzia, which consisted of armed young men travelling the countryside, entering villages and gathering young men asking to see proof of membership to the Fascist Party. Men not belonging to the Party would be beaten with sticks and forced to drink large quantities of castor oil, which caused rampant diarrhoea for many days. Such tortures would force many men to acquire a membership card to avoid future troubles. My father had difficulties in coming back to Lucca after the war afraid of reprisals. He lived in a hut in the mountains for a few months, armed with a shotgun, before going to Florence to live with his brother. Mother and I went to Florence to visit him. On the way, the bus caught fire and after the fire was extinguished, we spent a long time on the verge of the road in the sunshine. The group was discussing the danger from bands of outlaws roaming the Tuscan countryside. When we got to Florence, we saw my father in the distance, walking with my two cousins beside a canal. When we approached him, he hissed at my mother, "Why did you bring him?" He didn't kiss me.

When Father came back home, he worked as a civil servant in a government office. When he returned after work, he went straight to his room and listened to the radio in the dark, smoking.

If I had been naughty, I was made to learn poems sitting in the smoky room in semi-darkness. One poem was called *La quiete dopo la tempesta*. I tried to learn it while the radio announced the terrible diseases developing in Hiroshima after the bomb. Did I ever learn those poems? I do not remember!

Mother and Father fought a lot. Sometimes they came to blows. I heard them in the morning through the thin walls of the corridor, shouting hateful words. I put my Bakelite letter opener under the pillow to kill my father. When Mother got a swollen face, Auntie and Granny got mixed up in the row too, and Sister and I hid under Granny's four-poster bed, having taken Parmesan cheese crusts and bread and imagining we were large mice in a nest.

Father was closer to my sister. She was cuddled and admitted to his room; I was always sent away. One night, years later, Mother and I went to the theatre – a circus tent outside the walls of the city and, on coming out, we saw Father on a bicycle going towards the river. Mother became suspicious and excited and had my father followed by a neighbour. Apparently, he had a lover whom he visited regularly with the excuse of going to the bar after dinner. A few nights later, Mother dressed in dark clothes and, accompanied by the local Carabinieri, found Father in bed with the cashier of the local cinema. They separated. There was no divorce in Italy at that time.

By then, I was about ten and living with three women, which presented many problems for an already disturbed boy like me. There were often arguments turning into quarrels, and I tried my best to keep out of it. I realised that Mother suffered from PMT as often Granny and Auntie made allowances for her and were tolerant during certain times of the month. I could not ignore those times as there was a basin of water in the toilet where linen towels smeared with blood would be left to soak before washing. A strange female ritual for a boy to witness! Mother had manias regarding cleanliness and spent a long time mopping the brick floor of our large apartment. God forbid anyone stepping on her wet floor! I got beaten on several occasions because of that. Once while riding my wooden scooter, I strayed on a wet part of the brick floor that Mother had just mopped. She got very cross, shouted and grabbed me and the scooter and I got thrown across the floor. I was not hurt but the smooth handle of the scooter splintered. Auntie was not married and was moody and capricious. Granny was very tough and did not forgive mistakes in others. When a big quarrel happened, they all had ways of showing they had reached their breaking point. Mother would shout that she was going to give herself a lethal injection, even reaching the point of getting out a syringe and needle and starting to draw some liquid into it. She never finished the task! Auntie Bice's choice of death was tablets, and she would scream hysterically shaking a bottle of sleeping pills. Granny would open a window and try to reach the sill without much success, being very short. My Sister, Ughetta, and I had to witness such operatic outbursts, numbed and shocked unwilling spectators to this strange family play.

In the sitting room, we had a console with a wooden base and a high marble top. I sat on its lower part and liked sliding on the smooth curved base, pulling on the two fluted columns supporting the marble top. I spent a long time under there and wrote rude messages under the rough underneath of the marble top with coloured pencils. I drew a female organ, looking much like an upright eye. In the local dialect, it was called 'Topa', the feminine for mouse, and the word decorated many walls in Lucca, accompanied by the rarer 'Fava' or broad bean in the shape of a male organ. I sat on my low throne under the console, looking at the legs of the people passing by, protected by the sacred marks under the marble top.

Every year in the autumn, the wood for the fire would arrive. We had a black terracotta fireplace in the corner of the living room, with relief figures of temples and gods. I liked playing by the fireplace, smoking rolled newspaper cigarettes, filling thimbles with sweet chestnut flour and cooking it in the ashes.

Since we lived on the third floor, the wood was carried upstairs in tall baskets by surly men with red faces, wearing cord trousers and heavy leather boots, smelling of the acrid smell of fires from the mountains. The wood was stacked in our summer room called a 'stanzina'. I liked the way the logs were arranged against the wall, every year slightly differently; the smell of the new logs and the feel of the moss on the older logs, slowly browning. I played with the wood, trying to split it with a small blunt axe.

In the summer, I loved to play in the great marble sink in the kitchen. It stood empty at mid-morning before Granny, having come back from the market, started to use it to prepare lunch. I would put the brass plug in, it fitted smoothly in the brass-lined hole. Then I turned on the shining brass tap. Sometimes, if not turned fully on, it would start to vibrate and whine. The sink would fill slowly, while the strong sunlight from the window above it sent watery reflections around the kitchen. The sink reached my chest and was now full of water, ice blue against the marble.

Once I found a lot of courgettes in Granny's straw bag. I looked for the right shape and floated the chosen one in the water. Its green reflections and movement reminded me of when, at the fish market, I found a small pike still alive among the eels in the shallow tank. I begged Granny to buy it and ran home to put it in the sink, where it swam with sharp bursts. I felt the green and yellow skin of the pike. It looked like a crocodile. I touched its hard snout and it bit my finger, hanging on with its needle teeth. I washed the small beads of blood in the cool water. The pike, swishing around, turned the water pink. I stood mesmerised looking at the creature's mean eyes. It smelled of the sunny marshes of Massaciuccoli with its water lilies and bull rushes rustling in the wind.

The courgette settled in the water, and I scored a faint line above the waterline with a tooth pick, cut along it with a long knife, then hollowed out the soft centre with a spoon, leaving only the hard skin like a green canoe. It floated, bobbing along the sink. With toothpicks and paper, the canoe acquired masts and sails, and I blew it around the sink, dreaming of pirates and desert islands. Granny eventually reclaimed the sink, and the courgette ended up being fried with the others in olive oil, having been filled with moist bread, basil and tomatoes.

Uncle Nanni didn't like washing in the small ceramic basin in the toilet, and during breakfast, he would come to the kitchen wearing only his pyjama trousers – he smelled like the bear I had seen at the travelling show. He washed his hairy chest and arms under the tap, splashing and making strange humming noises or singing funny, dirty songs of his own composition. He shaved with an open razor, looking into a small mirror hanging above the sink. I sat at the marble table dunking bread into the caffe latte and trying to match the scraping noise of the razor on Uncle's face by scratching the rough marble surface under the table. Often, I could predict the exact length of the scrape and match it.

Uncle Nanni had not volunteered in the war because of his hernia, but he was captured with his red Guzzi bike by the fleeing German army. He somehow managed to escape from a town up north by stealing a German motorbike, a Zundapp, but having to leave behind his beloved Guzzi. Uncle was a great friend of the owner of the Togni Circus, and I had free access to the shows. I made friends with Bagonghi, the dwarf. He was shorter than me but very strong. He laughed a lot, throwing his head back, opening his large mouth and shaking his whole body. He was famous among the children of the circus people for his large cock, which he showed to anyone who asked to see it, holding the large brown flopping 'sausage' with tiny hands and laughing. His partner was a large German lady who looked after the horses and other animals. They had a child of normal size of about my age. He owned a parrot that could swear in many languages and could sing the national anthem.

I fell in love with the Amazon who danced on the back of a large white horse. She was French, always smelled of perfume and pinched my cheeks. During rehearsals, I crouched low beside the ring trying to see under her frilly short skirt but managed only to get sprayed with sawdust from the horses' hooves. Uncle Nanni was very fond of the Amazon too. He had his best flashing smile for her and bought her flowers and perfumes. I saw them kissing and rubbing together in the tent where the hay was kept. I was very jealous.

One afternoon, with Bagonghi's son, I climbed on the wheel of the bearded lady's caravan to see if she was hairy all over. The lady had a beard, long and soft, and she once let me pull it to see if it was real. Balancing on the wheel and holding on to the window sill, we peered through the curtains. She was standing by a basin wearing only a bra and pants. She did not appear to have much hair on her body, apart from very bushy armpits. She took her bra off after long contortions with the strap at the back. Her large breasts with dark nipples, fell forward and were carefully sponged and then dried, while she sang softly to herself. Her skin was very dark and her large behind was barely contained in very skimpy pants. My friend and I, still balancing on the wheel, kept smiling nervously and winking at each other. The lady stood on one foot and raised one leg, beginning to take off her pants when, in the excitement, I lost my balance and grabbed my friend. We were lying on the grass laughing when the door of the caravan opened, revealing a very cross bearded lady about to throw the basin of water on us. We ran before she did so, following by her invectives in the Venetian dialect.

Uncle was renowned for his capacity to eat large quantities of food. With his friends, they'd book a table at 'Baralla', the local osteria, and the first to give up eating had to pay for the rest of the party. Uncle often farted to the irritation of Auntie Bice who considered him coarse and below her. He also smelled terribly when he went to the toilet, and I always covered my nose when passing it.

At meal time at home, a large black cat sat on Uncle Nanni's shoulders and he was fed morsels from his plate. I liked this cat very much, but it refused to play with me so I ended up hunting it in the afternoon after everyone was resting, using small wooden skittle balls as missiles and imagining I was stalking a tiger in the jungle. This cat, possibly to avoid me, spent a lot of time on the roof. Having jumped on the window sill of the corridor, it would then jump to the top of the column which belonged to the church outside. It would rest there nervously flicking its tail and licking its paws before leaping out. It was suspended for an instant in the air, then, with a flick of its body, it turned mid-air clearing the gutter and landing on the roof.

When the cat eventually died, I wrapped it in a newspaper and, armed with a shovel from the fireplace, took it to the fields outside the walls of Lucca for burial, accompanied by my sister, Ughetta. The cat was stiff and slippery, and it fell out of the newspaper in front of the bar in the Piazza Santa Maria. It made a strange hollow thud on the paving stones. The men at the bar stared and laughed nervously. A black cat brings bad luck! We re-packed the cat in the newspaper and quickly moved on. Outside the walls, between the canal which was part of an old moat and the earth fortifications, the rope makers were at work carding the strips of hemp and spinning them into rope with wheels and hooks, the shining new long ropes of different thickness drying on the grass.

Digging a hole with the brass shovel in the sun-baked earth proved difficult and so I decided to give the cat a burial at sea, floating it into the swift canal on a raft made from twigs and the folded newspaper. It floated, turning in the current, past the washing place under the plane trees where the washer women stood in a trough, bare-armed, washing, soaking, scraping on the smooth long stone which was level with their wobbling bottoms.

They stopped as the cat passed by in the choppy water. Some crossed themselves. We could hear their voices rising as they saw us by the road, pointing and shouting until Ughetta and I ran towards the walls and the massive entrance door, the marble panther on the façade blinding white in the sunshine. We passed under the cool shade of the gate, then up the slope on the stony curved path to the top. We climbed the parapet and saw the black shape of the cat floating in the canal, running parallel to the walls. We followed the cat with our eyes till the bend of the next rampart when it disappeared, gently bobbing, hidden behind the long grass.

I loved hunting flies, stalking the buzzing bluebottles around the house. Granny Armanda believed that a bluebottle was a sign for something new, a visitor or good news, but that did not put me off my pursuit. Armed with a sprayer made from a hand pump and a can filled with DDT, which had just arrived from America, I sprayed furiously; my hands and forearms covered in the smelly oily liquid. My quarries slowly twitched and dropped off the walls in the lethal fog. Nobody told me how dangerous my game was!

I had my sister to play with, but she was four years younger than me and had a way of deciding that she had had enough in the middle of a game that made me very cross. We played under Granny's black metal bed, keeping our treasures on the smooth dark planks that supported the metal springs. To annoy Granny, we plucked the springs, producing a low droning noise, and she tried to evict us with a broom. Granny and her three children were born in that bed. It had a pastoral scene painted on the headboard; a ruined castle by a lake, with trees and mountains in the background, set in an oval bordered with mother of pearl.

Our neighbours lived in an apartment that was still connected to ours by a communicating door. Their house was always very untidy and it smelled. Their Grandmother Ulia was bad tempered and her whiskered face and puffy cheeks reminded me of a tomcat. She was often grumbling and cooking in the large dark kitchen with the high ceiling and a skylight, like the kitchen of the giant in my fable book. Her daughter Tina was small and dainty and used to hug me. Tina had three daughters. Her husband, an impoverished count, was a gambler and left her many years before going to America.

Luana, the youngest daughter, was a few years older than me, and I had a passion for her. The middle daughter, Ania, was very pretty and very good at drawing beautiful ladies in the style of the pin-ups in Hollywood or Grand Hotel, the glamour magazines of the time. The older, Lidia, was very dramatic and always dressed in smart clothes with high heels and stockings. The family was quite poor, and after the war, Tina and Lidia started to go to Tombolo, dancing at the American base established near Livorno, bringing back nylons and Lucky Strike cigarettes. I heard people talking about Tombolo as a den of sin, and I caused a quarrel when I asked Tina about it. She said, "You must have heard about Tombolo from your family, and it's none of your business what happens there." Lidia had many American boyfriends; they listened to jazz on the radio and danced together in a small boudoir with lots of cushions and a small bar near her bedroom.

Luana acted older than her age, had long curved nails like her mother and used them on me when we quarrelled. The loft to her house had been hit by a bomb too, and we used the roofless room to play in. We looked for hours at magazines, and she pointed out the glamorous actors of the time and made me jealous. Her favourite was Tyrone Power – mine was Rita Hayworth. We made necklaces and rings from peach stones that we rubbed with water on the gritty brick floor until they were pierced. Luana had a cat called Pussy, named by one of the Americans, and I used to chase it along the echoing corridor and down the stairs. Luana always refused to kiss me. She called me 'gattomarcio' or rotten cat, but once she let me go into the toilet with her and let me take her pants off and look.

Not far from my house in Via Fillungo, there is a large square, but more than a square it is a large triangular space with many roads leading to it. It had on one side the walls with three massive gates leading to the roads in the north. The square is called Prato – field – and I remember it as a dusty area with grassy slopes leading to the walls, with shops selling baskets and barrels on one side and trattorias and a bar on the other.

In the middle, surrounded by a rocky low wall and a high evergreen hedge was a café – I remember sitting with Granny Armanda at a rickety wooden table in the summer evenings, waiting for the fireflies to arrive on the grassy slopes by the walls, drinking sweet lemonade, holding a jam jar, its metal top pierced with holes I had punched with a nail. Granny sipped her coffee, the sound of the radio in the distance talking about the Korean War and the 38 parallel disputed over by the American and Korean armies. The evening breeze from the river finally entering the square. Then, in the darkness, the first flickers appeared on the slopes. Grabbing the jam jar, I ran towards the walls on new sandals that were still stiff. I ran to catch the magic flickering insects, so delicate I could only partially close my hands around them. Once inside the jar, I looked at them climbing the glass, their pulsating bellies emitting a greenish light. If you damaged their soft skin during the capture, a sticky liquid would stain your fingers and continue to flicker faintly, smelling of a strong metallic smell.

Then I returned to the café with my jar, the air cooler now. Granny tried to dry my forehead with her lacy handkerchief that smelled of stale perfume. We walked home, the street still warm from the sun. At home, I put the jar on the marble top of the bedside table and went to sleep looking at the fading lights reflected on the walls of the jar. In the morning, I emptied the jar out of the window into the garden below, the fireflies still moving a little. Did they sleep during the day? Were they dying? Did they manage to fly back to the slopes by the walls?

The buses stopped near the Prato too, and during fair days, the people from the mountains of Garfagnana descended on Lucca, recognisable by their heavy boots, clothes and dialects. Every year, the strong man Maciste would come too. He lived for a week or so in a green caravan with his name on the side, a skinny horse tied beside it munching on the sparse grass. On a dusty carpet spread on the ground, surrounded by people, Maciste performed feats of strength helped by his woman, Delilah. The strong man was large and hairy and moved with grace on strangely small bare feet. He spoke with a northern accent. "*Signori e signore*, I am ready to perform a fantastic act of strength seen for the first time in this town. A flagstone weighing several hundred kilos will be placed on my stomach with the help of *lor signori* and will be broken by a volunteer with a sledgehammer. Do not be afraid," he announced, taking off his shirt and revealing a massive hairy chest and belly. Maciste paraded around, puffing out his chest and pulling up his baggy and dusty leotard. Then, having got everyone's attention, he lay on the carpet with a blanket on his belly. Wearing lots of silver bangles on her arms, a long skirt and embroidered blouse, Delilah invited the strongest-looking men to remove their jackets and roll up their shirt-sleeves and take part. A large flagstone was put on Maciste's belly by four men and one chosen man broke it with a sledgehammer.

One autumn, Delilah took me by hand, which was hard and coarse, and I was asked to jump on Maciste's stone, which was already balanced on his chest, while a man was chosen again to wield the sledgehammer. I jumped up and down on the stone with Maciste looking at me with sad absent eyes and a faint smile showing his gold tooth under his moustache. The stone was broken with a single blow of the sledgehammer, which made a muted thud, and the two pieces slid off Maciste's blanketed belly and rested on the ground. Delilah skipped around with the hat, announcing the next marvel, "Fire eating *Signori e signore*, Maciste will eat and spit fire."

I ran to buy an ice lolly and came back to see Maciste blowing huge puffs of fire from his mouth, having filled it with an evil smelling liquid from a straw-lined flask. He blew on a torch which he held at arm's length and produced a long burst of fire. The people stood back, and he repeated the feat in every direction, the fire reflecting on his shiny chest. Having spat and rinsed his mouth with a glass of red wine, he prepared the chain.

Again, four people were chosen to pull at the heavy chain to prove that it was sound. Maciste puffed and pumped his biceps, and then with the help of Delilah, he wound the chain around his chest and fastened it with a padlock. Red in the face, having taken a big breath, the chain sank into his flesh and veins appeared on his chest. Maciste tensed and strained until the chain broke and dropped on the dusty ground with a metallic ringing noise. During the clapping and cheering, Delilah went around with the hat. I went to drink from the fountain in the corner of the square. When I came back, the people had disbanded and Maciste was sitting on the steps of the caravan holding a massive loaf of bread and biting on a salami. He winked at me, sucking on his teeth. The horse was grazing on the grass of the fireflies' slopes.

One year, Maciste came back without Delilah but with a newly painted caravan announcing 'Fritz the

Great Grizzly Bear Wrestler'. He wore leather shorts and wrestled stiffly with a large brown bear. Somehow, I could not take the new show seriously – the wrestling was more like a slow dance. When the bear stood up, he was taller than Fritz and his great clawed paws left red marks on Fritz's shoulders. At the end of the wrestling match, while Fritz refreshed himself with great gulps of red wine, the bear squatted like a dog and after a few grunts produced a large pile of shit, which smelled so terrible that the spectators were left laughing and pinching their noses. I gave a last look before leaving the square and saw Fritz, his shoulders drooping, walking towards the caravan followed by the bear who ran after him like an enormous dog.

*

Life at home was becoming more difficult. Having come back from his brother in Florence, Father spent more time in his bedroom smoking in the dark.

Uncle Nanni had gone to live with his lover, a skinny lady with a raucous voice, in the house near the abattoir. They now had a child, a girl called Amanda, who looked like Granny but was disliked by her.

Auntie Bice, my mother's sister, worked as a civil servant in the same office as Father and was nice to me – reading me poetry on summer afternoons. Her favourite poet was Dante Alighieri. I remember falling asleep to the sound of her soft voice reading La Divina Commedia '*nel mezzo del cammin di nostra vita…*'

Mother and Father fought a lot, and I felt often alone and miserable. At about that time, I discovered a way to get rid of painful or unwanted thoughts, caused by scoldings or quarrels by grownups. I would count, often tapping my teeth to the rhythm in my head, in a numerical pattern of increasing complication, which distracted me from thinking about anything painful. Counting could also be applied to defuse the increasing desire to enact crazy thoughts that came to my head. I developed compulsions, like looking at and counting the four sides of my shoes – point, outside, heel, inside – standing on one foot in the street and counting 1, 2, 3, 4 left foot 5, 6, 7, 8 right foot. Perhaps I did it as a reassurance of being there in my shoes, feeling the streets. Sometimes I felt detached from my body as if I was above looking at myself.

I touched the rails of the stairs going down but only every other one. If I touched two at a time, I had to start again. I had complicated patterns of touching and sometimes spent a long time going downstairs. I became maniacal about objects or toys and worried they would break or deteriorate. I acquired a large ball bearing from the engineering firm where Mother worked as an accountant. I kept it in my hand even when I slept. There was something reassuring in the heavy smooth logic shape – it added needed security to my life. When the ball bearing started to rust, I got so worried that Mother took it to work and had it chromium plated. I spent hours looking at the world and my face reflected on that ball bearing.

I had a small wooden garage and a few model cars that I played with, polished and examined for any sign of damage. I also had a shining, heavy model of a plane, a Boeing, that I loved and polished admiring its smooth symmetry, until I discovered that the tail was slightly twisted. I soon discarded the imperfect plane.

Sometimes my sister Ughetta and I were given similar presents like games or books. I soon discovered a fault or an imperfection in mine and swapped it for hers. Often her presents under scrutiny had even more imperfections so I had to swap again.

When there was a thunderstorm, I went to sleep on Granny's bed. She was also afraid of thunder and seemed to communicate even more fear to me. We prayed together, our words muffled by the noise of the storm, thinking that the next lightning would hit the house. We reached a paroxysm of fear and ended up with pillows over our heads still feeling the low rumble of thunder vibrating the springs under the mattress.

In the early fifties, a large number of miracles and apparitions started to happen. Some said they were orchestrated by the church to instil the fear of God in people and trying to stem the popularity of communism, in view of the imminent elections. Every town had several crying or moving Madonnas. Often, we congregated after dinner into somebody's house where a sacred statue or image had performed, waiting to see it for ourselves.

Such visits occurred again a few years later when the lucky families attracted friends and visitors to stare at the newly arrived flickering lights of television. I spent hours in various churches, staring at pasty faces Madonnas illuminated by candlelight. The lights and the staring bringing tears to my eyes, being afraid to blink in case I missed a movement or a teardrop! Fervent old ladies in black praying aloud and occasionally seeing a miracle!

I went to a school run by nuns in an old convent. I remember a large garden and eating lunch under arches in the cloisters, the sunlight playing in the trees. The classroom was up in the attic overlooking a canal outside the old Roman gate. I was expelled from the school for showing my penis to a girl outside the toilet.

I was then sent to another school also run by nuns. It had a courtyard near the walls full of huge logs from ancient trees cut after a bomb hit a park nearby. I liked running and jumping from log to log during the break after lunch. Once during play inside, I was pushed against a glass door, a sliver of glass shaped like a dagger sheared off and fell embedding itself on the back of my calf. I turned in surprise and removed the glass, looking at the gash filling with blood, strangely without pain.

Auntie Barbara was my father's auntie, and I had spent the first few years of my life with her in Garfagnana when Father was in the war and Mother had to work. I remember little of those years – the smell of Auntie Barbara like warm chestnut flour, her shape undressing in candlelight, her large breast soft against me. Auntie Barbara often came to stay with us in Lucca. Her hair was dyed with the help of walnut water.

There was always a saucer with walnut husks macerating in water. Auntie applied the resulting brown liquid to her white hair, turning it to blond. She had a sweet disposition that somehow had the power to make me misbehave. It was as if I wanted her to get cross like the rest of the family when provoked. Her patience infuriated me.

Once, she collected me from school and while walking home, she expressed disgust at the piles of horse and dog shit in the road. I had to enact it immediately. This time even counting did not help. I picked a cane from a window box, dipped it in some shit and tried to touch Auntie Barbara's coat. The more she screamed and begged me to stop, the more I teased her. I would touch her quickly on her back with the clean end of the stick, reversing it rapidly when she looked so that she thought she had shit on her back. I felt she was in my power and followed her all the way home, dipping the cane in shit as we went along to keep her frightened.

My memory of Christmas was food and more food. We had a capon stuffed with chestnuts, panforte, panettone and many types of wine. The use of Christmas trees had not yet arrived from America and instead I built a crib complete with its surrounding landscape on a table, using scrunched newspaper covered with brown packing paper to simulate hills and rocks. Using moss and cotton wool for vegetation and snow, a hand mirror surrounded by pebbles for a pond in an oasis of paper palm trees. All of this populated by antique terracotta shepherds and magi all looking towards the paper grotto with a crib illuminated by a small battery-operated bulb. We lost the old baby Jesus and its replacement was far too big, dwarfing Joseph and Mary. La Befana, on the 6th of January, was an old hag with a similar role to Father Christmas. She would bring presents to good children and charcoal to bad ones. On one occasion, I desperately wanted a cap gun with a leather holster and belt, but, to my disappointment, I got a skittle game. The night before Epiphany, the adults had a good time throwing around the room nuts and chocolate coins, making it look as if they came from the chimney thrown by La Befana.

The Sword

During the night, there was a heavy snowfall. On waking up, I could see the light from the snow through the shutters and when I opened the window, I tasted and smelled the snow on the windowsill. The noises of the town seemed to be muffled, even the sad sound of the sirens from the factories outside the walls.

It was carnival time, and I was on holiday. My sister was at a friend's house. After a warm bowl of coffee and milk, I walked out with Granny Armanda. On the stairs going down, I ran ahead not bothering to touch or count any railings. By the outside door, there was no need to step down as the snow reached up to the top of the step. The snow had added bits to the relief marble carving of the devil with virgin and child high on the wall beside the entrance. The devil that generally frightened me, looked benign, almost funny – a turban of snow covering his horns and curls. I pointed out the devil to Granny, but she frowned, hurriedly crossed herself and pulled me along towards Piazza San Frediano. We walked fast. The snow was reaching almost to my calves, but I felt warm in my thick green socks hand knitted by Auntie Barbara.

People's faces seemed red against the white background. Granny went inside the baker shop, and I waited outside. The old dog, belonging to the bar in the piazza, walked by on stiff legs, his penis trailing in the snow. He stopped to pee by the corner with the obituaries on the wall and left a neat yellow hole all the way to the stones below.

Granny came out with a piece of hot focaccia for me, and we walked with the crunching sound of compressed snow underfoot. In Piazza San Frediano were just two or three cars covered in snow and few footprints crossing the square. I ran all the way to where the steps of the church had been, now a slope of snow was there. We climbed carefully and entered the church through the tall door. Inside in the darkness, the familiar smell of the church – a strong smell almost like sweat and onions mixed with incense. Granny offered me the tips of her finger wet with the holy water from the tall marble font with the yellow rim and I crossed myself. We sat and I resigned myself to the long boring service. I kept playing with a sharp shard of wood sticking up from the pine bench in front. It looked like a small sword. I put my nails under it and pulled and let go, making a clicking noise. Granny slapped my hand.

During mass, I thought about carnival, and I tried to remember the colour of all the pierrot costumes Granny kept in the wardrobe. When the priest lifted the shining chalice, and the bell rang, I looked instead of lowering my head and the chalice catching the light of the candles made me think of the sword.

I had found it last year when I helped Granny to unpack the costumes from the large wardrobe where the tiger's head had been. I kept the thought in my mind during the service, but then it became too much.

"Granny, Granny," I whispered, but she kept her head down. "Granny," I said again pulling the sleeves of her thick coat. "Granny, can I have the sword?"

She gave me a reproaching look, and when I called her name again, she said, "Later."

Mass finally finished with the magic words, *ite missa est* (this mass is finished) to which I always added 'thank God'. We walked slowly out of the church in the blinding white square. "Granny, the sword I found last year…"

"What sword?" she said blinking in the strong light.

"The one I found when we unpacked the costumes. Don't you remember? Can I have it this year?…I am older."

"We'll see. If you are good," she said. Trying to climb down the steps, I ran all the way home lightly and silently imagining galloping on my white stallion in the snow.

I stopped by the green door of our house waiting for Granny. I was trying to leave a neat footprint in the snow without any flakes falling inside. A perfect footprint! I heard the door of the Milani barbershop rattle and saw the red nose and white moustache of the barber. "Can you collect some snow from the ground? I need to shave the devil!" he said seriously, handing me a brass bowl. When I did not move, he started to laugh. "Come in, come in, it's too cold outside," he said letting me in and patting my back. The shop was warm and smelled of patchouli and soap, the tiled floor covered in sawdust. Carlo, the young apprentice, shaving one of the neighbours, winked at me – the great open razor gliding on a shiny soaped ruddy face.

Carlo was much friendlier now. Last summer, he saw me spitting from the top window on the customers waiting on chairs outside the shop. When he caught up with me and I tried to run upstairs, he gave me such a kick up my arse that he lifted me onto the front steps.

Granny passed in front of the steamed-up window, and I left the shop. I took Granny's bag and walked slowly upstairs counting the steps. "When shall we unpack the costumes?" I asked at the top.

"Later, after lunch," Granny said breathing heavily. "You are impatient!"

Time passed slowly until lunch. Mother and Auntie Bice and Father came back from work and we had polenta with cheese, while listening to the radio. Father ate in his room. After lunch, I played near the fireplace in the corner. I branded logs with my initials using a red-hot poker and made cigarettes of newspaper and posed at the console mirror looking through the smoke like the actors on cinema posters.

Auntie Bice left for work wearing a new heavy brown corduroy coat in a trail of perfume. Mother left later after the washing-up, always in a hurry tip tapping in her high heels all the way to the front door.

"What is this smell?" said Granny coming from the kitchen. "Stop playing with the fire. The room is full of smoke. Let's go and unpack the costumes." I jumped up, and we walked together to the tall wardrobe in the corridor. Granny opened it with some effort, with the large dark key she kept hidden under the umbrella pot.

Inside, the wardrobe everything was neatly packed in boxes and paper parcels and there was a smell of camphor and mothballs.

Granny chose a large worn cardboard box and opened it. Its corners reinforced with metal straps. It revealed the Pierrot costumes neatly folded. A green one with a yellow collar and a tall flattened felt hat, another all red and a completely white one. They smelled of dust and faintly of perfume.

When Grandpa died of a heart attack aged 50, Granny opened a shop selling haberdashery and renting costumes. Now only these few costumes were left.

"You will have to wear this one this year," Granny said placing the red one against me for size. "The green one will be perfect for your sister." She started to move another package from the back of the wardrobe when, against the brown paper liner, I saw the black leather scabbard with the silver point.

"Look, Granny, the sword, the sword." She moved a box and exposed the dark steel hilt, the finely twisted wire of the handle with the shiny pommel.

"Be careful, it is a real one. It used to belong to my great grandfather. He was a dragoon of the Grand Duke of Tuscany. He was killed by the brigand Musolino," she said. I knew the story so I grabbed the sword. It was heavy, and I went to my room. Only after I closed the door did I draw the sword. The blade was still shiny and the point keen. I had to use both my hands and fought with it in front of the oval mirror. The blade swishing, I fought against pirates and brigands. Later, when I got tired, I took menacing poses and made speeches. My sister opened the door, started to giggle, and I sent her away with a growl. The sword made me feel secure, invincible. I wished I had it years ago when I was frightened of the Gargantua on top of the wardrobe! I hid the sword under the bed, but during the evening, I went back to my room to look at it.

Drawing it, I liked the metallic ringing noise of the blade when I pulled it in and out of the scabbard. The way it bent and flicked when I pressed its point against the wall. The blade had crosses, ancient marks and foreign letters still faintly gilt. I got the shoe polish box from under the kitchen sink, and I polished the scabbard till I could see my face in it.

That night after dinner, it started to snow again. Mother came to my room with the trabiccolo, the upside-down wooden basket containing the terracotta scaldino full of coals to warm the bed. I got the sword out to show her, but she did not like it too much. She opened the window to close the shutters, and I saw the falling snow. A few flakes melting now on the brick floor. She kissed me goodnight, and I slept with the sword, cold and hard against my body. I dreamt I was Fra Diavolo with my sword, swirling cape and horse.

*

The snow melted slowly in the garden below and green shoots appeared. The dark leaves of the magnolia tree shined in the warming sun. Swallows came back to the nests under eaves of the Stanzina, their happy shrills waking me in the morning.

Easter came with sunshine and wind, the ritual of visiting seven churches on Good Friday and wearing new clothes on Easter Day. Easter Monday was called Pellegrino or Pilgrim Day, and we went for a picnic. Uncle Nanni would arrive in his rickety buggy drawn by a horse. We all piled up on the leather seats. Auntie Bice complained about something like flies or the smelly horse. Ughetta and I, sitting beside uncle, would invariably get the giggles when the horse started to fart in time with his trotting. Uncle would get annoyed, and eventually frustrated by our giggles, he slapped our legs with his heavy brown hands. We found a place on a green windy hill near the river. The horse was unhitched and tied to a tree, free to eat the luscious grass around him. We had the picnic sitting on blankets eating boiled eggs, stuffed tomatoes and wine. I was in charge of making coffee on a chrome little machine with a spirit lamp that heated water and made four small cups of coffee. I loved it when the bubbling started and the dark oily coffee dribbled slowly into the cups with the final hissing when empty. After the meal, my sister and I would chase each other, and I let her catch me or she would stop playing. Then the journey back, tired, our faces red from the wind. Uncle clicked his tongue in his special way to make the horse go faster.

The Slippers

It was hot that morning and school had ended. I lay in bed listening to the sounds of Granny Armanda lighting a fire, breaking the charcoal into small pieces, then the smell of coffee roasting in the shiny copper pan. Granny called, asking me to mill the coffee – she knew I liked the smell of it freshly ground. I filled the old grinder with warm coffee beans and turned the squeaky handle. I checked often by opening the little drawer below the grinder. I hated knocking over the brown pyramid of ground coffee forming there. Granny made coffee for herself in the Neapolitan machine and prepared a bowl of barley and milk for me, and I dunked bread with jam into the bowl with green dragons on the rim, trying to keep the flies away. Granny joined me at the marble table with her small cup of coffee. "Today, we'll go to the lady by the walls who makes slippers – I need a new pair," Granny said looking out of the open window. The morning light was dazzling on the pale cracked wall of the House of The Guinigi, only a few feet away.

We went out, Granny always in black, wearing light shoes of brown leather fastened with buttons which she told me her grandfather had made in a shoe factory he owned. He had made shoes for Puccini and also for rich noble people of Lucca. She wore her white hair in a bun.

I wore sandals with no socks and my white linen shirt, darned under the chest pocket where it got burned by a spark when I was blowing on the fire. I was made to wear blue shorts in the English style, just above the knees, made from an old pair of Uncle Nanni's. I hated them! They made my legs look so skinny. The stones of Via Fillungo already felt hot under the light soles of my sandals. Quartuccio, the local taxi, passed us in his open buggy, pulled by the old grey horse – he touched his hat, and Granny nodded in reply.

I heard the light bell-like sound of the stonemason, bent over a marble bust in the shade of his shop. We passed the shop selling ropes and baskets, with song birds in tiny green cages stacked outside, sacks of multi-coloured seeds and feed and a large barrel full of grey-green, smelly, sticky substance made from mistletoe berry, called vischio and used on sticks to snare birds. At the bar on the corner, we saw the familiar faces of the regulars at the tables under the green canopy, playing cards and shouting. Granny stopped at the delicatessen, with its salty smells of dried fish, barrels of herrings, dried hams and salami hanging from the dark ceiling. The ladies inside were all talking at the same time.

On the Prato Piazza, the carts and horses were waiting in the sun, and I heard the bells of the cyclists and the roar of a car speeding on the road at the top of the walls. We followed the slopes of the walls, full of daisies, butterflies and crickets. I picked up a stone, ready to throw it at a lizard, but I did not see any. Granny entered a dark doorway, and I threw the stone hard against the rusty iron-lined door of the walls. I liked the echo, reverberating along the empty vast space of the fortification. Granny called me from inside the shady hall with arches. It was cool and there was a garden with drying sheets, billowing white in the sunshine.

We climbed the damp smelling stairs to the second floor. Granny knocked on a door and a smiling middle-aged lady opened it and let us in. "Is this your grandson? He looks so tall!" Granny smiled, exchanged greetings and asked me to sit on a chair with a straw seat, near the open window, while she went to get her feet measured. I was alone in the almost empty room with crumbling plaster that left a sprinkling of white dust on the brick floor along the wall. I drew my initials with the point of my sandals on the dust and then crossed them out. The scrapes left did not look right so I rubbed the wall with the side of my sandals till the falling dust covered them.

I stood up and went to look at the dresser that displayed many types of slippers in various colours. They had the names of the clients written on small pieces of paper pinned inside the heel. Velvet, linen, leather – some made from carpet materials and others with the rubber soles made from old tyres.

I heard the voice of the slipper-maker talking to Granny in the other room and the smell of glue and burnt rubber coming from the door that was ajar. I touched some of the slippers – they felt stiffer than I expected, reminding me of the toy boat that I was given the summer before, which was made of light wood painted red. I went to the window and put my naked arms on the warm stone windowsill. I looked down and saw a well near the house in the garden below. I could see, in the deep dark water, my image at the window with the white shirt, my long face and uncombed hair.

I threw a few shards of stone from the sill into the well, and each time I did this, my image in the water disappeared and slowly reformed. I was there; I disappeared. I looked for something else to throw into the well, but I could not find anything. I approached the dresser again and took a pair of red leather slippers. A strange impulse made me take out the pin and throw it into the well, then the tag with the name fell slowly against the wall. It got caught on a spider's web near the mouth of the well. In a panic, I threw one of the leather slippers then quickly the other, trying to dislodge the tag, but I missed. The two red slippers floated, bobbing in the dark water like my toy boat. I threw some carpet-covered slippers in a panic, but only a large one with a rubber sole hit the web and the tag fell slowly into the dark water that was now full of colourful slippers. I threw another pair of large ones with great force trying to sink the others, but in vain. I began to sweat, thinking about what I had done, and I sat back on the straw chair. The dresser in front of me, now deprived of many slippers, seemed to accuse me. I stood and re-arranged the remaining pairs, spreading them to fill the gaps. It was as if someone else had thrown the slippers and I had only been a spectator. The wind felt cold on the shirt stuck to my sweating back.

Granny re-entered the room with a smile. "Come, I still have to go shopping," she said taking my hand. The smiling woman opened the door, tussled my hair and we left. The same evening, the slipper lady, not smiling anymore, came to our house and spoke gravely to Granny in the kitchen. Hiding behind the door of the dining room, I listened. "I am sure your grandson threw the slippers into the well – nobody came after you. Many pairs are ruined, unglued and discoloured. You will have to pay."

I heard Granny calling me, shouting my name. I ran to the front door and left, closing it gently behind me. I went to the field outside the walls. The grass was still warm, and I saw many lizards, even a large green one with a yellow belly, called a Ramarro, but I did not pick up any stones. I sat on the grass, numb. After the sun went down, I made my way home, resigned and sure of a beating.

*

I remember touching myself a lot. I don't know if I did to relieve a continuous itch or because I enjoyed the feeling. Mother and her friends noticed my habit, and I was taken to a doctor. He was old and had extremely cold hands when he examined my penis, making it almost disappear, and he told Mother that my skin at the end was too tight to be pulled back for washing. "You can leave it and when he reaches puberty it will stretch naturally. Or you could have it circumcised," he said smiling at me and pulling my foreskin hard between finger and thumb.

It was decided that the touching could not continue and I had to be circumcised. I was taken to a clinic in Via Dei Fossi. Father's insurance would pay for it. From the window of my room, I could look into a garden and became friendly with a girl my age – the daughter of the doctor and clinic owner. I wrote messages on the headed notepaper and sent them floating to the garden below. She threw notes at me wrapped around pebbles. She asked me what was wrong with me, and I vaguely pointed to my tummy.

The operating room was dazzling white. Everybody was smiling stupidly at me, and I saw the steaming, shiny surgical instrument in a tray.

When I was under anaesthetic, I dreamt of white deserts in the sunshine, vast expanses of sand, or was it snow? I felt its ridges and shapes with my whole body as I floated just above it. I woke up with a terrible taste in my mouth, and after throwing-up a few times, I remembered about my penis and looked inside my pyjamas. It was wrapped up in bandages, and it hurt. When I tried to pee, the bandage got wet, and it really stung. I did not want to pee for the rest of the day, so a lady nurse with a vast bum and a moustache showed me a catheter she would have to use on me if I did not pee. It was thicker than my penis. I still refused but then my father came and was unusually sweet, encouraging me to try till I finally managed to pee in a bedpan. After the initial burning, it was all right.

Mother brought me comics and a bunch of bananas. The girl in the garden below refused to look up at my window. Maybe she had found out about my operation.

Seminary

During the summer in the late forties, I spent several weeks with Auntie Barbara in Pieve Fosciana. She was very religious, and we often went to church together. After mass, I was introduced to Don Angelo and became involved with learning the ritual of serving mass. Don Angelo wore heavy studded boots, summer and winter, had bad breath and walked bent forward from the waist.

It all started because of this damned book. The thick cover bound in green velvet and leather with silver corners and a clasp set with a red stone. Inside the book, in gold and vivid colours, were pictures of saints and devils.

One summer evening, after catechism, I asked Don Angelo if I could see the book again. "Do you like it so much, more than football?" Don Angelo asked, lowering the great missal onto a bench for me to see, then walking towards the sacristy.

"Yes," I said lifting the heavy cover and exposing the thick pages with the beautiful writing. At the top of every page, the first letter was in gold adorned with scenes from the bible in amazing colours. "You can have a book like that you know," said Don Angelo approaching.

"How?" I said turning another page full of more wonders.

"Do you have the vocation? Would you like to become a priest?" said Don Angelo, his hand touching mine, wet with holy water from the stone font.

"Yes," I said crossing myself mainly to avoid Don Angelo's bad breath, the floor of the church was ablaze with the colours of the stained-glass window in the sunshine. I pushed the spring door and went out in the strong light, across the square and down the narrow dark street with the tall medieval buildings, passed the dark carpenter's shop, the swishing noise of the great wooden plane and the smell of sweet chestnut shavings.

I passed the first and second fountain splashing in the light, through the small square, the dark stain where they killed the pig was still on the stones. I passed the house of my uncle with its new door at the bottom of the courtyard. Then Auntie Barbara's house, low and pink in the darkening evening light. Through the green gate, up the uneven stone steps, under the pergola with the strawberry-flavoured grapes, almost ripe. In the house, the smell of apples drying on the long low chest. Inside the kitchen with the darkened fireplace and the Madia chest for making bread.

I went to look if any slugs had come up the pipe to the stone sink. I drank from the blue enamel ladle immersed in the zinc pail. I liked the noise the ladle made hitting the side of the pail full of water. Soup was cooking in a blackened cauldron on the fire, and Auntie Barbara walked into the kitchen.

"How did you do at catechism?" she said. She wore dark clothes and her hair was a strange colour; she must have run out of walnut husk water! She had a pale, resigned face and very few teeth. I told her about the missal, and she got cross. "Did you tell Don Angelo that you put straw up toad's bums and inflate them? Vocation! And what about all the lies you tell, eh? Eat, it's getting cold," she said putting soup on the table.

Summer passed slowly. We built dikes in the river and swam. I wrestled with Nonzia, the miller's daughter. She was stronger than me! The strawberry grapes were ripe, and when I want to poo in the ditch, I always carried a bunch with me. Then it was time to return to Lucca.

A letter arrived explaining about my vocation and that there was room for me at the seminary in Bergamo. Mother had mixed feelings about it, but we did not talk about it very much. A priest arrived with dusty shoes with a silver buckle and a bald head that he kept wiping with a blue handkerchief. Mother cooked a good meal, and I was told I would be leaving with the priest the next day. My sister was laughing too much, and I kicked her furiously under the table.

Father stayed in his room. Granny asked me if I was sure I wanted to go and Mother cried. I was not sure of anything; it was as if all this was happening to somebody else. I just thought of receiving an illuminated book like the one at Pievefosciana and shoes with silver buckles.

We left the next day by train, and Mother bought me a comic book for the journey. She waved furiously disappearing from view. Soon after leaving the platform, I felt happy enough and made a start on the thick sandwich Mother had prepared. We travelled most of the day and the pale priest hardly spoke. He smiled at me and dried his bald head. I looked out of the window or read the comic.

We left the train at Genova, took a bus and on the winding mountain road, I felt sick. I held onto the lowered vibrating window, spraying the side of the bus with my vomit and smelling the dust and the fuel. The priest wiped my mouth with his sweaty blue handkerchief and told me that we were going to a village to collect another student.

We got off the dusty bus, and I got a dirty look from the driver. Old men sitting in the square, catching the last of the sun, looked at us curiously. Later, in the old stone house, I met Martino the other student. He was twelve like me, small and wiry with spiky short hair. His mother gave us some milk, dark bread and butter, and we ate staring at each other across the marble table. She opened a bottle of red wine for the priest.

"Come, we'll go and see the 'mad one'," whispered Martino. Outside, the light was fading, Martino took my hand and we ran past a stone arch with a statue of the Virgin Mary. Martino crossed himself rapidly without stopping. Outside the village in an old stone hut set against the hill, lived the 'mad one'. He came out immediately, moving rapidly with a side shuffle. As we approached, Martino took my hand again and warned me not to go too near. The 'mad one' really looked mad. His hair was long and matted, his eyes close together. He wore an old grey coat and wooden clogs and kept looking rapidly at us and away again. Then he reached inside his coat, got out his large penis and started to play with himself, his face twisted with a sad smile, his eyes moving rapidly sideways. He was still doing it as we started again up the hill towards the village.

That night, Martino and I slept in a large bed at the top of the house, with the smell of apples and grapes drying on cane trestles all around the room. We talked and ate large amounts of drying fruit before we slept, hiding the apple cores and grape rasps under the bed.

In the morning, we sat again opposite each other at the marble table, dunking bread in large bowls of milk. The priest drank his coffee in silence looking out of the window.

We arrived at the seminary late that night. A fat priest opened the large wooden door and started to talk rapidly and cheerfully to us in the local dialect. He took our cases, and we walked along cold, dark corridors. He put his finger to his mouth telling us to be quiet and opened a rattling glass door into a dormitory full of beds in rows, white in the dim light.

We were showed to our beds, and I waved to Martino before taking my clothes off and getting into a cold bed. I felt alone. The rough clean sheet was hard and with an unfamiliar smell. Soon I started to cry, silently in the dark. I woke up during the night with a terrible tummy ache, got out of bed, but without knowing where the toilets were, I fought the urge to shit but soon had to do it some in the bed and some squatting beside the bed near my shoes. I woke up with the sound of a bell and the insistent voice of someone telling us to get out of bed. Something was wrong; there was a smell of shit – I had been lying on it. Under the cover, my white skinny body was smeared with it. I put my head inside the covers to hide my face.

A young priest uncovered me and a look of disgust came over his face. I covered myself again. I heard muffled laughter, someone tried to uncover my face again, and I was hit by several pillows. I stayed inside the sheet, flushed with shame until the sound of shuffling feet, giggles and whispers died in the distance as the dormitory emptied.

I peeped in the direction of Martino's bed, and to my great relief, he was there in bed looking at me. "Told you we had too much fruit," he said laughing, and I felt better. The rattling door opened and the fat priest came in shuffling.

"And what do we have here?" he said in a cheerful voice. "*Mon Dieu, mon Dieu*," he kept repeating. We were taken to a cold room with several showers. The water was hot, and we were given soap and towels. When we returned to the dormitory, the beds had been stripped and long dark cassocks of rough wool were on the beds. Stitched on the breast was a cloth heart with the symbol of the Passionist Order.

Martino and I were teased mercilessly by the other boys about our first night's mishap. During recreation time, we were given drilled shiny seeds, which we fashioned into rosary beads with pliers and thin brass wire. During the long tedious church hours, I thought of the mountains of Garfagnana, of Lucca and my mother, and tears often came to my eyes. On Sunday, we were taken on foot to the vast plain beside the River Serio to play football. It was a popular spot for the local hunters;

armed with shotguns, they hid inside dugout hides, camouflaged with branches and waited for the larks attracted by mechanical lures posted outside and covered in shiny bits of mirror.

We played football on the cold gravel plain, a priest acting as referee, his long cassock flapping in the wind and the noise of the guns near the river.

Time came when a certain feeling of rebellion came over me. I knew the feeling well; it was an old friend – a demanding but loyal friend. 'He' kept whispering to me, "What are you doing here? You don't want to be a priest. What do these priests dislike most? Begin to swear, tell other children the bad and dirty things you know. They will send you back home."

During service, with the pungent incense smoke in my nostrils and the singing, I tried to remember the bad words I knew. From that moment, I tried to use as many swear words in my conversation. The children, even Martino, looked at me as if I was a rabid dog. Conscious of my new found power, I swore and explained to the curious children the meaning of the Tuscan swear words.

During another service one rainy evening, again intoxicated with the smell of incense, instead of singing I started to say 'Topa, topa, topa' till the singing ended and I repeated 'Topa, topa'. The drone of the organ slowly fading, faces stared at me.

At breakfast, while eating sweet polenta with milk, I was approached by a priest and taken to see the head priest. He sat me in a dark wood-panelled room smelling of camphor and told me gently that because of my behaviour he had decided to send me home. The priest sat me on a chair and, having placed a fat warm hand on my head, told me that he was going to eradicate the demons from my head. In a low voice and with the help of an old book, similar to the one that attracted me to priesthood, he pronounced the many names of all the devils and princes of darkness – Lucifer, Beelzebub – and summoned them to leave my head. This lasted a long time, and I nearly fell asleep with his monotonous voice.

I looked around the room at the sad neat grey bed and the spare cassock hanging from the nail on the wall – the library on the other wall full of old books and the window from which I could hear the children in the garden below.

I travelled with a priest to Bergamo and was put on a train to Florence where arrangements were made for me to be collected by Uncle Nanni. On the way, early in the morning, we travelled along the plain by the River Serio, silvery in the misty sunlight, reflections on the barrels of the guns in the hides ready for the day's killing of the larks.

II Pennino (The Nib)

My stay in Lucca was very brief after the expulsion from the seminary. Mother and Father continued to fight and Granny found it too difficult to look after me.

That autumn, I was sent to Collesalvetti, a Salesian boarding school near Livorno. I hated the place. Being too young to study at the boarding school, I went to the school outside near the church.

I liked the lady teacher – she was friendly and had many children of her own. Our classroom was high up in the school building, cold in winter and hot in summer. We had to run all the way to the ground floor to go to the toilet. The teacher was a great follower of the cycling tour of Italy, and in early summer, she would bring a radio and we all listened to the races. The legendary names of Coppi, Bartali, Bobet, Magni, Koblet were familiar to us like the ones of historical figures.

I liked being at this school outside and was sad to return to sleep at the gloomy boarding school nearby. I sick of the long echoing corridors, the smell of stale food, the bare courtyard where we played football and the church where we spent long hours every day among clouds of incense and boring rituals.

One day during mass, very bored, playing with my hands I discovered that if you closed the index finger against the base of the thumb making a small circle and placed the tip of the thumb against the top of the middle finger, you could make a rude representation of female parts. I showed it to the boy on the bench next to me, but I had to explain what it was; we giggled and by the time the mass finished, the boys around us knew all about it. The day after, at lunch, in the smelly noisy refectory among the din and scraping of metal plates, the head priest stood on a raised pulpit by the entrance. He clapped his hands and the chattering children became quiet. "There is a wolf among us that must be denounced and shamed," he announced in a dramatic voice. Then to my surprise, he called my name and said that I had been doing profane and lurid signs belonging to the devil during mass. I stood, my face red in shame, my heart beating furiously. I felt faint. "No more cinema for you this year," the priest announced, pointing a finger with a righteous look on his face.

The only thing to look forward to was the cinema on a Sunday, but I had been banned. They were showing a film about a poor fisherman who had found a large pearl and became rich. I was made to learn a poem by heart in an empty classroom with the verses still repeating in my head. I went exploring the empty boarding school. I ended up near the toilets and then upstairs in the new classroom. Its walls freshly painted and with new wooden desks not yet varnished, new inkwells in white China set in the wood and a large bottle of ink in the corner.

On an impulse, I opened the bottle and poured ink delicately on the walls and benches, careful not to splash myself. When all was covered, I threw the bottle out of the open window to the vineyard below. I was almost in a trance with the smell of ink, like blood, slowly spreading out and leaving a reddish halo around each spot.

Still repeating the poem in my head, I went back to the study room. I always denied it was me who splashed the ink, even when I heard one teacher saying that I was the only one they thought capable of such a deed.

We were taken for long boring walks in the pinewoods near Collesalvetti. Once I saw a wild boar crashing through the holm oaks followed by her spotted piglets. One of the student priests looking after us, a fat sweaty youth with red hair, had started to touch me during study time, and once during a walk, he took me into the bushes and touched my penis looking at me with staring eyes, sweating and breathing heavily. I wanted to run away, but he held me whispering that he would help me with my maths. The smell of his sweat made me feel sick.

Once on a walk with a friend, we decided to run away and try to reach Livorno and take a train home. We planned and talked and counted pocket money, even saving the lunch sandwiches. But when we reached the top of the hill covered in green bracken and with the teachers struggling after us on the slope below, we could not run and sat sadly eating our lunch. We fell in with our group and never spoke of the plan again.

On a windy day at school, the classroom windows rattling and the poplars bending in the wind, our teacher told us of things making the news. A young man, a few days before in Livorno, had filled a sock with gravel, used it to rob a man and clubbed him to death. I was thinking how simple it would be to fill a sock with gravel while I was picking my teeth with a loose new nib.

A Pelikan nib, one of the best and ideal for making darts with paper fletching. I sucked in and tasted the sweet smell of decay on one of my back teeth then bit my tongue and let my mouth fill with saliva, diluting the taste. I coughed, lost the nib and panicked thinking I had swallowed the nib. "I swallowed a nib!" I shouted, blood pounding in my head. The teacher approached, and I began to sweat and had an urgent need to pee. I was sent downstairs, and when I bent forward to unbutton my flies, I saw the shiny nib embedded just inside the chest pocket of the long black cassock we all wore. I picked it up and hid it in my pocket.

Outside, I was told I would be immediately sent home and my mother would be telephoned. I could not say anything now, the idea of being sent home was too tempting! Back at the boarding school, I was given bread and potatoes with oil so that the nib would be coated and not puncture my intestine. Someone drove me to Livorno and my mother met me at the noisy station, her face tired and worried.

In Lucca, she took me to a doctor, and he put me behind a screen and looked for the nib with his x-ray machine, the screen cold on my bare belly. "My dear lady," he said to my mother. "A nib is made of metal and would show clearly on an x-ray. I am sure there must be a mistake." On the way home, Mother held my hand and asked me to explain. It started to rain, and I ran home.

Everybody was less sympathetic than before, and although I didn't say anything, they all thought I was lying. My father refused to see me and stayed in his room, smoking and listening to the radio in the darkness.

Escape

The next year at Collesalvetti, I started to study in the boarding school itself, having become too old for the outside school in the village. I hated the long hours studying in silence, having to memorise long boring prayers and ridiculous pieces from the scriptures, the sour smell of the refectory and the sordid advances of one of the young priests.

One Sunday, I was in the courtyard doing running competitions with the boys. I had just been beaten in a race and felt low. I looked through the gate and saw Mother waving at me. She looked beautiful in a yellow dress with blue dots. We sat on a bench outside, and I ate the ham panino she got out of her bag. "Are you unhappy?" she said stroking my hair. I carried on munching and counting the dots on her dress.

"I am not happy," I said. "I hate the priests; I hate the school, and I am sick too." I bit another piece of bread and Mother looked at me with a worried expression. "Yes," I said, "every time I go to the loo to have a poo, blood comes out of my bottom." I don't know why I said that but it seemed to me a secure sign of a terrible disease. She took my face in her cool hands and looked at me straight in the eyes. "You are not sick; I have just seen you running. Tell me the truth." I looked in her eyes, still chewing and slowly started to laugh. Her look relaxed, and she knew I was lying. I cried when Mother left.

I somehow felt I had to find a way to leave the school. Some days, I had the feeling I had to escape. That night, the feeling was very strong, a physical sensation that started in my legs and went to my stomach tensing it.

The classroom where we studied was hot, and it smelled of young unwashed bodies. I tried to concentrate on the poem, but the verses made me feel even more restless: *stormi di uccelli neri, come esuli pensieri, nel vespro migrar* – flocks of dark birds like migrating thoughts in the evening.

I stood up and approaching the worn wooden desk, asked the young priest's permission to go to the toilet. "Oh, it's you again." He gave me a hard look and waved towards the door. "Be quick!" The long green corridor was dark – down the stone steps, feeling the cool iron handrail with a curl at the bottom. The toilet had been modernised and was white with red tiles on the floor. The door to the playground was locked. The bolt slid easily but hit the stopper rattling the glass door.

I walked silently outside, breathing the cool evening air. The gate was closed. Shall I go back? I looked at the steamed-up classroom window above and then reached for a branch of a tree near the wall. I kicked a few times against the slippery bark, then I was up on the wall and saw the light of the village in the distance.

I jumped and landed on the cobbles of the road below. The noise seemed to echo along the wall. My heart was thudding, and I felt so excited I had to have a pee against the mossy wall. Then I started to run on the cobbled uneven road going downhill towards the ford, slowly at first, gaining speed in the semi-darkness, legs spinning almost out of control. I reached the ford splashing in the icy shallow water. The road started to climb, and I stopped, exhausted. With the noise of rushing blood in my ears, I entered the wood. I knelt on the mossy floor, breathing in the smell of the wet wood around me. Feeling cold, I ran again slowly and deliberately, wet branches slapping my face. I ran for a long time, falling and running as if in a dream. Across a field with dark soil sticking to my shoes, towards the road in the distance, passed a few rows of vines. I jumped across a ditch with heavy feet.

I walked silently on the hard road until there was no more soil under foot and my feet began to tap to a song inside my head; I happily ran over a bridge and passed a village with a barking dog and a church dark against the sky.

Just outside the village, a white house stood by the road. A lady standing against the open lit door, looked at me and said, "Hello." I answered without stopping, and she called me back. Her voice was soft with the local dialect. I turned, and she invited me inside. There were smells of cooking from the black pot on the open fire. I sat down by the fire. "You must be cold. Take off your shoes. That's it! Are you hungry? Where do you come from?" I sat silently sniffling with my head down.

"I have come from Collesalvetti…I am at the boarding school there, and I am going home."

"I see. Here, have some soup. It will warm you up. Do you want some bread? Yes?"

"Yes, please."

She left me by the fire. I placed my steaming feet close to it. I was tired and while eating the soup I closed my eyes. The door opened and a large wet dog almost knocked the bowl out of my hands. Then I saw the man. "Come here. Sit!!" said the man. He was tall and wore a cassock under an old corduroy coat. He did not look like a priest and was carrying a shotgun. "What is your name?"

"Leo," I replied.

"You came from the boarding school at Collesalvetti, yes?...I will have to take you back." The priest didn't smile, but I was not afraid; I felt safe.

I finished the soup, put the bowl on the stone sink and thanked the lady. She nodded, smiling and touched me lightly on the head. I knelt to put my shoes on, trying to stop the dog licking me. The priest showed me out of the house. It was colder now.

He told me to wait and came back out of the dark with a bicycle. The woman was at the door. He said 'goodbye' and sat me sideways on the cross bar. On the downhill road, the dog running beside us, the priest talked to me slowly in a friendly murmur. When the road started to climb, with his fast breath smelling of grappa, I started to talk. I talked about my family and my father and my cruelty to animals, my misery at being at boarding school…

It was like a confession, an open-air confession…I had been crying and my face felt raw in the wind. Then for a long time, downhill, only the purring of the free wheel and the dog's nails on the road. The priest spoke to me in a calm soft voice. I cannot recall the words; they made me feel good about myself – I felt absolved.

When we got back to the school, the tall priest, holding me by the hand, pulled the bell by the entrance – the sudden noise saddened me. I heard echoing steps getting near and the door opened. The familiar smells hit me, and I felt like running again. I looked at the face of the priest; he nodded at me; the dog licked my hand. I walked along the corridor, up the stone stairs holding the iron railing with the curl at the end.

Everyone was already in bed. I entered the large, dark dormitory and undressed in the dark. I heard a few whispers, but I did not answer. Cold in bed, before sleep came, I thought of my conversation with the priest on the bicycle, but I could only remember the feeling of it, no words, and with that feeling, I went to sleep.

Lucca

After a final escape from boarding school at Collesalvetti, I was sent back home where I spent two years before my next boarding school at Mutigliano. In that golden period, I was happy at home. I had been introduced to a priest, Don Renzo, from the Church of San Frediano. He was young, dynamic and travelled everywhere on a 'mosquito', a motorised bicycle. I learned to serve mass in San Frediano. The church was connected to a large building occupied by refugees from Pola. They lived in vast rooms, camping in makeshift little cubicles built of different colour material and blankets on ropes. Their children were friendly and spoke with a strange northern accent. It was possible to walk from the sacristy to the 'camp', and I often wandered the building taking in the smells and voices so foreign to me.

The sacristy smelled of incense and its large dark wooden wardrobe contained the richly decorated silk and linen robes for every occasion in the yearly liturgy.

I liked serving mass; I felt clever at being able to remember all the answers in Latin and the precise movements. I wore a strange black cassock with a white embroidered cape on top. I enjoyed filling the crystal bottles with water and wine and the silver cask at the end of the chain with the hot charcoal ready for the incense. I felt I belonged to the church of San Frediano, and I needed to belong somewhere. I met other children there, and sometimes we played in the empty church among the altars with darkened paintings above. We ran around Romanesque fonts and marble statues. The noise of our running echoed and drifted higher towards the shafts of light of the stained-glass windows.

Don Renzo took me with him for the benediction of the houses before Easter. We walked carrying holy water and an asperger. In a week, we visited nearly all the houses of the parish. I became aware of the myriad of different smells of each house we visited, from palace to filthy room. The smells remained in my memory connected to the climbing of stairs, the opening and closing of dark doors, the brief Latin prayer and the noise of the silver brush being immersed in the pail of holy water. The families stood stiffly to attention, and after the ceremony, they sometimes offered us biscuits and vin santo.

I went to school in Piazza Santa Maria Bianca. Mother walked me there in the morning, always in a hurry, on her way to work. In the afternoons after school, I went to the walls where I met my school friends. It was possible to climb down the 12-foot wall using holds on the bricks accessing the area where the cannons had been kept and the vast labyrinth of subterranean interconnected vaulted halls. The first time I tried to climb down the wall, I was scared and got stuck halfway. I was teased and left dangling off the mossy wall. I started to sweat, gripping the wall. Then I realised where to place my foot sideways on the adjacent wall and which hold was best. Climbing up was tougher, and it required strength. But after a few weeks, I mastered it. Some of the older children climbed down the 40 foot outside wall. I looked admiringly at the wiry bodies hugging the massive brick wall but never dared to try. Each baluard had a different shape belonging to a different quarter of the town and to a different band of children. One day, having saved pocket money for a few weeks, I managed to buy 10 metres of brand-new hemp rope. The old man in the shop measured the rope and counted aloud, sniffing and retrieving, at the last moment, the shiny drop from his nose, while the black and white cat played with the coils. The rope had a reassuring sour hemp smell.

The children liked the new rope, and we decided to use it to descend a bit of smooth wall that stopped us from reaching a vast cave-like vaulted room, which we had observed from the top of the baluard through a large grill. At night, a number of bats flew out of it.

One of my best friends, Benso, was slightly older than me. His father came from the same village in the mountains as my father. Benso lived in a house in the middle of town so he did not seem to belong to any baluard. He was tall and thin and already had a large, curved roman nose. He was slow and ponderous and had a calming effect on us. Benso and I had spent long afternoons hunting lizards on the walls of Lucca and outside at the foot of the walls. Armed with catapults, we stalked the beautiful lizards and shot at them with round pebbles. We had laboriously made the forked part of the catapult using boxwood or ash. Boxwood was easy to find. We had reached inside many ornamental hedges looking for a perfect fork of wood. When the fork had been found, we cut it with our pocket knives, peeled the bark off it and, having tied the two top branches together and created a curved shape, we gently cooked it on a fire to dry and preserve the shape. We ended up with a beautiful darkened smooth fork to which strips of rubber, from a bicycle or car, according to our strength were attached with sturdy string. A rectangular piece of leather with two holes was fixed to the other end again with string. The catapult was capable of propelling a small pebble over a hundred yards with good accuracy. I had seen children hitting pigeons on the wing with it. In retrospect, our activity was cruel and misguided, and I wonder if good advice from our peers would have curbed our hunting instincts.

We decided to find the room from where the bats came. One day, armed with the new rope and a sack of newspapers, we descended the wall leading into a shady arched area full of tall weeds. Under the arches, there was a low curved tunnel descending into a lower room in complete darkness. The earth floor was covered with rocks. Water was dripping from the ceiling, and there was a strange damp smell. We twisted many newspapers into torches and advanced to the end of the room where a small window at floor level led into the main room – its vaulted ceiling ended with the grille, which we had seen from above. The small window had the remains of rusted iron hinges to which we tied the rope. Benso was the first to descend into the room about 3/4 metres below. The rest of us followed slowly. There was a sour smell of bats and the floor was, in part, covered in grey mounds of droppings. Blinded by the shaft of light from the gate above, we lit some more torches and now we could see the bats hanging from the ceiling. They moved slowly along the cracks disturbed by our noises. We decided to light a large fire with the rest of the newspaper to which we added lots of the weeds growing on the floor. The smoke and heat rising towards the ceiling disturbed the bats that started to fly around the room and out of the grill. The fire lit on top of the droppings started to produce a thick, horribly pungent smoke and soon we were pushing each other in the semi-darkness towards the rope. I was one of the smallest in the group, and I had to wait, trying not to choke on the terrible smoke. Half way up the rope, my hands slipped, but I pushed with my feet against the wall, and with Benso encouraging me, I found myself at the top where I was grabbed and pulled over the window. We sat choking. Having used all the newspaper, we had to find our way in the dark over the rocky ground towards the entrance to the curved corridor. I got a gash from a rock and felt the blood sticking my foot to the sandal. Red eyed and choking, we reached the end of the curved tunnel and the fresh air.

Inside the walls and painted yellow, stood the cigar factory. During the summer after swimming in the canal, we used to group outside the entrance sitting on the low brick wall of the canal that crossed Lucca and looked at the hundreds of women dismounting their bicycles for the afternoon shift. They arrived in groups chatting and laughing in the summer breeze, dressed in light dresses.

They wheeled their bicycles towards a row of wooden parking slots. We sat observing the women and commented on their shape and riding styles.

The large matrons with their enormous behinds stopped slowly, placing a foot on the ground, lifting the other leg over. Then after parking the bicycle, stood pulling their trapped knickers from between their buttocks, chatting, laughing, drying sweaty faces and armpits with their handkerchiefs. The young faster girls, rode the last few metres standing on one pedal and skipped lightly off the bicycle.

We had our favourites, and we got to know them by the nicknames we gave them. One of them 'La Pupporona' was very slim and dark but had enormous breasts. She stood combing her dark hair holding pins in her mouth, her breasts almost jumping out of her dress with every stroke of the comb. She often waved and smiled at us. 'Nilla Pizzi', named after a singer of the time, always arrived singing the latest song. We heard her before she turned the corner. Then we had 'La Signora Pelo' – she had the hairiest legs and bushes of dark hair under her armpits.

Looking after the bicycle was Golia, an old man wearing a cyclist's hat, a Toscano cigar between his lips. We called him 'Golia' because he was always ready to offer us kids small dark liquorice drops wrapped in twisted paper called 'Golia'. He had a tool kit in the seat of a chair and repaired punctures and small breakages in the shade of a plane tree. Golia was an expert at sniffing saddles. "I can tell everything about a girl from sniffing her saddle," he announced wheeling a bicycle and quickly bending for a sniff. "This one is still a virgin, sweet as milk." He encouraged our little group to try the saddles and we did, running from one to the other looking for our favourite. "This one is always wet; I bet you anything she is not wearing knickers," Golia would say laughing knowingly.

We sat on the ground playing marbles trying to catch a glimpse of the girl without knickers. Golia was in love with the 'widow' – a mature large lady always dressed in black and sad looking. Her hair was black and pulled into a bun. Golia said she had lost her husband in Russia. The widow never rode with the other girls, and Golia was always ready to take her bicycle, bowing and smiling. When the widow had gone through the gate, he would lovingly and knowingly sniff the shiny saddle. "The best, the best," Golia would announce winking at us. He would prop the widow's bike against his chair and got jealous if we tried to sniff it! "This is special, only for me. Have a Golia," he would say.

Sometimes on Sundays, after long hours of washing of floors and ritual cleaning, Mother would take my sister and me by train to Viareggio. We always went to the same establishment, Bagno Balena. Mother knew the lady owner, a fat lady with gold teeth, always shouting! When Mother and Sister slept in the shade of the umbrella, with other little boys I squeezed under the wooden floor of the raised changing rooms, and crawling on the cool sand, we looked through the gaps in the floorboards of the various cabins. We waited for ladies to change and had great views from below of big bottoms, bushy pussies and bouncy tits. That, roughly translated, is how we described them but also 'culone pelose' – big bottom hairy ladies. Sometimes we got the giggles, but we couldn't laugh too loud. We also had to be careful that the sand on the ladies' feet did not drop on our eyes through the gaps. Some of the boys said they were frightened by the view of such hairy ladies, but I liked them. They had something animal like and powerful that appealed to me.

One day that summer, I invited a girl a few years younger than me into my bedroom and asked her to take her knickers off. She did so giggling, and I looked at her and briefly touched her fanny with a hesitant finger. Later on that evening, a very large irate mother demanded to see me, and I thought she was going to squash me with her tits. She stood so close! Mother was horrified, and when she asked me why I had done such a thing, I found I could not explain. "I just did it," I said.

Lucca had a large population of unhinged people. I always had a fascination for crazy people, probably recognising in them some of my own madness.

Carretto was a middle-aged gentleman looking like a clerk and always neatly dressed. I had been told by other children that if you shouted 'Carretto' (cart), the man would go berserk. I experienced the transformation myself when one day after we spotted Carretto and shouted his name, he leapt in our direction brandishing an umbrella and shouting obscenities against our mothers and sisters. He never seemed to recognise us at other times and behaved as any respectable middle-aged gentleman till the triggering word. I asked but never found out why he behaved that way.

Troncausci (or door breaker) was the local prostitute. She was thin and pathetic looking and always wearing very red lipstick and a feathered hat. She walked slowly and after shouting 'Troncausci' at her, she would immediately retaliate by shouting always the same words at us. "You are nothing but dust, tuberculotic sons of whores." And she repeated the insult over and over again till she calmed down and resumed her slow walk. Once we called her 'Troncausci' in the cinema and she stood up and repeated the same words against us, unconcerned by the rest of the audience trying to make her sit down.

Slow witted and full of tricks, Elfo was the son of an ice cream shop owner and, with little persuasion from us, he would shout at the top of his nasal and distorted voice, the praises of cunnilingus and other sexual practices. If we asked him, he would start touching women in the street, darting surprisingly fast from one to another, touching a breast, a bum with mad eyes and tongue out of his mouth.

Bandoni was a social security clerk. He was very thin with a black moustache, always dressed immaculately with grey spats and endowed with great strength. He was always expounding his strength and virility. I heard amazing stories about him – the time when he single-handed moved a huge filing cabinet that four men had not been able to budge. Or the time when, in the local brothel, he made love to six different girls. He could beat anybody at arm wrestling. We looked admiringly at the little dark man moving fast and lightly in his grey spats.

Enrico, a boy older than me, kept rats as pets. Having trapped them by the canal outside the abattoir, he tyrannised over them, torturing and experimenting on them and calling every person he met 'talpone' – rat. He kept them in bird cages. It was terrible to see them standing up, their little hand-like paws on the bars. Enrico injected them with evil concoctions. We all thought he was mad. A few years later, I met Enrico again. He had heard of my passion of sport and exercise and invited me to his house to look at his new set of weights. His mother opened the door; she looked tired and waved towards Enrico's room without speaking. He was on his bed reading a body building magazine. He looked hot and excited. In the middle of the room stood a new shiny steel bar, the discs painted black. I looked admiringly and tried to guess the weight of the set, maybe 70–80 kilograms? I approached the bar and put on my hands on the cold steel. Enrico jumped towards me and removed my hands. "No, no you are going to damage it," he shouted.

"What?" I said. "Don't you use it? Why do you have it?"

"Oh, I don't want the discs to rub together and scratch the paint. Also, the bar will rust." He had grabbed a cloth and was rubbing the steel where my hands had touched. I heard later that he suffered from depression and ended up in Maggiano, the local mad house. 'Jesus' was a longhaired character living in a cabin in a wood and occasionally came to town. He was a vegetarian and his leather sandals showed very dirty feet with long claw-like nails. He wore a sort of woollen robe in summer and winter. He always recognised me and patted me on the head. He spoke in a loud voice about his apostles and his miracles as if he really thought he was Christ.

Magua was a man with a strange twisted smile always riding a lady's bike. He called himself a Puntatore (pointer). He spoke with a distorted voice through almost closed lips. He wore a raincoat over trousers with an open front and without underpants. He hung around crowded places and having partly opened his raincoat, would point his penis to ladies' behinds during processions or festivities. He had been beaten, even arrested on several occasions, but he carried on 'pointing'. He told us children, with a sad smile on his twisted face, that he had started to go 'pointing' outside Lucca. He was too well known here.

Carts pulled by horses with large wooden barrels on top were often to be seen in town, emptying the septic tanks of Lucca. Bottino was one of the men doing the dire job. He was often to be seen in the area of San Frediano where I lived. He was a small man dressed in rags. Very animated, he would speak to every passer-by. He would light a fire in a metal basket under the cart to disguise the smell and then, still laughing and joking, he would try to lift the round stone manhole giving access to the tank. Many times, he would beg men passing, to give him a hand. Bottino's expertise was in his ability to judge the maturity of the liquid in the tank. He would immerse a very long bamboo pole ending in a wooden bucket in the tank, and after mixing it, he would retrieve the bucket and dipping a finger in the mixture, pass it rapidly along his lips with a sucking sound before pronouncing aloud his judgement. *"Come caate bene a Lucca* (how wonderfully you shit in Lucca)." Then with really deft movement, still laughing and joking, he would empty the tank slowly into the barrel on the cart and then drive outside the walls to the farms for the contents to be used as fertiliser – as it had been done since medieval times.

Piazza Dell'Amfiteatro is a wonderful oval amphitheatre that had, through the centuries, become inhabited. Roman arches and columns had been bricked up and houses built on the terraces. Only very little marble remains were visible. The amphitheatre square was used as a fruit and vegetable market and inhabited by the Piazzaioli (people of the square), a derogative term for the merchants and sellers filling the square with carts and stalls full of the produce of the season. They were a colourful lot and had a reputation for violence and drunkenness and were considered socially inferior. The king of the Piazzaioli was Castagnino, a tall, handsome man with curly hair, a moustache and a red kerchief around his neck. He was very dark and dressed like a gypsy. He always had a toscano cigar in his mouth. He had a reputation for being a fantastic fighter and always carried a knife in his sash. He looked like Clark Gable in *Gone with the Wind*. Many of the women in Piazza Dell'Amfiteatro had kids by him, and you could tell his progeny by the flashing eyes, dark skin and curly hair. Once I saw him in a fight. I had just handled a prickly pear from one of the stalls and got painful stinging hair in my fingers. I was trying to bite them off when I heard some agitated voices coming from near the fountain. Castagnino was surrounded by three men; swear words were exchanged. One of the men grabbed Castagnino by the throat from the back. In a flash, he elbowed the man in the stomach and floored him. A few more punches and the other two men went down. The cigar had remained in his mouth. He then elegantly took his red kerchief off, approached the fountain, drank from his cupped hand and wiped his lips, winking at the crowd. I saw the magnificent Castagnino in the course of many years, getting old, grey and somehow shrinking and always wearing his red kerchief, his cigar between his lips, the fierce defiant look never left his eyes.

Ruffo was a short, thickset man with an enormous nose in charge of the few parked cars in the square where the Banca Toscana stood. He acted very politely, almost deferently to every client, bowing and cleaning windows, expecting a tip. My friend Nino, the son of a Sicilian policeman, and I enjoyed teasing Ruffo. Nino's father was very cruel and, as a punishment, used to handcuff Nino to an iron bed in a room of his house overlooking the Piazza San Michele. He told me that, after many hours, to relieve the frustration and boredom he would masturbate again and again till his penis bled. Nino and I would vent our frustration at Ruffo. '*Non ce l'ai*' (you haven't got one), we would shout hiding behind cars. Apparently, he was very well endowed and could not stand the affront of our taunting. On one occasion, after our usual shouting and having tried to catch us, he ran with his strange shuffle into the entrance to the bank where he kept a chair and a few possessions.

He came out exhilarated, brandishing a painted piece of wood in the shape of a large penis with a red head. Ruffo ran around the parked cars, shouting, "Bring your mother, bring your sister and I will show you." A local lady, having witnessed his antics reported him to the bank, and he had to give up his wooden toy. Why were we so cruel to the poor man? We drove him mad with our ways! We lit newspapers under the cars, and once, we found a dead cat and put it underneath the cushion on his chair inside the entrance to the bank. After a few days, having spied from behind cars, we noticed people entering the bank covering their noses. Only poor Ruffo did not notice the rotting cat under his cushion. One day, we came back for a dose of power at Ruffo's expense, and after shouting our usual taunts, he chased us and got out of his jacket a folded piece of cardboard in the shape of a large penis beautifully painted. Years passed, and Nino and I remained friends. One summer, after swimming in Viareggio, we drove back to Lucca in Nino's new Citroen looking for a place to have lunch, and looking for a parking space, we arrived at Ruffo's square. He was still there looking grey and came out smiling and shuffling. His face clouded for an instant as he recognised us, but he smiled again and greeted us. We patted him on his shoulder and laughed, apologising for our past ways. I could not resist asking him if he still had his folded cardboard. He looked at me with his sad eyes and said, "I don't need it anymore!"

La Maestra

I ran with the sound of my studded sandals on the black and red tiles of the corridor towards the glass door on the left. I opened it and smelled the classroom.

"Always the same, always late, go and sit," said the teacher with a raucous voice among the chuckles of some children.

I sat at the single desk at the back of the class. I kept my head down looking sadly at the familiar names scratched on the pale wood of the desk, smelling the ink in the white inkwell. The teacher stood up from her desk and went to the blackboard. She began to write rapidly, making a scraping noise. Her blue pleated skirt bouncing with every movement of her arm, uncovering her tense muscular calves.

She wrote for a long time. I listened to the scratching sound of the chalk on the blackboard and the bells of the church nearby. It was nearly summer. I began to daydream, looking outside the window at the grey wall of the palace opposite, counting the pigeons on the roof in the sunshine.

I thought of running on the grass outside the walls of Lucca. I ran for a long time till, out of breath, I fell in the long grass, and I lay on my back looking at the ever-changing shapes of the clouds.

The iron fingers of the teacher around my ears brought me back to the class with a jerk. I was made to stand and was guided towards the teacher's desk. She sat down, adjusted and patted her skirt with rapid movements and signalled to me to come nearer. She grabbed my ear again and pulled me towards her. I felt the warmth of her thigh through the skirt against my naked leg.

Although my head was kept pulled to one wide, I managed to see my marks on the register before she closed it with a thump. They were bad! The teacher let go of my ear and began to dictate to the class a series of numbers to be divided. She wrote them for me too, on the back of a used orange office envelope. Being so near to the teacher, I noticed she was sweating and had dry white saliva at the corners of her fleshy mouth. "Here it is, do these divisions for me," she whispered to me almost gently, then she shouted to the class, "Do not dare to raise your eyes from the paper. You've got fifteen minutes."

I began to divide the numbers on the orange envelope, but I soon got distracted and wanted to look at what was written on the other side. "You are already in trouble, aren't you? How many times have I shown you how to divide, but you cannot do it yet!" The teacher spat the words into my face with a sickly breath through her sparse yellow teeth. I did not answer; I knew what was going to happen now; it had happened before.

The cool hand of the teacher was on my thigh. She moved under my shorts, wriggled through my pants and found my shrunken testicles and slowly, almost gently began to squeeze them. She seemed to follow the tension of my body and my breathing and stopped always before it got too painful. I felt waves of nausea rising towards my stomach. I had tears in my eyes, and I could not see the numbers on the orange envelope. "Come on, write," the teacher whispered holding me close to her. "Why don't you write," she said touching the pencil I kept under my sweating hand flat on the desk.

With an overpowering desire to vomit, I ran from the desk with shaky legs, reached the glass door and left without closing it. In the toilet, I threw up soaked bread and caffe latte into the squatty bowl, splashing on my sandals and white socks.

I put my hot forehead on the marble windowsill of the open window. Outside, the swallows had arrived and were building their nests of shining soft mud between the dry, grey, dusty beams of the school roof.

Mother asked me many questions about what happened on that day. When I eventually told her, she got furious. She spoke to the headmaster, having learnt from other mothers what the teacher had done to their children and got her expelled from the school.

I saw the teacher again in the street in Lucca. I had heard she had started to work from home as a dressmaker. I always crossed the road when I saw her; she stared at me with a nasty smile on her face.

La Pieve

Nearly every summer for a few months, I was sent to live in Garfagnana with Auntie Barbara. I remember those months of joy away from school and the women in my family.

The smell of the first fires in the cool air of the evening, the bells of the cows walking back to the stables among the tall medieval buildings towards the courtyard of the Fosciana. They were a large family living in a medieval fortified farm at the edge of the village. The entrance was dark like a cave and protected by an enormous door with iron studs.

The Fosciana children were large and smiling. We played in the tall barn, jumping on the hay in the dust, kissing girls and fighting boys, stopping only when out of breath to rest on the hay, eating apples. The girls smelled of milk and wood smoke.

One morning, a runaway horse came galloping from the mill. I could hear the shouts of the people following it. Amidst the noise of the hooves on the cobblestones, the horse appeared around the iron cross bend, frothing at the mouth and trailing his harness and chains. I stepped into the road without thinking – I was going to stop him! Auntie Barbara shouted for me to get out of the way. The horse approached. I was in the middle of the road, and I knew I could stop him. He stopped a few feet away from me, his eyes dark and wild, his mouth covered in white lather, his sweet-smelling breath heavily on my face. They grabbed his reins from behind and turned him towards the mill.

I got more confident after that, and it led to one day when, strangely and miraculously I thought I had become omnipotent. Just before I went to Auntie in Garfagnana, Mother gave in and bought me a cap gun with a rotating cylinder and a leather holster. I adored that gun and spent hours polishing it. I loved putting the shiny copper caps onto the spikes of the cylinder and the noise and smell when firing them. I showed off my gun to the children of La Pieve, especially Franco who showed a lot of envious interest. He asked me what came out of the barrel when I fired, and I explained that fragments of the cap shot out and could hit anything you aimed at. He seemed unconvinced, went inside the mill and got an apple and placed it on a low wall. "Hit it," he said. I aimed the pistol, other children stood around covering their ears. I fired and quickly ran to the apple, managing to make a dent on the skin with one of my nails. When I showed the apple to Franco, he looked almost convinced. "Let me try," he said. He fired several shots, and naturally, there were no marks left on the apple. He looked at me admiringly as he handed me back the pistol. Later on, our little group went to the river. Franco had always been very good at throwing stones. He placed several flat ones on top of each other and offered me a round stone. "See if you are as good at throwing stones," he said challenging me. It was warm from the sun and heavier than I had expected. I threw it, and I felt as if it would hit the target even before it left my hand. It did and I was almost as incredulous as the other children. They cheered. Even Franco patted me on the shoulders. Later, we roamed along the river and all threw stones at various targets, trees, large rocks, and I always hit them. They all looked at me in surprise. I had never been good at anything before, and by now, I felt invincible! On a low bridge higher up river, there was a long reinforcing rod spanning the arch. Franco started to go across on his hands suspended over the stony shallow river. Halfway across, he started swaying, lost his grip and, amongst our shouts, fell in the water. We laughed, and he sat on the riverbank removing his wet tennis shoes. "Try it," he shouted at me, his face red and cross. I knew I was not as strong as Franco, but today, I was invincible! I reached for the iron rod and started to cross on my hands. I found a rhythm and moved along quite well, the rough, rusty bar hurting my fingers. I reached the middle under the bridge, the bar bent slightly with my movement. The smell of the river and the noise was stronger here. I stopped to catch my breath then carried on. I heard the children cheer. I knew I would do it! My fingers started to open, but with my last bit of strength, I managed to reach the soft mud bank on the other side amongst the shouts of the children. I wish my day of omnipotence lasted, but the next day, I became a mortal again.

Once by the river, I stood on the jagged bottom of a green broken bottle sticking out of the gravel. I stood there not daring to look, having heard the grinding of the glass deep in my heel. Blood was pouring on the sand. I walked home leaving red marks on the trail. I was rushed to the chemist shop where the old pharmacist stitched the gash and told me how brave I had been.

On another occasion, with Mother and Father by the river on a hot heavy day, while playing, I ended up in the water. I stumbled, did not shout for help and was gently carried away. The noise of rushing water, the peace of the scene broken only by the splashes and shouts of my father grabbing my body! The coughing, spitting and shaking my back on the hot stones, I was almost sorry for having been taken from such a peaceful ride.

Uncle Ado had been telling Auntie Attilia in front of me, of how her brother, Ismaele, had spent a fortune ordering his new shotgun from Florence. One evening, Ismaele arrived at Uncle Ado's house while I was in the garden playing with the pigs in the pen. I put sticks up their noses while they were eating – they seemed to like it at first. It was difficult to aim at their nostrils, as they never stopped twitching their noses. When both sticks had been inserted, the pigs had difficulties in breathing while eating and would become annoyed and squeal, jumping around the pen.

Uncle opened the door to an excited Ismaele. He was carrying a long cardboard box, which he put on the kitchen table as we stood around. He removed the top and there, wrapped in brown paper, was the shotgun, blued and shiny with the wood beautifully marked. Ismaele opened the gun and made Uncle Ado and me look inside the shining barrels smelling of oil. The gun closed and opened with a series of lovely clicks like a well-oiled bolt.

Coffee was made and the gun was left in the open box on the table. I touched the cold blue steel, the gold bead at the end of the barrel, the smooth wood and sharp chequering. They drank the coffee and all three of us walked towards the river. There was a tree near the iron crucifix by the mule track that led to the mill, that Auntie Barbara called *L'Albero Degli Uccelli* – the bird's tree. It was an old yew tree and every evening became home to flocks of birds when the light faded. We approached the tree and Ismaele broke open the shotgun and loaded two red shells. He stood against the fading light, aiming the shining gun at the dark mass of the tree full of singing birds. There was a boom and a yellow flash from the gun, then silence and ringing in my ears. Ismaele stood looking up, the gun smoking in his hands, birds falling slowly from branch to branch at his feet, drops of blood black against his white shirt, the noise of the shot still echoing in the hills.

While hunting by a lake near La Pieve Isamele looking in the rushes for a duck he had shot was bitten by a rat. He got leptospirosis and died in hospital a few days later.

Uncle Ado lived in the house that my Grandfather Pietro had built on returning from Glasgow where he had emigrated with my Granny Egidia at the turn of the century. He had gone to Glasgow to meet a small group of men from Garfagnana already working there. Pietro was a small man with strong arms, weak legs and a handsome wife taller than himself. I have a yellowing photo of them in their best clothes staring stiff and startled at the camera. Grandpa Pietro had polio as a child and to avoid him collapsing on his weak legs had been kept in a barrel so he could hold himself upright. His legs remained weak and his arms got stronger.

He never learned to speak English properly. They spoke a sort of language mixing English and Italian and Italianised English words – so 'pictures' became 'piccette' and 'fish supper' was 'fisopa'. They worked hard, had four boys and saved money.

When there was a fight with the local rough crowd in Gowan, Pietro was called and brandishing an empty beer crate, re-established order. Eventually, they had their own fish and chips and ice cream shops and returned to Pieve Fosciana rich.

My father and Uncle Beppe were the only ones of the four who did not go to school in Glasgow, therefore, never learned English. The house Grandpa Pietro built looked towards the mountains and was one of the largest in the village. It smelled of apples and wood polish. I never met Grandpa; he died of typhoid after eating too many wild strawberries in the woods shortly after returning to Italy.

Granny Egidia, his wife, was the illegitimate daughter of a sea captain from Garfagnana and an oriental lady. He brought back his daughter and Auntie Barbara's family, the Franchi, adopted her. Barbara lived in Pieve Fosciana in a small pink house near the chestnut wood overlooking the river. The previous stone house had been destroyed by an earthquake and had been rebuilt by Barbara's brother, mainly out of wood.

Auntie Barbara had spent a few years in Brazil as a nanny to a rich family from Pieve and had been to Scotland and looked after the children of a relative from the village.

From the house, I wandered down the mule track to the wood looking for insects, hairy colourful caterpillars and lizards.

At the bottom of the sloping wood, there was a mill, then the river. The mill was cool and dark under the great chestnut. The water ran fast and silently into the cavernous opening under the mill house to the wheel. The rumble of the stone mill seemed to come from inside the earth. The sweet smell of still warm chestnut flower filled the hall. The miller was a tall, fair man with bushy eyebrows and was always covered in a film of flour, giving him a ghostly appearance. He had a large family and one of the boys Sandro, Franco's brother, was older than me, tall and muscular and had already driven the horse and cart to Castelnuovo by himself.

In the long afternoons, after lunch, I would say 'goodbye' to Auntie Barbara who was grumbling, busy washing up in front of the stone sink and, having grabbed an apple, I closed the green wooden gate with a reassuring clunk. Down the cobbled street passed the house of a rich relation from Scotland with his neat landscaped garden and down the winding mule track paved with pale cobbles from the river. At the bottom, the smell of the tall buddleia bushes and the butterflies in the sunshine – the noise of the bees and the drone of the mill stone always working.

A whistle and Sandro would come. After my day of glory the year before, we became good friends. We would wander by the river and other boys would join us. Sandro was always laughing; he could throw a stone further than any of us and get shiny trout from under the boulders in the water with bare hands.

The river was clean, swift and had its own smell, different from other rivers. Its noise too seemed different, and I learned to recognise and love it. It had cut its way through ancient hills leaving behind enormous boulders bleached by the sun in its wide sandy bed.

The riverbanks had been turned into vegetable gardens, interspaced by patches of wild vegetation. Each garden had its own dry wall. The place had a great attraction for us boys. Black cherries and figs in summer, grapes, walnuts and hazelnuts in the autumn.

Franco would direct his small band of boys at will. One day, guiding us to the dike through the overflow tunnel, dark and dangerous, or to the cemetery where the parapet wall had collapsed into the river, searching among the gravel for bones, looking in vain for gold jewellery or jumping into a deep pool with a sandy bottom, hunting birds with catapults. At sunset, he would take us silently following couples courting by the river in the evening. We learned a lot from our evening expeditions and soon this became our favourite activity.

During the day, we discussed what we had seen the evening before, and we all became excited. Sandro was the final arbiter of any discussions. He had already settled questions like 'was he putting it in her navel?' and 'why do they make strange sounds as if in pain if it is supposed to be fun?' Sitting on boulders in the sun, our bare feet in the water, shouting against the noise of the rushing river, we talked for hours about the lovers we had seen. Sometimes in the afternoons, we went to a shallow cave noisy with the crickets and with the smell of wild garlic in the air. Our backs against the cool rock, we would masturbate like in a secret ritual.

I played with myself imitating the other boys, trying to conceal my red penis looking like a mushroom after my circumcision. Sandro was the only one that could come, and when he started making certain noises and moving faster, we gathered around him on our knees to see the miracle of the white liquid shooting from his penis. Thinking back, a strange ritual to witness but completely devoid of any sexual feeling; on our part, only something to witness hoping it would start to happen soon to us too.

We knew of a large lily-shaped flower that grew by the river, and we would rub the vulva-like flower on our penises till irritated by the juices of the flower, they would grow larger than normal. Intoxicated with our enlarged organs, we would roam the river like dogs on heat.

We discovered a clay bank by a tributary of the river near a spring. Naked, we wallowed in the warm, muddy water. We made holes in the soft slippery clay and made love to the earth. We created a primitive life size figure of a woman in the clay with open legs. Her nipples made of cherries and her pubic hair of moss. In turn, we made love to the warm clay, holding our bodies up not to destroy our clay goddess.

We chose enormous pumpkins from a walled garden and cut neat holes in the skin exposing the soft flesh and made love to the pumpkin – brown boys' bodies against pale pumpkin. Sandro told us to put back the plugs we had cut out of the pumpkins carefully. He said they would heal and grow again.

Infinite

I don't remember how I learned the meaning of the word 'infinite' – maybe at school or from the radio. The word entered my head, like other new words, but slowly, it started to worry me. The idea that something could be infinite, without end gave me a hollow sick feeling in my stomach. When, during religious lessons, the word became 'infinite hell', I really got worried. I learned to push the thought back by thinking quickly of something else, letting the word 'infinite' settle under the weight of other thoughts.

One hot sunny afternoon, I woke from my after-lunch sleep with the word in my head. I opened the green wooden shutters of one of the tower room windows and the heat and light entered the room, almost like a sound. I pushed the shutters against the flaking outside wall and placed my forearms and chin on the hot stone windowsill. I started to spit, slowly, onto the terrace below, trying to aim the drops of spit on one large dusty stone. *Infinite*, I thought, letting the spit fall from my lips and starting to focus on the word.

The door of the terrace below opened out slowly and the bald head of Serafino, the servant of the Guinigi family, started to turn up. I quickly stood back and went to sit on the bed. The bells of San Frediano Church started to ring, slowly as they always did on Sunday afternoon. I opened the rattling shutters of the other window facing the church and saw the golden triangular mosaic, catching the afternoon sun.

The window had a wrought iron grill, close to the wall at the top but bulging out at the bottom, like a belly. I climbed the window and sat on the ledge dangling my legs in between the bars, kicking my bare heels against the crumbling wall. I remained there suspended outside over the Guinigi garden sending flaking plaster flying over the laurels stretching below me, looking at the gravel path curving around the great magnolia tree as high as the house. I managed to close the window against my back. The air now reverberated with the noise of the bells. I shut my eyes and rested my forehead against the hot iron bars.

Again, the word 'infinite' came into my head and my throat tightened as I tried to think of something that was infinite. The stone windowsill, I was sitting on, was cracked and flaking, the iron bars rusty against my sweating hands; yet something could be infinite, lasting forever. I was now approaching the painful, yet strangely delicious moment, when having fully understood the meaning of the word I could apply it to something frightening. I tightened my grip on the iron bars and tried to think of infinite hell, often mentioned by priests as a punishment for sinners. Was I a sinner? Yes, I was. Forever, I repeated with the bells, without end. Forever and ever and ever. Slowly, rhythmically with the pounding of the bells, I beat my head against the iron bars. The thought burned in my brain till I could not bear it anymore, trembling almost without breathing holding tight onto the bars…with frightening silence, suddenly the sound of the bells stopped, and through the ringing in my ears, I heard again the cries of the swallows and the noise of the town.

I rested, my eyes closed. The window behind me rattled with the wind of the door of my room opening. "Where are you? You're not outside the window again, are you? How many times…" The window opened, I turned and Mother stood there, a glass of water in her hand, her brown eyes smiling before her mouth did. "One day, you'll fall off. Look you are covered in sweat." She touched my forehead with her cool wet hand. "Come inside, it is still too hot out there." She walked away, and I jumped back inside the room and sat on my bed drinking the water. "We are all going to the Walls for a walk and ice cream," said Mother smiling. "Get ready – okay?"

I remained on the bed, drinking the water and feeling it resurface on my skin, looking at the window through the glass in my hands. I stood up and poured water from the enamel jug into the bowl with the blue frieze of nymphs being chased by satyrs, or were they devils? I liked the noise of the water falling in the bowl. I poured it gently till it reached the necks of the nymphs – anymore water and they would drown. I washed my face and kept it in the water, then sponged my body with the large sour smelling sponge. I learned that Christ on the cross was offered vinegar to drink on a sponge like this at the end of a cane. I could tie the sponge to the cane Granny used for beating mattresses, I thought. I dried myself with the rough linen towel looking at the nymphs dancing with the water in the bowl.

The 'word' tried to resurface, but I rapidly started to count the splashes of water on the red brick tiles evaporating fast in the shaft of sunlight. I put on white stiff cotton socks with my new black patent leather shoes and a white shirt with blue shorts.

We went out into the blinding afternoon sunlight. Granny in her black Sunday best, my sister in a white and pink dress, skipping and posing and Mother in blue with blue and white matching shoes. I placed my feet carefully not to scratch my patent leather shoes as we walked along Via Fillungo, on the shady side, the cool air coming from the open grills of the cellars at street level smelling of cats and dust. We met a few people and talked with the sound of our feet echoing on the stones. Piazza San Michele was white in the sunlight, pigeons flying in the still air. In Piazza Napoleone, few cars were competing for shade under the trees with the Carrozze – the horses were tapping the stones with pointed hooves and shaking flies from their heads deep into feeding buckets.

On approaching the walls, we felt a cool breeze rustling the leaves of the plane trees. At the ice cream parlour, we sat around a rocking aluminium table and had cassata. We ate in silence, the ceiling fan whirring overhead, the sweet sticky smell of vanilla in the air. I put my chin on the chequered tablecloth and looked at the distortion of everyone around the table through the glass of water in front of me. Outside, I pulled at my sister's dress – the chair ropes had left red welts on the back of her legs.

We ran up the sloping avenue to the walls, the huge knotted roots from the plane trees emerging from the gravel, like the tails of dragons. We stopped, panting at the top to look at the white marble lion with the curly mane, smiling benignly on top of his pedestal. Mother and Granny followed slowly, and I hid behind trees throwing pebbles at my sister. I could smell the tobacco factory – a fine film of dust had formed on my patent shoes but no scratches.

We walked past cool 'baluards' and the high walls of the prison, and I saw a guard with his rifle, smoking in his tiny turret. We descended from the wall behind San Frediano. The bells started to ring again. I covered my ears against the noise and climbed the low parapet wall followed by my sister. We descended slowly towards the huge grey and white tower.

When we got near to our house, I ran up the stairs, smelling the food cooking inside the apartments. At the top, I met Dora's husband wearing a vest and shorts, his white skinny body shaking with coughs, a cigarette butt in his mouth. He winked at me and twitched his great nose. "I am repairing the film projector," he said in a croaky voice. "I have an American cartoon to show you." He closed the door of his dark attic workshop smelling of glue and oil. Behind the wooden gate, I chased a cat to the end of the echoing corridor. I stood by the front door, one foot and my back against the wall, looking down at my dusty shoe. The 'word' came back to me but the chatter of the others climbing the stairs distracted me. I bent down and drew a cross with a finger on the dusty shoes for protection.

I read the encyclopaedia for children in my room till supper and kept the 'word' weighted down with the story of an early Polar exploration in great wooden ships, crushing ice, polar bears and Aurora Borealis.

During supper, Auntie Bice came back from the café smelling of perfume and smoke. She was in a good mood. We ate melon and a sort of a salad niçoise, and I put all the anchovies on the side of my plate. We listened to the radio at some silly play about a journey by train to Venice. Without saying 'goodnight', I went to my room. I closed the heavy wooden shutters, the garden dark below. I saw the darting shapes of the bats against the paler sky. I went to bed and turned to face the large dark wardrobe which Granny said had been built with spruce from Moscovia.

Slowly, I let the 'word' into my mind with the cool linen sheet pulled tightly against my shoulders. I let myself imagine again hell forever. I saw great devils with dark shining bodies, clawed feet and horns. They had smiles like Uncle Nanni when I saw him in the stable near the abattoir, doing 'it' with a woman in the straw. The devils were spearing poor sinners and tossing them into boiling cauldrons of oil, with pits of fire all around…the smell of burning flesh and screams of pain.

I was afraid now, sweating in the darkness, thinking about the unmitigating, relentless idea that something so dreadful could be infinite. 'Forever, forever' I repeated in my head. I was trembling, crouched in a ball, the muscles in my stomach cramped, teeth chattering.

After what seemed a long time with the hissing of my troubled breathing in my ears, I opened my eyes to face the shape of the wardrobe. I fanned the sheet to cool my sweating body and felt more calm. I was conscious that I had finally reached the core of my fear. I understood the 'word' and had no more reasons to fear something I understood and finally accepted. A feeling of tiredness and a sense of peace came over me.

Just before I fell asleep, Mother came in to kiss me goodnight. Her lips on my hot forehead! I dreamt of the marble lion with its curly mane, smiling in the sunshine.

Sometimes on Sunday, I kept Mother company. We went to the house of the Fortuna family when they were away on holiday and Mother had extra work to do. I liked exploring the huge luxurious house – the room where Raffaello kept his vast collection of shoes all highly polished and stretched flat with shoe trees; the vast fridge in the large kitchen with many cold drinks; the room where the guns were kept in racks gleaming in the darkness of the glass fronted mahogany cabinets. In the library, I sat on leather armchairs reading avidly medical books and encyclopaedias finding anatomical photos and details about sex and reproduction. My curiosity was insatiable!

My stay in Lucca did not last long. I was quite a handful, and Granny often complained she could not cope with looking after me.

I had made a blow pipe from a discarded waterpipe. Hiding behind the window of the corridor outside the front door, I chewed wads of newspaper and blew them aiming at the unfortunate passers-by. There was something satisfactory in pressing a ball of chewed newspaper neatly down the tube with my thumb. Taking a big breath, lips pressed hard against the tube opening. Taking aim, the tip of my tongue against the wet ball! Then suddenly pulling the tongue back, a hard blow of air sending the ball out of the pipe. With a hush and a thud when hitting the mark – I loved it!

One of the clients from the barbers got hit on his bald head and complained. The barber knew exactly who the culprit was. He came upstairs to talk to Granny. I was in my room sitting on the bed making round balls of newspaper ready for the next expedition. Granny caught me, and I could not deny anything. "I will tell your mother," she said, "you are incorrigible." I didn't say anything but stopped making balls. I went to the basin in the toilet and rinsed the taste of chewed newspaper out of my mouth.

Later, hoping Granny would have cooled down a bit, I approached her. She was in the kitchen shelling beans. "Can I do it?" I said.

"You can," she said coolly, "but I still will tell your mother." I shelled, for a while, the squishy light beans accumulating in the bowl. When I finished, I approached Granny again. She was washing greens in the marble sink. I put my arms around her wet apron.

"Come on, Granny, please don't tell Mother," I begged. She shook my arms off her waist and turned.

"I will. You never learn. You are impossible."

I left the kitchen, just behind the door by the open window stood Granny's Singer hand sewing machine, sitting in a mahogany box shining in the sun. "Promise me you won't tell Mother or I will throw the sewing machine out of the window," I shouted.

"I will tell her," she shouted back, her worried face looking around the door. On an impulse, again as if someone else had made the decision for me, I picked up the heavy box, stood it on the windowsill and let go. It balanced, and I almost hoped it would stay there. Then it slowly disappeared, following by a crash and a metallic ding on the stone courtyard below. I looked down. Serafino, the servant of the Count Guinigi, came out of the kitchen rubbing his hand on his apron looking up. The smashed broken box showing the shattered cast iron body of the machine! Granny stiff and pale stood beside me, looking down. She was speechless! That was how I ended up in Mutiliagno.

Mutigliano

Mutigliano was an agricultural school, which was founded to take the orphans of WWI and the odd disturbed child like me, and there was an eagle there.

My first memory of Mutigliano was the sight of the iron cage with the green bars showing red bubbles of rust, and inside, the eagle on her olive wood perch sadly preening and picking with her great yellow beak at her scaly clawed feet. The rancid smell of her droppings against the back wall of her cage, like an abstract painting, and through the bars, sight of the pinewoods and the olive trees on the distant hills.

We were taken twice a week, marching down the dusty road, bordered with cypress trees, to the woods where there was a sort of a shrine with columns topped by marble eagles and slabs with heroic poems dating from the First World War. Some of us played football on a clearing by the stream. I preferred to explore the woods looking for newts in the ponds and learning to recognise mushrooms. One of the boys caught a mouse and kept it in his pocket, feeding it bread. I nearly swapped it for an electric torch, but the mouse died before the exchange.

It was autumn, and the boys knew how to recognise mushrooms, which we grilled on sticks on an open fire. Using wild rye grass, we made long snares and caught the black and yellow salamanders with red crests from the ponds. The first time we went to the woods, I found myself wandering with an older boy called Mario, along the shallow stream. We took our shoes off and looked for fish and water snakes. The stream smelled of hidden damp places and fish.

My companion was friendly, although I noticed he had a strange fixed smile showing darkened teeth and close together eyes. On our return, there were smirks and nudging from the other boys. I understood that Mario had a predilection for boys and preyed on the new children. I hated to be derided by the children and before sleeping, cried at the injustice of the situation. The news of my adventure must have reached the grown-ups looking after us.

One evening, I was ordered, together with Mario, to clean the small cinema that was under the dormitory building. It was used at weekends by the villagers for film shows. I found myself becoming suspicious of the open projection slot. I felt as if somebody was observing us. The air was full of dust as we moved along the rows, lifting wooden seats, sweeping the floor full of debris from the night before.

"You know," I shouted over the sound of the seats being lifted, "the boys have been teasing me over our walk together by the stream. They have been saying, you know…that we did things together. You know it's not true. You should tell them."

He gave me his fixed smile and bent to pick up a cigarette end to be smoked later. We continued to lift seats and sweep in silence. I was sure the hidden observer had heard our conversation.

There was a bakery with a wonderful wood oven where the bread for the school was made by the children. Focaccia was made too, if you had money or you could barter. It tasted fantastic dripping in olive oil!

Near the bakery was a small cobbler room operated by the older boys. The shoes made there, for our use, had high leather lace-up top nailed to a wooden clog. I often went there to gossip and to cut with shears the long thin strip of metal from used tomato cans, which was rested against the leather then nailed to the wood.

We had an ambulance with a faded red cross from WWI, which used to make errands to Lucca and a large cart with a grey horse to take the produce to the town. We made wine, oil and cheese and had a large chicken pen.

Once a week, on Saturday, we collected our kit and towels from the dormitory to have a shower. We changed in a room full of logs which were used to heat the water in the boiler in the next room. I used to hate to show my circumcised penis looking like a pink mushroom, and I quickly wrapped the towel around me on the way to the showers.

We had a barber's shop in a wooden building with a grand sign Barbitonsore. A dentist armed with a pedal drill would torture us in the same room, once a month. The cooking was done by nuns in the building where the girls and young children lived. The wardens ate with us in a long refectory room on a raised platform at the end and had tablecloths and good food. We had marble tables and one litre of wine amongst eight children but rotten food.

There was a prison room under the chapel – Heaven and Hell! Mass in the morning and prayers in the evening were the most boring times.

An American friend of my mother's gave me a flying jacket with real sheepskin inside but with a manmade outer. I spent the time in church chewing on the cubes of sugar always in my pocket and dreaming my jacket was leather and I had a good pocket knife. Mother was coming to visit me every Sunday. She brought me eggs, one kg of sugar cubes in a blue box and a salami. She arrived on a bicycle, her black hair frosted in winter and dusty in summer. As I saw her, I felt self-conscious in front of the other boys.

I remember the sounds of the bells on Sunday. A sad sound coming with the wind from the village, sometimes missing a toll like my heart missing a beat! Why did Sunday have to sound so sad?

The boys at the school, mostly orphans from WWII, were a tough bunch. We were made to work in the fields digging, sowing and pruning. When I joined, the school was involved with the reclaiming of a few acres of hill and rock, clearing the forest and digging the rocks. In the vineyard, along the vines we used a spade shaped like an elongated heart with a stirrup on the side of the long wooden handle and capable of lifting long sods of soil that would be turned in the furrow green side down. The children were tough, and you had to fight to be respected. When I first arrived, tall and thin and not used to physical work, I got soundly beaten by some of the boys, some quite a bit smaller than me. I realised that work made you stronger, so when we were made to work, I worked harder. Every day, using the branch of a tree near a wall in the main square, I pulled myself up, becoming stronger. Soon I could look after myself and that made me feel more confident. When Mother started to come with a man she had met on holiday after separating from Father, some of the boys, and in particular a tall hard boy, made some remarks. We fought by the toilets for a long time. I was determined to win, and although I had received bruises on my face, I managed to throw a good punch on the boy's face. I saw the look of surprise before he collapsed, unwilling to fight any longer. I became popular after the fight and was accepted.

One of the tasks of every agricultural student was to collect insects, still very ubiquitous before the spreading of pesticides. We were given cardboard boxes, pins, labels and ether in a small glass bottle with a conical cork. We used this to anaesthetise the various captured insects and butterflies before pinning them on the boxes and labelling them. The smell of ether repulsed and attracted me. I started to sniff it secretly before falling asleep. I would put a few drops on a handkerchief and smell it long and deep. Sickly, revolting, delicious waves and tingles of pleasure reaching to my brain in an almost suffocating feeling. Then sleep, deep and sound blissful sleep. After that, I felt sick in the morning. It took a lot of will power to stop, having realised the addictive side of ether.

In the middle of the square was a squat marble column with a bronze eagle on the top. The inscription started with, *'Degno figlio di una stirpe prode e di una millenaria civiltà'*. The column stood on a tall plinth with four corner posts and a cannon on the side. You were considered strong when you could tilt the cannon forward using the handles it had on the front. I felt really strong when I managed to do it the first time.

We were punished for misbehaving by having to stand to attention on top of the main square columns of the monument, sometimes for hours. I spent a long time freezing or in the summer heat on top of those columns. One day, it was so windy that it was impossible to stand there so I was made to stand in the courtyard at the back instead.

We had a swimming pool with a net mounted on rails that would be used to limit the access to the deep water. I remember the excitement of the first day in summer when the pool was cleaned, then filled with water. The sound, the colour, the smell of the water, the exhilaration of that first immersion!

They decided to give us a uniform – a dark grey suit, sombre and smart. We spent long hours being fitted, but it took so long for the uniforms to be ready that most of us had outgrown them.

We saw a film called *Ivanhoe* and started to make wooden swords using the natural wide fork of an ash branch as a guard. With careful shaping and flattening with our penknives, they looked very realistic. We had long battles in the woods divided under different leaders. We were considered dead only when touched by the swords in a vital place. There were many arguments about this and often an argument was settled with fisticuffs.

I started to read books from the library mainly by Emilio Salgari, a writer very famous in Italy in the 40s. He wrote exciting adventures set in Victorian times in India and the Far East. I heard later that he wrote the books without ever leaving Italy. He gathered all his information from encyclopaedias and history books. The descriptions were vivid and colourful and helped me to forget my time at the boarding school. According to the last book quickly passed around, we became pirates or members of a secret Hindu sect killing with Kryssses. Names like Sandokan, Tremannaik, Kammamury still remind me of the daring adventures of the *Pirates of Malaysia*, one of my favourite books!

We were taken to see the Tour of Italy, which passed near Lucca that year. We waited in the heat, perched on a sloping grass verge on a bend of the Via del Brennero. Preceded by an open Lancia with officials and motorbikes with loudspeakers, the tour passed by in a multitude of coloured jerseys, the hissing noise of hundreds of freewheels. I saw Coppi, Bartali, Magni, Bobet, Koblet. The fantastic names so often heard on the radio went flashing by.

After that back at school, we drew circuits with chalk on concrete or scratched them in the gravel. We polished the bottom of bottle tops and pushed inside the faces of our heroes cut out of newspapers. We played for hours, flicking the bottle tops along the circuits and missing a turn if we flicked out of the circuits. I was always Bartali and my bottle top had pressed into it a portrait of his Roman-like face cut out of a colour magazine.

During agricultural practice, we were sent digging in the orchards or turning for hours the centrifugal handle of the machine that separated the cream from the milk. Then turning the churn barrel and finally pushing the golden butter in wooden forms with old designs of cows and milkmaids, which imprinted on the butter blocks. The smell of rennet and fresh cheese around us! We had to scrape the inside of huge wooden wine barrels and wash them, our eyes streaming from the strong smell. We also cleaned the large chicken pens, sucking fresh laid eggs as a reward. We pushed red and white cockerels together inciting them to fight. We got drunk on sweet new wine in the autumn on our return to school.

To warm ourselves on winter nights before going to bed, we made a long line of children holding each other firmly by the hand, and we ran in a straight line as fast as we could. The lead child would suddenly swerve sending the last few children flying in the air, amidst general laughter. After that, we went to our freezing dormitory, well warmed.

We had an odd bunch of teachers. The art teacher was a short, fat middle-aged lady that patiently taught us drawing and geometry. She was a stickler for precision and in a monotonous voice she would say, "First, you have to square the paper with the dividers pinned on the corner of the paper, draw a quarter of a circle then connect with a line the edges of the circles to create a frame." Our artistic and geometric skills were judged on how well we framed the paper. We sometimes approached the desk at the same time and the short lady would become frightened and would squeal 'bambini, bambini' in a falsetto voice, much to our delight. One of our favourite pastimes was to make a plane with a folded paper, set it on fire, before sending it flying towards the desk.

We had a music teacher that put us off music forever. He was blind, the skin behind his dark glasses puckered and greenish. We heard that it had been caused by some explosion during the war. He knew exactly where we sat and could tell if we moved places by rapidly calling a name and expecting an answer, which he would check on his Braille map of the classroom. We had to painfully read musical notes while moving our hands in solfeggio waiting for the inevitable clout if we made a mistake. We never learned much music or to play any instruments.

The history teacher was thin and tall with skinny legs. During my first lesson, she accused me of having made a rude remark, and although I tried to explain my innocence, she never forgave me. She used to stare at me with grey cruel eyes, reminding me of an adder we found under a stone by the stream.

The teacher of Italian was great fun, tall, fat and jolly. He taught us Shakespeare and Dante and made it interesting. He was preoccupied with his weight and weighed his food and his poo. We had fun asking him how much it had weighed that morning. He would answer seriously checking the small book he carried full of his strange calculations. He told us that one day after a binge of tuna and beans, he had an explosive accident before sitting on the toilet and splashes of shit had reached the ceiling.

The French teacher was dark and very shapely, and I was in love with her. She told me she thought I was disturbed because my writing sloped to the right and I stood too close to her when I was called to her desk. She wore tartan skirts and dark stockings. I had seen her shapely legs when hiding in the box hedge, saw her playing netball with the girls of the school. Her boobs jumping in her tight jumper! When she first arrived at the school, we all gathered around her desk to ask questions and some of us knelt under the open desk to look in between her legs. A cold windy January morning, the classroom full of smoke from the terracotta stove and the rattling window steamed up, I was looking at the French teacher standing by the stove listening to her voice reading to us in French, when she bent sideways and slowly sank to the floor having fainted. We all gathered around her. She had fallen with her legs slightly apart, her skirt lifted enough to show the pale skin of her thighs. She was breathing heavily. Before I thought of what I was doing, I lifted the heavy cloth of her tartan skirt enough to see her crotch. Her dark, copious pubic hair showing in wisps beside and through her white knickers! Her leg twitched, and I quickly covered her. We all had looked at her body silently and in wonder and now panicked and helped her to her feet. Did she realise what we had done? She gave no signs of knowing what had happened. I ran for a glass of water. She drank, combed her hair, her armpits showing patches of sweat. She started the lesson again.

The PE teacher was young and dynamic. He was also a good athlete and could jump over a metre and 70 centimetres, measured on the rope stretched between two wooden posts. We admired and envied his muscular body.

The practical agricultural teacher rode a motorbike at full speed along the uphill road to the school. I remember him arriving in a cloud of dust, red faced, flashing teeth and the largest hands I had ever seen.

The head of the school was a short elegant man with a diploma in agriculture, always wearing a suit and tie. He had one leg shorter than the other and wore a specially built shoe. He looked like the face on an old Roman coin and always patted me on the head till I got too tall for it. We had several wardens looking after us. Mr Bulian was a large man from the north, an ex-soldier. When he was in a good mood, he told us about his army days in North Africa, the black ladies he had loved and how many guinea fowl he had eaten in a single meal. He was fair but firm. In the morning, he did his exercises in the washroom before shaving and waking us up.

Mr Bianchi had been a primary school teacher and was quite keen on slapping us without much provocation.

Lucchesi had been an orphan from the First World War and spent all his life at the school. He was tall, dark and knew all the ways of the school; he could not be fooled! He still played football with us.

We had another warden who had been a boy scout. He showed us his beautiful German folding knife, the shining steel of the blade, beautifully engraved and the handle made of stag horn. Once, he wore his scout outfit, but we giggled, and he never wore it again. He was innovative and fair and open to discussing any subject with us. Unfortunately, he did not stay long.

A booklet describing the dangers of masturbation had been distributed among us, the scourges of blindness, consumption and insanity. We were scared! I had not started to abuse myself yet properly. Being circumcised, made it more difficult. We discussed the book with the boy scout teacher, and he wisely dismissed it, telling us not to worry too much. Certainly, we would not grow hair on our palms!

Sometimes I needed a day away from the noise and chaos of the school. I would announce, just before class, that I did not feel so well. I would be sent to the infirmary where I had to wait for the nun to arrive, generally red and flustered, straight from her kitchen duties. The infirmary smelled like a hospital with jars of chemicals on the shelves.

The nun would place a thermometer under my arm and, having joked at my state of health, rushed back to the kitchen. By rubbing the ampoule of mercury on my woollen plus-fours, I would bring the temperature to the required 38.5 degrees before replacing it under my arm. The nun would send me to the dormitory where I would have a full day of peace, a good book and food brought on a tray.

On one occasion, not feeling terribly well, I did the same trick and raised the mercury to the usual temperature, only to find to my surprise that when handed back to the nun it had reached 40.5. The nun was alarmed, and I was sent to the dormitory with an aspirin. Sweating profusely, I dreamed that the sheets, creased and wet on my naked body were like waves in the sea breaking all around me. There was a large threatening moon in the sky, and I somehow was inside that moon. The ridges of the sheets were like folds of wet skin and the moon was all around me, constricting and suffocating me.

That year before a maths exam, I wrote some formulas with pen and ink on my left thigh just under my shorts. They helped me during the exams, but the ink caused an outburst of painful large boils on my thigh. I had high fever and had to stay in bed and the old dream came back.

Every time I got high fever, I had the same dream. Years later, I became the friend of a young psychiatrist, the uncle of a friend of mine. During a conversation at a party, I found myself describing my recurring dream. The doctor smiled and asked me how I was delivered. I told him Mother had a difficult time and I was delivered with forceps. He nodded and smiled knowingly and explained to me that the dream was a manifestation of the subconscious feelings during my difficult birth. After that explanation, I never had the dream again.

*

One Saturday, I climbed the narrow steps of the villa where the young children and the girls lodged. The ground floor was cool with the familiar smell from the kitchen, a floor up and the smell of the nursery, a mixture of urine and talcum powder. I climbed slowly rubbing my finger in the smooth groove that generations of children had created against the wall – a narrow dirty mark all the way to the top floor. Another floor up and the smell from the girls' dormitory – a smell that always demanded my attention!

From the open window, I heard the noise of children playing, feet running on the gravel in the garden below, then the clean smell of ironing and the wide door leading to the laundry room. Inside were tall wardrobes with dark wooden cubicles all with a blue number on a white China oval tag. I was number 41 and I came here every week to collect my laundry.

That Saturday was a hot day in late June, and I was sweating, having spent the morning in the sun working on the landscaping of the new olive grove at the Montaccio. The large white table seemed to take up most of the space. My cubicle was in the right-hand corner near the floor, in the shade of the great table. Today, only Sister Domenica was there behind piles of linen, pressing clothes with the hissing large black iron filled with charcoal. She turned her red face towards me and smiled. She was stocky and rounded and almost looked like a little girl. She greeted me in her heavy jumpy staccato Venetian dialect. "Ah, Pieroni 41, how are you? I have just pressed your vests. You are really getting tall."

I tried to pass behind Sister Domenica, and I noticed that I was much taller than her. She pressed against the table to let me pass. I squeezed between her and the wardrobe, and I smelled the hot steam and the charcoal inside the great iron, mixed with the smell of her sweat.

For a long delicious moment, I felt the back of her tensing and pushing against my body. I felt excited and confused but could not move. I remained there without breathing with the blood pounding in my head. Sister Domenica put the iron on its steel base with a sharp metallic noise and having put her hands on the table she lowered her head. She pressed her soft behind slowly rhythmically against my body sending waves of pleasure through me. I put my hands around her rounded belly and breasts, and she began to breathe heavily. I saw part of her dark curly hair under her headdress, and I kissed her neck and tasted her salty sweat.

I stayed in that position a little longer my legs trembling then I moved towards my cubicle with the No. 41 blue on white in the shade. I knelt to pick up my laundry when I heard the soft light shoes of Sister Domenica near me. I turned, still kneeling and found her soft belly pushing against my face. She started to lift her black skirt, and I found myself under it in the dark. I searched with my face and my hands, and I found her coarse, wet hairs against my mouth. She parted her legs, and I started to lick her, avidly delighting in her smell. I licked her until I could no longer breathe. She pressed my head to her and tensed, trembling. She slowly relaxed and I felt the swish of her skirt passing over my head.

I slowly gathered my laundry and stood up. Sister Domenica was ironing again with her head down. She let me pass and without looking up murmured, "Please,

please do not tell anybody." Her bright eyes and red face finally turned towards me.

"I promise, I promise," I whispered, then louder, "thank you, Sister Domenica," I said with a croaking voice. I walked out towards the stairs with my bundle of laundry towards the cries of the children in the garden below.

Il Bottaccio

I heard other children speak about it; I felt I knew the way. It was early summer, and I knew I had to go!

The time came when the man looking after us children, during agricultural practice, cut his hand sawing logs on a circular saw. He had to be taken to the hospital. They said he would lose his hand. He was taken away, his face pale and worried, a cheese-cloth wrapped around his hand already turning red. The blood was never washed off the stone floor. I tried to scrape it off with the point of my clogs, but it remained there for a long time, shaped like a large question mark, dark, shining like glossy paint, to remind me of that day.

There was enough time before lunch, as our class had been dismissed. I drank from the tap in the covered courtyard where the agricultural machinery was kept. The cool water tasted of iron and gave my back teeth a sharp pain. The sugar cubes Mother brought me had made my teeth very sensitive.

I went down the long slope between the pens with the Livorno chickens white in the strong sun. I reached the vineyard and picked a cane from a row for protection. I had seen a snake there before and listened for a hissing among the long grass and the red poppy heads. It was hot and still now; the sound of the crickets was everywhere.

I walked along an overgrown lane till I reached the wood and stopped in the shade to cool down, breathing in the smell of pine pitch. I loved that smell, and I touched a long dripping line of pitch on a tree ending in a yellow soft tear that stuck to my finger. The poppy heads had stained my knees and thighs with black streaks. I climbed out of the wood, the pine needles springy under my feet and followed the path beside the crumbling dry stonewall with the darting lizards and the caper plants. I picked a wild fennel stalk and bit a piece off, keeping it in my mouth like a cigar, slowly chewing sucking on its juices.

I walked uphill for a while. A bell rang from the village at the top of the hill, a sad sound mingling with the continuous noise of the cicale in the olive trees, until I reached a narrow valley, a still place of long grasses with yellow butterflies and the smell of thyme in the air. I slid through a narrow opening beside a gate.

The farm stood ahead, silent, overgrown, a young fig tree growing out of a broken window. Part of the roof had collapsed leaving a cascade of red tiles and wood reaching to the long grass. The door was missing, and I walked inside. It was cool there, and in the shade, I saw tables and chairs peppered with woodworm holes. In another room was an old iron bed painted black, rusting, sparse long blades of grass growing through its metal frame.

I looked from room to room searching for something to pinch. Other children had found beads, knives even cartridges, but now everything was rusty or crumbling. I stood on a wooden drawer resting on a pile of soil, and it slowly collapsed under me, filling the shafts of light from the broken roof with woodworm dust.

I went out of the back door that was off its hinges and entered the orchard. The noise of bees was in the air; the branches of the cherry trees were almost touching the ground under the weight of large deep red cherries. You could smell their sweetness. I picked them in handfuls, firm and warm in my greedy fingers. I swallowed mouthfuls without spitting out the stones. They were sweet and squished against my teeth till I bit into them, their sharp juices sent pain into my jaws. I filled my pockets with cherries and walked out of the overgrown orchard, down the worn stone steps to the Bottaccio – the pool dug into the hill to keep rain water for irrigation and to power the olive mill downhill. It was round, lined with large mossy stones, the water deep green and still.

I took my clothes off, careful not to squash the cherries and saw the reflection of my white body in the dark water, like an apparition. I lowered myself slowly into the cool water, holding onto the slippery stones, closed my eyes, not daring to let go, then I pushed away and swam slowly. The water smelled like the mill in Garfagnana. I swam around trying not to make any noise; a large green dragonfly nearly landed on my head. I swam on my back with the sun hot on my face, no clouds in the sky. My stomach, full of cherries started to rumble and ache.

I swam for the side, put my hands up and tried to pull myself out, my feet slipping on the slimy stones underwater. I tried at many points around the pool – I was getting out of breath. The water felt cold now, and I could just support my weight with my skinny arms covered in goosebumps. I drew a long breath and shouted *'Aiuto, Aiuto!'* as loud as I could, listening to the sound of my voice echoing and dying down the slope, then only the chattering of my teeth and my breathing. I felt stiff and cramped and almost smiled at the ripples in the water around me, created by my shaking body.

Time passed, and I called out a few more times. I had to pee and felt a brief warmth on my belly. I thought of my body sinking, pale in the green water. I imagined Mother's face; she would be cross with me if I drowned. Would the children be allowed to come to my funeral and the teachers? No! It could not be like this. I coughed, sank in a bit and felt revulsion for the green water and its hidden depths. I saw a green frog moving slowly between the stones.

The shaking had become continuous; I panicked. In desperation, I kicked my feet against the stones lining the sides of the pool – it hurt! Then I felt my foot wedge between two stones, kicked up and managed to grasp a tuft of long grass on the edge. Out of breath, I waited. Then with a final effort, I pulled myself out the pool. I sat exhausted on the warm stones, watching rivulets of pale green water over my white body, my feet bleeding, scratched by the stones. Suddenly, a great surge of joy came over me. "I am alive!" I shouted defiantly like a madman and laughed.

Later, I grabbed my clothes and sat eating cherries and spitting stones. Shivering with the sun on my back, I watched the pale stones breaking the mirror surface of the pool, then slowly disappear in the murky water.

In time, I got hot and lay face down on the grass, soft and cool. I folded my arms under my chin and closely observed the skin on my forearms, now hot in the sun. The pores seemed to open in time with my heartbeat and shine briefly, till dried by the sun. Other pores opened, glittering, pulsating and fading.

*

I started to smoke cigarettes, cheap unfiltered 'Nazionali' that left a terrible taste in my mouth. Our smoking room was the outside toilet, a dark row of four cubicles with no doors, always overflowing and terribly smelly. We gathered there, safe from the eyes of the grownups. We bought our cigarettes, one at a time from the day pupils at our school.

One of the most enterprising providers was a girl called Mara. She always had a few packets of cigarettes in her bag. She was maybe fourteen with flashing green eyes and long dark hair. I joined a mixed class for my last year at school, and Mara sat at the desk beside me. I admired her, but she hardly ever spoke to me. She looked like a woman and I like a tall gangly boy! I bought my first cigarette from her just so that I would be noticed. I thought of Mara before falling asleep and often woke up with a hard-on and her on my mind. She rode to the school on an old-fashioned black bicycle, and she smelled sweet when she sat beside me, drying her brow with her sleeves. During Italian lessons, I tried to help her; she was not very good, and occasionally, I had a rewarding smile from her, her green eyes noticing me. I corrected her spelling putting my head close to hers, her breast on my arm but only too briefly!

The year passed slowly, and finally, I got my diploma and left Mutiliagno and the boys and returned home to Lucca for the summer.

About that time, I started to have doubts about religion. In the local church of San Frediano, there was a glass sarcophagus and inside the body of Santa Zita. Legend said that her body was uncorrupted and unchanged since her death. When I pointed out to the head priest the woodworm holes on the saint's face and her skeletal clasped hands, he told me I was mistaken and faithless. Suddenly, what I had believed in seemed like a fairy tale and what I had feared and felt guilty about made me laugh. I started to realise that the God that I had believed in was not so powerful anymore. An extremely liberating thought! I felt much stronger and secure now. I was in charge and stopped going to church.

When Mother realised I had stopped, she refused to allow me to lunch on Sunday, so sometimes I went back to mass, mainly to please Mother. So instead of following the ritual of the mass, I looked at people, made eyes at the girls around me and admired the magnificent Romanesque architecture of San Frediano. The more I listened to the words of the priests, the more I marvelled at the naivety of so many believing in them. That made me feel superior! I always sat on a bench in full view of a round font with a frieze of figures all around. The marble looked almost translucent glowing in the semi-darkness of the church.

I spent hours walking on the avenue on top of the walls of Lucca talking in my head and debating the benefit of my newfound freedom and the lack of guilt that I now felt.

Later on, during the summer, I went for the last time to a camp organised by the school at Mutigliano. I rode a bike to the school carrying a military rucksack on my back full of my possessions. Mother had bought me a new pair of blue Superga tennis shoes; they smelled deliciously rubbery! I had saved money in the last few weeks and bought a German hunting knife with a long shiny blade stamped 'Solingen', a brass guard and handle made of leather segments and stag horn with a pommel of aluminium. The scabbard of brown leather was finely stitched and smelled of tannin.

We left for the mountains in an old blue bus carrying tents and food for two weeks. We sang during the two-hour journey up to Piano Sinatico, a medieval village at about 800 metres surrounded by meadows and chestnut woods, perfect for camping. We erected the tents from the last war, grey and worn, a gift from the council. A large tent was used as a kitchen and refectory and many other individual ones in a circle. I made wooden pegs with my new knife and borrowed a rusty shovel to dig a channel around the tent in case of rain. We gathered straw from a friendly farmer's barn and made the inside of the tents comfortable. We were given old smelly blankets, but the inside of the tent smelled fresh like the inside of a barn. We ate mainly pasta that was cooked in a cauldron on the open fire. We were also given rations of peanuts, cheese and chocolate when we went on a walk.

On a gloomy day guided by a very energetic Mr Bulian, we left early, our cold hands in our pockets, we walked silently up a mule track. Lots of snivelling boys not wanting to walk so early in the morning! We drank from many springs beside the track. After a few hours, I felt better and more energetic. I had my knife in the scabbard at my belt that was the envy of many of the boys. The sky cleared, and I took my pullover off in the strong sun. We reached a high valley called Libro Aperto (open book) covered in flowers and with many small streams. We gorged on blueberries and had lunch of bread, cheese and chocolate. Later, climbing up the valley, we found a dugout from the war with lots of spent cartridges. The brass had turned green in the damp soil! I picked a few large ones, possibly from machineguns and polished them using sand. They left a green, smelly stain on my hand that would not come out with the cold water from the stream. Later, I exchanged a polished cartridge for half a bar of chocolate. We explored the valley and played games, especially the snake one where we would run in a long line holding hands then the leading boy at the head of the snake would suddenly swerve, sending the tail boys flying on the springy grassy floor of the valley. The soles and sides of my Superga shoes stained blue and green from the berries! On the way home, the sky turned dark; it started to rain with thunder and lightning all around. We covered our heads with jumpers and ran on the slippery stones of the mule track. Mr Bulian tried to keep us together shouting at the stragglers. The rain mixed with hail, stung our skin and obscured the way. We saw a grey farmhouse in the distance, smoke coming from the chimney. We repaired in the open barn and sat shivering, hands between our knees. An old lady in a green shawl on her head came out of the farmhouse and invited us in. We warmed up in front of the huge stone fireplace, steaming and giggling! I sat on the stone floor eating my bar of chocolate, drying my scabbard near the fire, flames reflecting on the shiny blade! The lady made hot milk in a cauldron on the open fire, and we all drank in turn from a copper ladle. We thanked the smiling, toothless lady and left. The sun had come out again, and a peacock stood on a haystack fanning his resplendent tail and calling eerily.

In the village beside the campsite, there was a small stone church where we went to mass. The inside had whitewashed walls and a dark wooden ceiling. There were wooden benches with no back rest and you knelt on the stone floor. The villagers wore sturdy boots, corduroy clothes and smelled of bonfires. There was a bar in the square where I discovered you could buy miniature bottles of liquor. I sampled quite a few flavours; my favourite was blueberry-flavoured grappa. Sometimes I went into my little tent drunk and put my knife under the bundle of clothes, used as a pillow, for protection.

The camping holiday ended, and after a few days in Lucca, Mother and I went to visit a friend of hers, Fernanda, in a mountain village called Coreglia, near Barga. We got there a hot afternoon on a steam train fitted with hard wooden benches. I lowered the window. Mother wore a cream linen dress and got covered in black specks from the locomotive. I tried to flick them off, but they left a black streak. She gave me a sour look! Fernanda was a jolly middle-aged lady with a gold tooth and large brown legs. Her husband had left her for another lady. Her son, about my age, was called Renzo and had a spotty face, spiky hair and was taller than me. They lived in a pink house by a church. Mother and Fernanda had many cups of coffee together and talked endlessly about their betraying husbands. Renzo and I did not get along at all. He was always picking on me, showing me how strong he was. We competed on everything, how many steps we could jump up, how many chin-ups we could do hanging from the vine pergola in front of the house! We were quite well matched, but he was better at throwing stones, and he teased me at my lack of accuracy and punched me in the shoulders. I tried to practise after lunch in the fields behind the house, trying to match Renzo's accuracy with stones. An afternoon with the drone of cicadas everywhere, I gathered a mound of stones and tried to hit a large tree beside a tall hedge some 30 metres away. The stones were round, heavy cobbles from the river fitting neatly in my hand. I hit the tree a few times with a nice thud, but some of the stones went past the hedge behind the tree. A scream came back! I ran to the hedge and looked through a gap. A tall man in a white beekeeper's overall, wearing a net mask was trying to calm a swarm of bees coming out from a damaged wooden beehive on the other side of the hedge. I ran back to the house followed by the man in white. Mother was alone in the kitchen baking a cake. I tried to explain, but the man arrived, banging at the door. He shouted at us, pale in the face, demanding repayment. I went into the kitchen, and while Mother went upstairs to get her purse I started to clean the cake bowl with my fingers still gritty from the soil on the stones. The man calmed down and left. Mother came into the kitchen and noticing smears of the mixture on my face, called me an idiot and having grabbed a piece of soap on a broken China dish by the sink, threw it towards me. I tried to duck, but I was hit on the side of my eye by the soap still stuck to its dish. The broken dish cut me, and I bled profusely on the pale wood of the kitchen table. Mother got scared, but I reassured her about my eye. She bathed the cut and put a plaster on it. She apologised and kissed me and made me a drink of fruit syrup and water. Fernanda and Renzo came back, and while Mother told them what had happened I sat with the drink in my hand, sticking and unsticking my fingers around the tall glass in time to a tune in my head. Finally, I got out of the room, and Renzo followed me, teasing, punching and laughing. I went and sat outside on the wall by the church. I put a long piece of rye grass in my mouth and chewed it, spitting bits out, counting how many pieces I could bite from a length of grass. The brown door of the church opened and out came a tall, young priest with a pink face and balding red hair. A flash of blood came to my head; he was the student priest that had abused me at Collesalvetti! I looked at him; he approached the open bell tower and started to ring the single bell. I walked back slowly to the house and went into my room, sat on the bed with the sound of the bells from the church through the open window! Renzo walked in, laughing and teasing and when he started to punch me, I stood up and threw a punch fast with all my force into his face again without thinking, as if someone else had taken over my action! Renzo fell on the floor and banged his head against the door. I went near him and knelt on the floor, blood poured from his nose; he looked surprised. I helped him up. I poured some water from the jug into the basin, and he washed his nose turning the water pink. He didn't say a word. At dinner, we all sat in silence, Renzo's nose red and swollen. We left by train the day after.

That summer, my sister, Ughetta, told me that Mother had met a man called Mario. Mother was still an attractive woman of perhaps 45. The previous year, whilst on holiday with my sister in the mountains, she met Mario. He had a small farm near Lucca and travelled everywhere by pushbike. I met him in September. He was a tall, big man with a moustache and a deep voice. He came for lunch and brought my sister a book and me a small green cage with a hawfinch inside. I loved the bird, its muted, neat plump plumage and its strong conical beak. Mario told me it could open cherry stones to eat the kernel inside. I kept the green cage outside the window of my room hanging on a nail. Once, while I was trying to insert its water dish he bit me with his beak and took a triangular piece of flesh from my finger that slowly filled with blood. I looked at my blood dripping on the stone windowsill, took the cage off the nail and opened the cage door. The finch jumped onto the crossbar by the door, looked around, seemed to look at me, then flew out fast towards the trees on the walls of Lucca and the mountains beyond.

Mario was pleasant and seemed to want my approval. He spoke with a country accent and sometimes mispronounced some words. I felt intimidated by the sheer size and bulk of the man and somehow tried to find ways of minimising his effect on me. I judged him a bit ignorant and thought Mother could have done better. I stayed at his farmhouse, and he took me out with his shotgun to hunt birds and showed me how to kill a rabbit painlessly with my hands. I had to hold both back legs of the rabbit in my left hand then with the edge of the right hand deliver a fast blow in between the back of the neck and the skull of the dangling rabbit. He had two sisters living with him that doted on him and allowed him the life of a gentleman farmer. They liked me too and cooked great dishes for us.

When deciding about the school in Pescia, if to be a boarder or not, Mario sided with Mother and told me I was too young to be out of the boarding school. I disagreed with him explaining how many years I had spent at boarding school already. Mother left us alone, and I told Mario that although he was a friend of Mother's he did not have any say in my education and should not interfere. "Mind your own business!" I shouted. He got red in the face and grabbed my shoulders and shouted in my face that he heard that I wasn't going to mass anymore. "What has it got to do with it?" I shouted. I saw the gold tooth under his moustache, his breath smelled of stale smoke. I lost control and pushed him back. We stood staring at each other a few seconds, then he grabbed his hat and left. Slowly, Mario stopped coming around, and Mother said he was not her type anyway. I saw Mario again a few years after. Mother had paid for me to spend a week in the mountains in some distant relation's hotel in a place called Dogana. I even took a dumbbell in the suitcase with me to do exercises. I had a small, cool room with no view set against the mountain face at the back of the hotel. At dinner, to my surprise, I saw Mario sitting alone in the corner. He nodded at me, but we did not speak. I had coffee at the bar later, and Mario joined me. I had grown as tall as him and almost as big, and I felt superior. He asked about Mother and the rest of the family, and we chatted politely for a while.

There was a small dancing place on a terrace overlooking the river at the other side of the road from the hotel. There I met a dark, vivacious girl called Gigi. She was maybe a couple of years older than me and had just started as a primary school teacher in Bologna. We danced under the watchful eye of Gigi's mother. We drank Coca Cola and talked easily about music and art. She had read more than me and told me she was fluent in French. We arranged to meet the day after and go for a walk. We met outside the hotel; it was windy, and she wore a red scarf covering her black hair. She looked stunning in jeans and black jumper. We walked, talked and drank from a spring. We found a spot away from the road, sat on the grass and kissed and touched. Then I realised that the wet around my mouth was not saliva but blood pouring out of Gigi's nose. I tore a handkerchief she had in her pocket and made her stuff bits up her nose. At the spring, I put some cold water at the back of her neck. But the blood would not stop and was now dribbling from the saturated red bits of material sticking out of her nose. We got back to the hotel. The flow had not diminished. Her mother looked very annoyed with me and decided to go back to Bologna in her Fiat 500 car to see if Gigi could be helped at the hospital. I kissed Gigi goodbye. "Let's keep in touch," she said in a nasal voice and pressed a piece of paper smeared with blood in my hand. That evening, I went back to the dance terrace. Mario invited me to his table where he sat with some local men. He offered me a beer and enquired, winking at me, about Gigi. I told him what happened, and he accused me, laughing in a vulgar way with his friends, of having been too rough with her.

I danced with a tall local girl, and when I went back to the table Mario said, "How do you manage to dance so close together? Don't you get excited?"

"Yes, I do," I said, "that's the whole point."

There was some envy in his voice when he whispered, "If it was me dancing like that, I would have already come."

I felt pity for him and said, "Maybe that's your problem." The men laughed at my remark and at Mario. Later, most of the single girls had left; the men around the table started to arm wrestle. Mario sipped his beer and looked at the men with an air of superiority. Then to my surprise, he challenged me to wrestle. We grasped hands, elbows on the rickety aluminium table, and to my surprise, after a few seconds, I managed to pull him down. He did not want to try again but congratulated me and bought me another beer. He left a few days later, and I only saw him again in Via Fillungo in Lucca many years after. Grey and thin, pushing a bicycle, he remained in my head as the image of what I would look like in my old age. I heard he died of a heart attack a few years later.

My father in his uniform, 1943

Me and my Father, Ugo

Me and my sister, Ughetta

Auntie Bice

My communion day

My mother Giulia and uncle Nanni on my confirmation day

At school in Mutigliano

In Rome doing my national service in the Army

A view of Lucca

Granny

6 At school posing with the Alpha Romeo belonging to a rich friend

Pescia

At the end of the summer, I moved to the boarding school in Pescia that specialised in olive culture. Pescia is a small provincial town beside the River Pescia, a small brown river meandering among grey pebbles and bushes. The soil there is very fertile, and it is intensely cultivated with ornamental flowers and plants, especially carnations. The town is dusty and grey with a nice old bridge over the river. The school was at the top of a steep, straight road flanked by large olive trees. It had been a villa and the front had fountains and grottos in the Italianate style of the 18th century – a double staircase leading to a wide balcony spanning the whole width of the villa!

Almost immediately, I made friends with Leonardo Guidi, a boy in my class. Having shown interest in science, we were given the task of reclassifying the mineral collection in the school museum. After lessons, we rewrote labels, emptied boxes full of dusty specimens, checking the hardness of minerals with the help of an old volume on Mineralogy and a Moss scale. When we were cold in the unheated room of the museum, we started to play fight. The rule was we could punch hard on any part of our body but the head. We discovered that there were parts of the body that would disable the adversary when hit. Like a point on the side of the forearm that when hit with the knuckles would become paralysed for several minutes. On a particularly cold afternoon near Christmas, having got bored with the minerals and labelling, we fought until almost out of breath with sweaty red faces. Leonardo missed a punch on my shoulder and hit me on the jaw. I heard a crunching noise and my jaw went sideways. I grabbed Leonardo by the neck and pushed, sending him towards a tall wooden cupboard set against the wall. We both hit the cupboard and heard the noise of glass breaking inside. We quickly opened the cupboard and found a few broken empty beakers and a bottle of mercury that, having lost its cork, was emptying on the shelf. Droplets of mercury running everywhere, alive, shiny, impossible to catch! We got on our knees and tried to push the smaller droplets into each other, forming larger pools reflecting our red, worried, distorted faces. We collected most of the mercury by pushing it on a sheet of paper and pouring it into the bottle, leaving only tiny spheres in the cracks of the green and red tiles to remind us of the accident. The morning after, I had difficulty in opening my mouth to wash my teeth and later, at breakfast, I had to drink the caffe latte from the cup sideways. Eventually, the jaw recovered, and I could open it, but for a long time, I heard a crunching noise when eating.

Leonardo and I were very different physically. He was short, stocky and very strong, I skinny, tall and fast. I borrowed the key to the gym and trained in the evening. I loved to climb the smooth, shiny, wooden pole to the dusty beam at the top. But then I discovered that when climbing the thick hemp rope and drawing my legs up to push, I often got an erection! Very distracting!

I was very interested in chemistry, and I fancied the middle-aged lady teacher. She wore very high heels and tight jumpers and wore her dark hair in a pony tail. She was very strict. I loved the dark mahogany tables with the Bunsen burners and the bottles full of colourful chemicals. The smell of the acid and its danger made me afraid in a crazy way that I would get the compulsion to drink some, that frightened and worried me. Eventually, I learned to control those thoughts, and they finally disappeared.

There was a pecking order at the school and the older boys performed a ritual of initiation on the new boys. Having filled a can with paint, shoe polish, glue and other nasty things like ink and sometimes pee, they would amass us new boys into the shower room and force us to take our clothes off. To resist was foolish because they would forcibly strip and beat you if you rebelled. A few months before, when peeing against a tree in the country, I had notice with pride dark, curly hair sprouting from my pube. Now I wish that had not happened as I knew that the foul content from the can would be brushed onto my prize growth. There we stood cold and naked surrounded by the bigger boys who were laughing and teasing, waiting for the brush. I got brushed and whilst I worried of how to wash the sticky mess off, I noticed a large, tall, pink-skinned boy that refused to take his pants off. He was pinned to the floor, his pants removed to reveal the smallest, pink penis with no hair.

To see such a small organ on a large body was very shocking and the older boys stopped laughing and let the poor boy go and get dressed without being brushed. He slowly started to sob and that put an end to the ritual! The boy carried on crying at night, appeared to be depressed and not to eat. His mother was called, found out about the ritual and discovered the cause of her son's malaise. He was taken to a doctor and given hormone treatment that brought forth puberty and normality to the boy.

Leonardo, my best friend, sometimes invited me to his house for lunch on Saturdays. His father, a young dynamic man, wore tweed jackets, moccasins, Ray Ban glasses and he was going bald. He would collect us in his new Alpha Romeo and take us to his modern house in Montecatini. His mother was attractive with short dark hair, high heels and always smiling. She loved feeding us! One Saturday after lunch on a walk near the house, Leonardo and I got caught in a downpour. Running and splashing on a lane beside a muddy field, we stopped under a fig tree. On the floor shining in the grey clay was an exquisite flint arrow head. Red in colour and shaped like an olive leaf, I washed it in the rain in my cupped hand, feeling the smoothness of the flint!

Our favourite word was 'amorphous'. We hated anything shapeless, especially people. Being a boarder at the school, I hated my lack of freedom and wanted to go daily like Leonardo. The food was very boring, mainly pasta overcooked with some sour tomato sauce. The kitchen was smelly and run by two middle-aged ladies. I liked one of them and often went to the kitchen helping to peel potatoes or polishing pitted aluminium pans with pumice. I would look at the cook's behind wrapped in a striped apron and brushed against her at every chance. She laughed at my gaucheness and blushed.

I read a lot and wrote poetry inspired by the works of Dante, Petrarca and Boccaccio we studied at school. Our Italian teacher was a priest from Florence. He was tall and skinny with a pot belly and wore black moccasins with red socks. His hooked nose reminded me of Dante Alighieri. He didn't think much of my efforts in Italian and told me, "*Sei pieno di vuotame* (you are full of emptiness)." But although he never liked me, he never failed me either. I didn't mix much with my fellow boarders. That did not go down well with a group of boys headed by a tall, red-haired youth called Vaccari. He was loud, funny and very bright. He looked like a gangly bird with mad blue eyes. His body was covered in freckles. His father was a tall hunchback always dressed in black when he came in his smart car to collect Vaccari.

I often walked in the countryside around the school alone. I had discovered bats in the vaulted ceiling of an abandoned covered well in the fields near the school. I liked listening to the shrill sounds of the bats. I could pick them up and wonder at the perfection of their tiny bodies. The small sharp teeth, the swollen breast of the feeding mothers with their babies and the almost transparent skin on their hooked wings. On a covered, oppressive, heavy summer's day, I met Vaccari and his little group. They started to tease me. "Always reading, always by yourself," they taunted. They managed to push me into a large hole in the ground used to burn diseased olive wood. Every time I tried to climb out of the hole, they pushed me down again. I got streaks of charcoal on my shirt and my tennis shoes covered in ash. After a few more tries getting out of breath, I sat on the ash at the bottom hoping the boys would get bored and leave. I sat for quite a long time, and when they started to pelt me with sods and soil, I found an incredible rage was building inside me. I took a running leap and managed to scramble up the side and run towards Vaccari. He was taken by surprise, and before any other boy got near us, I assaulted him with fists, kicked and bit his arm. I saw fear in his eyes and smelled his sweat. We were separated, and we walked in silence towards the school. I never got bullied again. Vaccari and I became friends. He was actually a great guy, a red-haired extrovert. Many years later, I learned from a school friend that Vaccari had died of a brain tumour at twenty-eight.

Another one of my friends was Vittorio, a boy from Torre del Lago, the village where Puccini had lived. He was tall, skinny and athletic. He told so many tall stories that I wrote a booklet mimicking the style of the Greek books on mythology describing the many heroic deeds of Hercules by using Vittorio as the protagonist. We called him Il Picchio Masturbatore or wanking woodpecker for obvious reasons. He became infatuated with a blond girl who worked in a bookshop in town. We were allowed on certain days to go to the shops and the cinema, and Vittorio spent hours inside the shop reading, not having the courage to speak to the girl. We incited Vittorio to write to the girl declaring his intention to meet her! The girl wrote a letter back explaining in a nice way that she already had a boyfriend. We intercepted her letter and replaced it with another inviting Vittorio to meet her by a shrine in a lane near the school. One of the butchest boys, Cavallini, with mean eyes and a broken nose, dressed as a girl having borrowed a blond wig and skirt from one of the cooks. Vittorio read the letter from the blond to us and boasted about his conquest. We followed Vittorio without being noticed to the meeting point. The sun was going down, and as he approached the blond figure in the skirt silhouetted against the reddening sky, she turned around and blew a large 'raspberry' at him. We followed with obscenities and jumped on him, patting his back and squeezing him. His face a sad picture of disappointment!

Cavallini, the 'blond girl' went with a prostitute during a visit home and caught the clap. He somehow managed to buy a phial of penicillin but could not find the courage to tell the lady in charge of the infirmary that he needed an injection. I volunteered to do it. I had seen Mother on her many suicidal attempts with her 'lethal injections' and had many vitamin injections myself so I knew what to do. I took the chrome metal box with the syringe and needle from the infirmary, put it in the pan of boiling water in the kitchen ready for the pasta to sterilise it and, in the dormitory, injected Cavallini's hairy spotty bottom. He recovered and gave me a large salami made by his family firm in Maremma.

Another boy, Angelo, was a good athlete. He moved with grace and made me feel clumsy. He was a very good gymnast. His father was the manager of a large farm in

Maremma belonging to the Prince Corsini. The farm specialised in the breeding of the large white Maremmana cattle. I visited Angelo many times during the holidays at the farm in Spedaletti – the original building had been used as a hospital by the crusaders returning from the Holy Land. One evening, Angelo collected me from the bus stop where I was left in the dark near a crossroad. I saw the light of a car approaching, going in and out of the hilly ground. Angelo arrived smiling in a red Topolino, 500 Fiat, with much dust and screeching of brakes. I jumped on board, we hugged, and I had a puff of his Nationale and held on. On a bend fording a small brook, a dark, fast shape came out of the bushes. A large wild boar stood framed by the light! His huge head was covered in shiny black bristles, his mouth open showing large curved tusks! Angelo tried to stop but could not on the wet ground. The car hit the hulking beast, softly with a thud that shook the car. The boar stepped sideways, shook its head and slowly walked into the bushes. We got out to examine the front of the Topolino. No damage, only a tuft of black hair caught on the badge on the Italian Automobile Club screwed to the grill.

We always visited the stables with the beautiful Chianina bulls with the gracefully curved horns – the tallest breed of cattle in the world. We played with the enormous Maremma sheepdogs, also white. One of them, a large male with mean eyes of different colour, jumped on me with his front paws and tore the front pocket off my moleskin jacket. It was strange that such arid infertile land bred such large magnificent creatures.

We had great meals on long tables. Angelo's family was large and noisy and the food amazing. After great chunks of roasted meats and huge trays of potatoes, we young ones went to the granary to dance, drink fierce local red wine and smoke French cigarettes. I danced with one of Angelo's older sisters; she was probably sixteen, quite intellectual, and I really liked her. There was real feeling in our entwined fingers and my quick kisses on her white neck.

I had been taught to dance by an older boy at school called Ficonero. He was dark and slim, had polio as a young boy and a leg shorter than the other with a misshapen foot. He always dressed neatly in dark clothes. He danced gracefully on his skinny legs and was the dancing 'master' of the school. He reminded me a white Sammy Davis. Once a year, near Christmas, there was a ball organised by the school in the local dance hall by the station. The girls from the town would turn up in colourful frocks. I spent a long time shaving the sparse whiskers I grew and plastering my short dark hair with Bryl cream. I wore my best blue suit and tie, and we danced to the slow tunes of the time. The excitement of approaching the girl I liked, asking her to dance, if accepted, escorting her to the dance floor, your hand on her swaying hips! Then dancing, staring into her eyes, holding her close, feeling the tingle in our hands, then neck to neck, face to face, sometimes kissing discreetly letting the side of our lips touch. Our bellies pressed together, the great sounds of the fifties guiding our feet. The look of Ficonero gliding past his pupils, on agile feet!

During the time approaching examinations, we pupils were allowed to go into separate empty classrooms to be alone and better able to concentrate. Chemistry was a subject I liked but had difficulty in remembering all the various tables and formulae. I had managed to forget my problems with my compulsions and fear of acid suicide. I still fancied the terrifying chemistry teacher who was dark and very shapely and to me, very sexy. She was also severe and unpredictable and threw terrible tantrums when cross. I sometimes got the giggles during her lessons, with other friends on the back benches and could not stop laughing. She looked at us with pity and called us 'stupid, stupid boys'. Her large breasts bouncing at every 'stupid' she shouted!

During revision in a locked classroom trying to memorise chemical formulae, being bored I started to play with myself. I had done this so many times before in bed in the dormitory, trying not to make any noise. I still had not managed to come and made my circumcised penis very swollen. This time, I played and played reading my chemistry book and thinking of the stern chemistry teacher. Something different was happening. I felt a stirring in my balls and a surge of pleasure. A shot of sperm went past my shoulder on the wall just missing the crucifix. Hallelujah, I was normal after all! I showed my friends, proudly, the shiny transparent stain.

We had a young geography teacher. She was pale, fair and fresh from university. I discovered that if I rolled a long thin piece of paper, chewed the end to soften it and put it up my nose, I could feel a tingle and a strange feeling of pleasure that started a serious attack of sneezing, loud and almost continuous that made the class laugh and annoy the young teacher. She could not do anything against such a natural action! Once, we made a plane out of newspaper, set it on fire and hurled it towards the blackboard to the amusement of the class. I found a small broken metal file and cut an opening on the brass tube on top of the urinals in the teachers' toilet. Anybody going for a pee would get wet trousers from the fine, invisible spray coming out of the tube.

I still had compulsions to do naughty things like putting a condom filled with water on top of the half open door to the teachers' room to break on the head of the first teacher to open it. Mr Pilucco, the head of the school, tried to find the author of the pranks in vain. From the top floor, where the dormitories and showers were, we looked into a large walled garden at the back of the school. Towards the end of the garden against the wall stood a small open wooden shed containing straw, fertilisers and tools for the gardens. I bought a catapult and some windproof matches from the town. One night, I went into the shower room, opened the window, tied the match onto a pebble with a piece of tape, struck the match and quickly put it into the leather of the catapult, flinging it towards the straw in the shed. Back in bed, I listened to the roaring fire and the agitated voices at the windows. Why I did it, I will never know!

I discovered that if you screwed off the chrome head of the showers in the cubicles and received the warm jet of water on the end of your penis, you would be able to experience a great 'come'. Soon, during shower time on a Saturday, the room echoed with strange sounds and even boys reluctant to take a shower, queued for it.

I became friends with a boy, Luigi. He was older looking and more physically developed than most of us. He looked like a cowboy in a western film. On a walk to Uzzano, the village on a hill behind the school, we met two girls. One well-developed wearing a tight green pullover and a pleated grey skirt, the other blond, slim and intellectual looking. After a few meaningful looks with Luigi, I found myself walking beside the girl with the green pullover. We talked about French cinema and our lives at the school, and I tried to impress her by talking about my poetry. We met several times in the countryside near the school and once at the station on our journey home for the Easter holidays. We kissed and petted lying on pine needles in the woods or on straw in secluded barns. She let me touch her, and she played with my penis patiently. Once, she let me rub my penis between her thighs, but I managed to get cut by the stud on her suspenders and stained her pale skirt. We spent a long time washing the red stain off with the water from the trough where the cows drank. Luigi told me that his girl did not want to take her glasses off when kissing and did not want him to go 'all the way'. The girls invited us to a ball in town. We knew we would not be allowed to go out at night so we hid our smart clothes in the gym for which I had the key. After everyone was asleep, we went silently down the dark stairs and corridors to the gym, got dressed using a torch, our bodies sending huge shadows on the white walls. We got out through the rattling French windows, scaled the orchard wall and walked in the moonlight, careful not to muddy our shoes. We got to the ball and had to call the girls to be let in. They looked beautiful in their ball gowns, and we danced, hugged and drank whisky and soda. I went to the terrace outside with my girl and while I was fondling her boobs the shoulder strap of her red gown broke. I managed to knot the ends together but one boob was higher than the other. We got back to the school before 4 am, exhilarated and tired. The director of the school, Mr Pilucco, a dark sour man from the south found out about our outing. He called us into his office. He kept smoothing the sparse hair covering his bald head with his flattened hand. His eyebrows were twitching, and he told us we had been seen in town. He stood up and his grey cat sat on a leather chair licking his private parts. Luigi and I got the giggles and could not stop. We were sent away and made to do a few more hours extra work pruning in the olive grove.

Baffino, so called because of his pencil thin moustache of which he was very proud, was an older boy of nineteen. He came from Bagni di Lucca. We went for walks in the watery sunshine of winter after lunch, and he told me of his visit to the brothels in Lucca. The girls, the smells, the rooms were described so vividly during our walk! I still remember the details as if I had been there myself. Baffino loved giving the girls oral sex, and apparently, he was so good at it that they let him in at a reduced cost. There is a photo of us, his hand on my shoulder, smiling with me putting on a tough face. He drowned after graduating the next summer in a pool of the River Serchio.

The first year passed, and I got promoted. I remember the feeling of the first days after school in Lucca: the leisurely breakfasts, the walks on the walls under the plane trees or lazing on the benches watching the girls walk by. The days passed quickly. I read in bed in the afternoon; I rode a bike with my friend Nino sitting on the crossbar. Often, we got the giggles about some silly subject and sometimes fell off the bike from laughing. I went fishing on the River Serchio and caught fish that Granny rolled in flour and fried. I ate a large amount of food and exercised with a dumbbell in front of a mirror in my room. I vainly liked to see my muscles grow.

Signor Fortuna, my mother's employer, invited Mother and I to the mountains in Pizzorna. He drove his Lancia very fast, swearing at other drivers and sweating. He spat when he got excited and the windscreen on his side was covered in dry spittle. He had a chalet and a special large net to catch wild birds to be eaten. In a space in the forest stood the net, perhaps 10 metres long, all neatly folded ready to be sprung with the use of gunpowder to cover an area where small birds were lured with food. Sometimes hundreds would be caught in a day, and after killing them, they would be sold to restaurants. I made it clear that I was not going to help with the killing of the birds taken alive under the net. Signor Fortuna was jolly, large, wore a diamond in a grey metal ring on his little finger. He had a very large mouth always open showing his sparse yellow teeth. He kept asking me, in his booming voice, if I had had any sexual experience, winking and slapping me on the shoulder. Preoccupied about my sexuality, he told me stories about his sex marathons in the brothels of Paris in the twenties and how he caught various venereal diseases and got cured by an Indian doctor who made potions for him and encouraged him to drink his own urine. Sometimes we sat in his study and drank beer. He liked showing me his shotguns, shining blue smelling of oil, closing it with a metallic sound. "Listen to this clunk," Signor Fortuna would say, "like poetry."

Luciano was Signor Fortuna's butler. He was skinny, bald and very funny. He looked gay and Signor Fortuna always accused him of being a 'poofter'. Luciano had the latest records and showed me how to polish shoes till you saw your reflection in them. One evening in Pizzorna, Mother had cooked great food and was playing cards with Signor Fortuna. Luciano listened to Perry Como's 'Magic Moment' over and over again on his gramophone. Later, we walked to the bar near the chalet. We drank beer and talked to the owner, a blond lady with the largest breasts. I could not take my eyes off her cleavage. I aligned my glass so that when the lady put her elbows on the counter in front of me, her face on her cupped hands staring into my eyes, all I could see were her breast enlarged and distorted. I laughed! She kept smiling and giggling with us, and Luciano told me she fancied me. We drank too much beer, and later, I was invited by a local boy to arm wrestle. We settled on the corner of the sticky wooden surface of the bar. The boy still had a cigarette in his mouth and was closing his eyes against the smoke. We clasped hands. I pulled hard, and to my surprise, I won. People gathered, and we did it again. The boy rolled his shirtsleeves and threw away his cigarette. We joined hands again, veins in our forearms bulging, and I won again! He paid for beer for everybody. The barmaid kissed me and smelled of alcohol and stale perfume. On the way home, we sang *Catch a Falling Star* loudly and then went to bed.

In the morning, after breakfast, we all went out for a walk in the hills nearby. It was very hot. Signor Fortuna looked like a portrait of Henry VIII; I had seen in a history book, with bulging calf muscles, shorts and a red T-shirt. He complained of not feeling very well. He looked pale and covered in sweat. We somehow helped him back down the mule track beside the wood towards the chalet. I had most of his weight on my shoulder and could smell the rosemary, fennel and thyme in the sunshine mingled with his sweat. The chalet did not have a phone. None of us could drive so Signor Fortuna had to drive his Lancia down the bendy gravel road to Lucca, breathing heavily. He did not swear once even when a bus in front made so much dust that we could not see the road. When he tried the water for the windscreen, nothing happened. He gave Luciano a dirty look for not filling it but did not say anything saving his rattling breath. Later, he was diagnosed having had a heart attack but due to his strong constitution, he recovered and lived a few years longer.

Later on, I went to the mountains to stay with Auntie Barbara. My friend Leonardo had lent me a science fiction book where sabre toothed tigers came alive and attacked people at night. Somehow, the story frightened me and after switching the light off, I tried to breathe without making a sound, listening for the growl of a tiger outside!

I met a boy called Carlo; his father managed an electricity station near La Pieve. I loved the noise of the water coming down the huge pipes from a pool at the top of the hill into the turbines, the hissing noise and the smell of electricity in the making! We swam in the pool at the top, the water cold and green came from the River Jara uphill. We swam naked and lay shivering on the concrete side of the pool in the sunshine. I was no longer ashamed of my circumcised penis. It did not look like a mushroom anymore. It had smoothed out and grown bigger. When comparing sizes with Carlo, they were about the same size. We were also the same age and built, but he was stronger and more daring. We used to do press-ups and chin-ups on the branches of a tree. We pumped our chests and measured each other using our shoelaces. We got brown and talked about girls. I was about fifteen and still a virgin. Carlo told me he had had a few local girls, but I am not sure he told me the truth.

We walked to Pontecosi Lake. There was an old bridge there by the side of the lake near a stone church and tower. Boys were jumping from the top of the tall bridge into the river joining the lake. The water was quite shallow, and Carlo told me that to avoid hitting the stony bottom you had to open your arms as soon as your feet touched the water. I felt afraid to jump, but I knew I had to do it. I spent long painful minutes sitting on the hot stones of the parapet nervously rubbing my nails on them, looking at the brown boys shouting and jumping. Carlo grabbed my neck from the back, his hand cool and wet, teasing me and trying to push me off the bridge. Among the cheers of the boys, I stood at the highest point of the bridge and having taken a big breath, jumped! I opened my arms too late and got a dark long bruise on the underside of my arms from the impact with the water. I jumped over and over again, and eventually, I managed the timing of opening my arms. It was exhilarating!

Carlo and I went dancing at the farm by the bridge near the power station. The girls were bold and strong and smelled of fire smoke and cheap perfume. We danced close together feeling our bodies against each other to the sound of an accordion, well into the warm night.

I started to fish again. I bought a nice cane rod connected by brass ferrules. I learned to tie flies on Auntie Barbara's kitchen table after meals. I made nymphs to match the ones in pebble tubes under the stones of the Jara River. Blue hooks wrapped in yellow wool for the body with the head made of black silk. I caught small trout and wrapped them in large Gunnera leaves growing by the river to keep them fresh. Auntie Barbara patiently fried them in an old frying pan. Every time she used the pan, she told me, "Never wash it. Only wipe it clean with newspaper." I always finished the sentence for her! One of the boys I met at the river, a blond boy with a large head, took me to a lake he knew and showed me how to make the best casts. After a few casts, I hooked a large trout. The rod was pulled down as the trout dived then resurfaced, jumping and splashing. Her body ghostly under the surface near the shore! Then on the shallow water of the sandy beach, beautifully shining, still pulling away, her body marked with the colours of the rainbow. I killed the trout using a long thin stone and felt guilty. She was so beautiful. The boy told me he had never caught a trout that large; I could see he was envious. That was the only catch of the day, and on the dusty road home, we did not speak. We never went fishing together again!

Auntie Barbara cooked, washed my clothes and was the usual warm supportive woman, solid and simple. Just before going back to Lucca and knowing that the train went through Bagni di Lucca, the town where Baffino my friend from the school lived, I sent him a postcard that if it was okay, I would meet him at the train station on my way back. I had heard from Mother that Father had settled in Bagni di Lucca and had had a child, a boy called Pietro, named after my 'Glasgow' grandfather. I somehow hoped I would meet my father in the town. Baffino was at the station, smiling his moustache as trim as ever. We walked to his house near the river outside the town, a turn of the century villa surrounded by a dark garden with large trees. His mother, a widow, owned a shop selling electrical goods in town. She made me very welcome and asked me about my family. When I told her my father and his new family lived in Bagni di Lucca, she seemed to be interested, but she did not know them. We had dinner of pasta with tomato sauce and a large trout that I deboned, showing off my skill. After dinner, we all went to the town centre to have ice cream, and I looked at the faces in the crowd hoping to see my father. We walked back to the darkened villa. I slept in a soft, fresh bed smelling of lavender. In the morning, we had breakfast at a table in the garden in the sunshine. "We could go fishing," said Baffino pouring coffee in the cups. "I have done a lot of fishing in Garfagnana."

"We can stay around here. I don't mind," I said.

"I know. We will go to the mountains near Castelunovo," said Baffino excitedly. "Last year on a walk, I found a cave. The access was blocked."

"What kind of cave?" I asked.

"A cave offering great shelter! It could have been inhabited," Baffino said spreading jam on his bread. "A collapsed rock is blocking the entrance. We need some tools, but I think we can open it up." We left in his mother's car, a dark blue 1100 Fiat armed with a spade, pickaxe, a torch and a picnic in an old grey rucksack. Baffino drove fast on the winding roads, and I held onto the leather strap to keep my balance.

"Are you still a virgin?" He teased me.

"Not for long, I hope. It has not happened yet, I tried."

"It will happen and then you will see how great it can be. The secret is to give pleasure. If you do that, you will get it back."

"Are you still going to the brothels in Lucca?" I asked.

"Not so much now. I have a friend in town. She is older, very experienced, and she cooks me great food too. Mother does not like her; she says she's common."

We reached Castelnuovo and stopped at the bar by the bridge for coffee. We drove again for a few minutes and then turned off the main road and took a dirt road following the river under a canopy of hazel trees. We stopped by an old mossy grey bridge, picked up the tools and rucksack and walked up a mule track, its stones smooth from centuries of use. We walked in silence uphill breathing heavily for maybe half an hour. We reached a rock face golden in the sunshine. Low hazel trees at its base among the boulders and a small stream tumbling downhill. Visible along the face was a large crack opening towards the base where a slab of rock had fallen, a small beech tree growing out of it. If you stood on the rock, you could just put your head inside the crack. The air felt cool there. We began to work to remove the tree. "Let's keep it," said Baffino. "I have got a book on bonsai; I think this will make a good one." We peeled back the stony turf, cut some roots but kept a ball of soil around the remaining ones. The trunk of the beech was thick and smooth as I grabbed it to put it in the shallow water of the stream. Its small leaves had started to brown with the end of summer. We dug some more and managed to rock the boulder till we levered it out with the pickaxe. We were hot and sweaty and drank the cool amber water of the stream. After a few more spadefuls of soil from the base of the opening were removed, we managed to enter the cave. Dark at first, the gravely floor covered in dry leaves, its ceiling ended in a pointed shape where a few bats hung making whistling noises disturbed by the torch. The cave was dry and cool and smelled of bats' droppings. In a corner, a pale rounded stone emerged from the leaves on the floor. We approached the stone and knelt beside it. We pushed the leaves aside exposing the fine gravel. I tapped the stone, and it sounded hollow. We scraped the gravel from its sides, and we both realised that it was not a stone emerging but a large skull.

"Maybe a goat died here," I said. "It's too big," said Baffino. We continued to scrape the gravel away with our fingers, excited when a large eye socket appeared, then the shape of a jaw with yellow cracked teeth and then a huge conical canine.

"I know," said Baffino, "I read about it in my encyclopaedia. They were all around the Appenines Ursus Speleo. Twenty thousand years ago, they roamed these mountains." I had read about them too, these enormous cave bears. I thought about the great grizzled hulks hunting and sharing these mountains with man. We dug in silence, the skull emerging from the gravel. We picked it up; it was heavy, the buried base darker. We shook gravel from the socket and the base of the skull, a canine fell from the upper jaw and dropped on the gravel with a metallic sound. I pushed it into its socket again. We rested the skull back on the gravel; it was magnificent, perfect! A large yellowing vertebra stood at the bottom of the hole.

"There is more buried down there. Maybe we should report it to Pisa University," I said. Baffino nodded. Then we looked at each other, and we knew we would have to leave the great bear where it lay. We walked outside in the sunshine.

"Let's have lunch," said Baffino grabbing the rucksack. We sat on the grass, took our boots and socks off and put our feet in the cold water of the stream. We ate our sandwiches in silence, the last sunshine of the day on our faces. Baffino finally spoke, still chewing his sandwich. "I think we should go and put the skull back as it was. In a way, I am disappointed about the cave. I thought there would be more chambers. But the bear, what a find! I think the bones had been there so many thousands of years they deserve to be left in peace. No palaeontologist from Pisa!" I agreed and we shook hands. Baffino produced from the rucksack a little bottle of grappa, and we took a swig each. We stood up, shook hands and patted each other on the shoulder, fortified by the grappa. We dried our cold feet on the grass and put our socks and boots on. We went back inside the cave. The light had changed and a shaft was flooding the end of the cave where the skull lay. We pushed back the gravel where it had been and covered the sides of the skull as before, and it looked undisturbed. We looked at it in the light for the last time and left. We managed to roll back the boulder and packed it with soil. I put a few old beech nuts in the soil – maybe a new tree would grow! We washed our hands in the stream, now in the shade and put the small dripping beech tree in the rucksack. We walked downhill in silence, the noise of our boots making hollow sounds on the stones of the mule track. As I said before, Baffino died in a pool of the Serchio River the next summer. He managed to plant the beech tree in an old stone trough, which he carried upstairs and placed on the terrace to get the sunshine. I have, on occasion, called Baffino's mother. She tells me the little bonsai is still alive and facing the mountains where it came from.

I went back home and soon noticed how different the women in my family were. My sister had grown, but she was tall and skinny and very moody. Mother was not very friendly and blowing hot and cold according to her moods. Auntie Bice, dissatisfied with her work and critical. Granny was aggressive and sometimes bitter. We got a phone installed, and Granny was afraid to use it. 'Work of the Devil', she called it.

I phoned Leonardo in Montecatini, and he invited me to spend the weekend at his house. I went by train – steam was starting to give way to diesel, and I travelled on a new Littorina. Leonardo was at the station, and we walked towards his house looking at the smart shops in the town. I bought a pale blue Lacoste tennis shirt with mother-of-pearl buttons and the crocodile logo on the chest. They had built a restaurant bar with a swimming pool on the hills near Leonardo's house called Le Panteraie. We went there to swim the day after. His father had a season ticket. The large poster at the entrance announced that the beauty contest for Miss Toscana would be judged by Steve Reeves, Mr Universe. We swam in the pool competing with each other. Leonardo had become hairier and more muscular. He told me my chest was larger but my legs still skinny. We sat by the pool and ate toasted sandwiches and drank beer.

In the evening, I wore my pale blue Lacoste shirt and went back to Le Panteraie in the car with Leonardo's parents. We sat near the stage looking at beautiful girls parading, posing and being interviewed. They wore one-piece swimsuits with frills and had not shaved their armpits. Leo and I kept looking at each other and made appreciative movements with our eyebrows and mouths.

Steve Reeves arrived with a lady interpreter. His bulging biceps and chest straining his white linen shirt! His massive legs showing through the light blue trousers. He spoke almost shyly with a voice too delicate for his size, and the interpreter translated. A girl was picked out by the judges, and Steve kissed her on both cheeks showing his teeth. During the shouts from the crowds, he took his shirt off. We gasped at his size, muscles rippling as he posed, his gold Rolex glinting in the floodlights! Leo and I looked at each other when his mother applauded excitedly. I thought the interpreter girl was much more attractive than any of the Misses. In the strong floodlight, you could see her nipples and the slight bulge of her dark pubic hair showing through the white dress.

*

There was a small club called the Le Nove Muse in Via Buia. I climbed the stone stairs with the sticky iron rail, and I entered a small corridor where I paid a fee to a skeletal man with a greasy bow tie and a Nazionale in his mouth. He never spoke or looked at you. Then through a worn curtain, careful not to ruffle my combed hair! Inside the larger room in a corner were a small band of old grey men playing accordion, drum and piano. In another corner was a small bar with a short curly-haired blond girl in attendance. The windows were always shut and the room smelled of smoke and alcohol. On the chairs against the wall sat the girls, generally servant girls from the countryside and older ladies with too much makeup. The few men looked around with suspicious eyes. I was the youngest one there and always went by myself.

"Would you like to dance?" I asked the girl with thick ankles and large breasts.

"Yes, with pleasure," she smiled. She had very pointed teeth. They were playing La Cumparsita. "I am not very good with the tango," she said taking my hand and putting her heavy hand on my shoulder. Other couples joined us on the floor. The light was low. We danced. She kept looking at my face, and I said 'What?' smiling. "How old are you?" she asked looking at me sideways.

"Seventeen," I lied.

"You look younger."

"You come from Garfagnana," I said to change the subject.

"Yes, from Gallicano."

"What are you doing in Lucca?"

"I work in the kitchen at the Count Tegrini," she said.

"What do you do in the kitchen?" I asked.

"This and that. I help with the cooking. They are a large family. They have gone to Spain now." We danced, talked, and at the end of a particularly slow tune, we kissed and stayed close together as the music ended. We left before 11 pm. She told me she had to be back by midnight.

"Like Cinderella," I said. She giggled. I accompanied her to the dark entrance of a large old building. Cats were caterwauling in the garden behind the iron grate. A large stone staircase led to the count's apartment and her room was through a small door in the corner. She did not want me to go inside; she was too scared of losing her job. I put my hand on the wall behind her, and we kissed. She was warm and firm, and while I touched her she unbuttoned me and played with me until I came in her hands. I stood with trembling legs and kissed her with gratitude on the forehead. She laughed in the dark, cleaning her hands on a handkerchief from her bag smelling of lavender. We kissed again. "Ciao," I whispered.

"I am happy to have met you," she replied and gently closed the door. I went to Le Nove Muse a few times more, but I never saw her again.

During that Summer, Mother decided that I should learn French. "The tongue of gentlemen," she said. The year before, she had decided to take piano lessons with an old school friend now teaching music at the conservatory in Lucca. She would come back from the lessons flustered and bad tempered carrying the music scores under her arm. When I asked her how it was going, she frowned, shook her head and was very vague. After a few weeks, she was advised by her teacher to give up and save the money as it was impossible to become proficient at her age. So instead, she decided to send me to a private tutor to learn French. The teacher was the daughter of an Ethiopian lady married to an Italian who had brought them home after returning from the war Italy had waged against Abyssinia on a foolish attempt to colonise North Africa. The teacher was golden skinned with pale brown eyes, and I fancied her immediately. "Bijoux, Caillou, Hibou," she would pronounce pouting her full lips and urging me to repeat.

If I pronounced something wrong, she patted me on the arm with her beautiful soft hands with long unpainted nails. The rapid movement reminded me of a cat at play. She sat close to me in the hot afternoons. I could feel her heat and her smell, and I had to stop myself reaching out and touching her honey-coloured breast and the soft rounded knees visible under the table. At the end of every lesson, to my surprise, she complimented my progress and standing escorted me to the door allowing a full view of her rounded bottom like two melons moving under her summer dress. Many times, I thought of how I could tell the teacher of my desire, after all she was only a few years older than me, but I never had the courage to do so. A few years ago, in my sixties, I saw her in Piazza San Michele. I followed her. She wore a scarf and an old grey coat. An old lady carrying a bag! I introduced myself. She looked surprised but a smile came to her face when she recognised me. I took her supermarket bag. The plastic had dug into the skin of her aged red hand. Gone were the long nails! We walked, and she asked me about my life. At the end when we reached her house, I said how much I had fancied her all those years ago. She smiled, colour came into her face, her eyes lit up, and for a moment, she looked young again.

Every year in September, Lucca has a festival with a huge fair in the fields outside the Mura. The wall of death with tough tattooed men revving shining bikes demonstrating on rollers outside, bumper car circuit and stalls everywhere selling food, watermelon and drinks amidst the noise of loudspeakers and music! One evening, out with my sister, having won an ugly brown monkey at the shooting booth, I felt a hand on my shoulder. I turned around, and Mara was there, more beautiful than I could remember. She wore high heels and a voluminous skirt with a tight jumper. She was with a few other girls, and by the way they chatted and looked, I got the idea they liked me. Mara told me she had got a job in a store in Via. Fillungo selling wool. "A tenuous connection with agriculture," she said laughing.

"It's close to my house," I said. "I will call on you."

She gave me a peck on the cheek and left saying, "I'll see you." My sister looked surprised, and I felt proud to know such a beautiful girl.

After siesta one afternoon soon after, I decided to call on Mara. I wore my favourite pale blue Lacoste shirt. Crossing the road, I saw my reflection in the window of the Art Shop. I could see the outline of my chest under the pale blue shirt. The wool shop was crowded with middle-aged ladies all talking animatedly, and Mara told me to wait for her at the new bar near Piazza dell' Anfiteatro. She arrived in a trail of perfume, smoking a cigarette. It took time for me to realise the new way she saw me – I had changed; I was not the skinny boy sitting beside her anymore. I ordered a beer for me and a Coca Cola for her. "How is your life at boarding school?" she asked.

"Not terribly free. I would like to live outside. I have almost convinced Mother to let me rent outside."

"Have you got a girlfriend?" she asked smiling.

"Not really but I have met a few girls since Mutigliano." Her interest in me made me daring. "Do you know when we shared a desk at Mutigliano, I really fancied you?"

"Did you? How sweet," she said and drank some coke quickly. The gas went up her nose, and she sneezed, laughing. I drank my beer. She offered me a Peter Stuyvesant. We smoked in silence smiling at each other. We could hear the mixed noises from the fair outside the Mura.

"Would you like to go to the Mura?" I said.

"Okay," she said while pulling her hair in a ponytail, a hair band ready between her strong teeth. I paid, and we left.

We walked up the road leading to the walls. Behind the church, I took her hand; it was cool in mine. She walked swinging her hips making her skirt swish. We stopped; the sun was going down. I sat on the grassy parapet. She was close to me smiling, the sun in her eyes. She tried to shade her face behind my head, and I moved sideways teasingly then I kissed her. Her lipstick tasted of watermelon. The lips parted and her tongue searched my mouth. I pressed my body to hers, and she hugged me. I kissed her and bit her earlobes. Her neck smelled of perfume and tasted terribly bitter. I excused myself and spat on the grass. She found that terribly funny and laughed and laughed. We kissed again, more seriously now. She took my hand, and we walked towards a tall wall in the fortifications hiding us from view. The area smelled of pee, but we were too excited to worry. I rested my back against the wall and pulled her towards me. I put my hand between her thighs, and she did not stop me, so I pulled aside her knickers and touched her there. She was hairy, moist, and she bit my ear. We kissed. I kept exploring the inside of her vagina, so soft. I tried clumsily to unbutton my fly, but she stopped me. "Enough," she whispered looking at me with worried eyes.

"Why?" I said.

"It is not the right place. I feel uncomfortable. We will meet again some other time," she said. She rearranged herself, and we left the walls looking towards the noise of the fair below.

I met Mara again by a wood near her house outside Lucca. I went by bike and travelled the few miles in a state of anticipation. She came walking through the trees swinging her hips and smiling. She had red lipstick and a yellow T-shirt. She stood looking at me, hand on her hips. I felt hot and self-conscious, but I put my hands on her waist and kissed her. Her lipstick still tasted of watermelon and her tongue touched mine. I tasted her sweet saliva. My leg softly pressed the gap between her thighs. I pushed hard against her belly, and she hugged me, threw her head back, and I kissed her neck, no perfume this time. She took my hand, and we walked through the trees. We sat on the sparse grass behind a pine tree and kissed long and hard. I touched between her legs, and she did not stop me. I put a finger inside her, and she moaned kissing me. I pulled down her knickers past her knees and looked at the black triangle of hair and the pink flesh of her opening when she parted her legs. I unbuttoned my jeans, but she stopped me again. She kissed me and said that it was enough. I got suddenly cross, stood up and walked to my bike and left her sitting picking bits of grass off her T-shirt. I never saw her again!

I had grown a few inches that summer and Auntie Bice, as a confirmed hypochondriac, diagnosed that I was suffering from hyperthyroidism. She took me to a specialist and a very tall doctor with a large nose looked at Auntie as if she was mad. A young nurse made me breathe into a tube and did various other analyses. I liked the feeling of her cool hands on my skin and her soft voice. We spoke, and I realised she was the older sister of a friend. A few years before, I had gone to see a cowboy film with her. During the long film, I tried to pick up the courage to kiss her, but I felt too shy to try. *When the Indians attack, I will kiss her*, I promised myself, but the attack came and the film finished, but I didn't kiss her. A few days later, I heard from friends that she had said she thought I was gay because I had not tried with her. The results from the exams were negative and Auntie Bice relaxed.

The nurse was called Carla, and I met her again in town. Later, we went with a group of friends by bus to Torre Del Lago. We visited Puccini's villa and had 'pane e salame' by the lake and hired a rowing boat. Later on the way home, the bus was so full that we ended up standing in the aisle. Carla's soft behind pressed against me. She moved gently; standing on tiptoes, she pressed rhythmically against my penis. Entering the Mura of Lucca through the enormous gate, I came, my hands against Carla's waist, in bursts, silently, my penis pressing the softness of her arse, my face buried in her scented hair. Descending the bus, I noticed the wet patch on my light gabardine trousers. I took my pullover off and carried it on my arm in front of me. We walked towards Carla's house, but we stopped by the fountain in Piazza San Martino and tried to wash the stain off, making my trousers even more wet. We went back to her house, and she told me her brother and parents were away and would not come back till after dinner. We kissed in the kitchen, the coffee machine hissing on the gas. We went into Carla's room and listened to the Platters *Only You* on the gramophone, close together, breathing each other's breath and kissing until stupefied. We lay on the bed and touched each other in the semi-darkness. We kept our clothes on, but she pushed my head towards her pussy and kept it there firmly. I pulled her panties down and kissed her there, her wetness stinging my shaved chin. We heard the front door rattling and voices. Shit! I left through the French windows, stumbled into terracotta pots and bushes, climbed the front wall and went home.

Years passed, and during a summer holiday from England, I went to the hospital to visit Granny. She was almost a hundred, and she looked so small in the white bed. She wanted me to put the flowers I had brought her into a vase, and I went into the corridor to look for a nurse. The door of a room was ajar and a nurse came out; it was Carla, still attractive and smiling. She told she had got engaged a few months before and was happy. She took a picture with my camera of Granny and I sitting on her bed in the hospital. I still have the picture with Granny looking so small, like an old little girl.

Pescia (2nd Year)

I managed to convince Mother that I did not want to be a boarder anymore. I appealed to her explaining how much part of my life was spent boarding. I heard that a relation of my director from Mutigliano rented rooms in a large apartment near the school. A few days before school started, I went with Mother to a smart shop, and we bought some wonderfully expensive clothes. Jackets in muted colours, trousers, woollen shirts in grey, Bordeaux and black to match! I felt smart and looked good in my new clothes. Even the shop assistant said so. My body had started to fill out with exercise and good food. I spent time looking at myself in the mirror in the poses of the actors of the time. I cut my hair like Marlon Brando and had started to shave regularly.

A few of the boys from the boarding school joined me in the rented apartment. Angelo arrived from Maremma on a new Guzzi bike with a bag full of salami from his farm. Marco was already there and was the hairiest guy I had ever seen. He paid me to shave him. He was hairy all over, his beard joined hair on his neck and down to his chest, the same on his back. Hair everywhere! Zalum was a Jew from Livorno, and he spoke English well. Vittorio arrived with a tape recorder and told us that last summer in Torre Del Lago he caught a pike weighing 13 kilos. Cristiano was another boy in the flat. He was tall, thin with dark curly hair. He was a count and looked like an Etruscan warrior. His father ran the Military Office in Lucca where the conscripts had their medical examinations. Cristiano had a very long penis and showed it at any occasion.

We made friends with a group of girls working at the Olivetti typing pool. We were invited to parties where we drank and snogged a lot. At the local bar, we made friends with an older gentleman in his sixties. He always wore a black shirt. He had been very active during Mussolini's regime and had been a high ranked member of the Fascist party. He now ran a small office for the MSI, a party trying to revive fascism in Italy. He offered us his small office to have parties. Equipped with a gramophone and records, we became well known among young people for 'good time' parties in Pescia. Vittorio used his tape recorder to record songs from the radio. We listened to *Coconut Woman* from Harry Bellafonte till the tape wore out. Zalum translated for us. We recorded our voices with all the dirty words we knew in our local dialect. I marvelled at how different they sounded!

During chemistry lessons, I learned how to make smoke bombs by mixing potassium chlorate, sugar, charcoal and sulphur in a small plastic bottle. The fuse was made with the long head of a windproof match. We exploded the bombs in various parts of the town causing great clouds of smoke and worrying the locals. We sat on the steps on a small dusty church in the town centre, smoking, eating peanuts and looking at girls. I went to the gym in the local town hall in the evening. Nobody was there, an empty dark room; I lifted weights in silence, only the sound of clinking iron and my breath. At the apartment, very little studying was done. When one of us was found working, he would be rapidly dissuaded by the boys and taken out of the house to roam the town. The food was cooked by the lady upstairs and was very appetising. One of the boys, Giovanni, was very fussy about food. Once he found a hair in his pasta and from then on always checked his plate. We borrowed a monkey's skull from the museum at the school, put two olives in its eye sockets, put it on Giovanni's plate and covered with spaghetti alla Bolognese. Giovanni did his usual turning of his plate to inspect it, started to fork the spaghetti and ate a few forkfuls, our eyes on him, then hit something solid and the grinning skull appeared among the pasta. The olives in the socket staring at him! He rushed to the loo next door, and we heard sounds of retching.

We slept in two rooms with three beds each separated by the dining room. At night, before falling asleep, we took turns in telling stories. One of the stories I remember is when Marco, the hairy one, told how in desperation, not able to find any girls in his village willing to sleep with him, went to his barn. He climbed on a milking stool placed near the back end of a cow, pulled his pants down having wrapped the swishing tale of the cow around his neck. At the moment of entering, the cow shat filling his lowered pants. The door opened and his father came in. Oops!

Angelo had fallen in love with the daughter of the landlady upstairs. At night as the door to the apartment was locked, he would go to the courtyard at the back, climb an old wisteria and reach the window of his beloved. He would descend in the morning pale and bleary eyed and go straight to bed missing lessons.

To try to build up my body, I consumed large amounts of food and drank milk. I have a photo of all of us at dinner in the house. Everyone is posing swigging from a bottle of red wine but mine is milk.

When we were flush, we sometimes went as a group to a club in Montecatini. There we met a man, Sansone, older than us, maybe in his thirties. He was very well dressed and sophisticated. He bought us cocktails we had never tasted before and introduced us to older girls. We realised he was a homosexual, and he loved to be seen with us. He was a great dancer and moved with grace, looked very manly and we wondered why he was gay. He was the owner of a large plant nursery employing many people. He drove a large Lancia car, and sometimes we all piled in, the six of us. He took us to Florence and Pisa. He liked to stop at places where prostitutes congregated either in town or in lonely woods by the road. He knew how to talk to them and offered to pay if we wanted one. I never took up the offer. Maybe I was shy? Marco always went and told us the details in the car on the way home. Sansone asked him questions and appeared amused at the answers.

We drove to Viareggio during the carnival. We wore masks he bought and had a great time throwing confetti and squeezing and kissing the girls. He smiled at our antics and took us to many bars. On the way back, Marco vomited inside the car. Even that did not seem to worry our benefactor. He shook his head and smiled. We stopped at a garage, and he bribed the pump attendant to clean the car while we had coffee and pastries in the bar. He bought a bottle of Atkinson's lavender from the kiosk to sprinkle inside the Lancia.

He never made a pass at us or mentioned his homosexuality. One Christmas, he bought each of us a beautiful Dunhill lighter in a velvet pouch. He was like that, generous! He disappeared from our lives as quickly as he had appeared. Some people said he had gone to Morocco, some said he went into a monastery. We never knew the truth.

One evening, after a trip to town, I did not feel very well. I had a pain on the right side of my belly and went straight to bed instead of having the usual swig of grappa and conversation. The boys jumped on my bed to try to rouse me. My pain got worse, and I had to go and vomit. Finally, they got worried. I was sweating profusely and refused to play with them. They called the landlady upstairs, and she phoned for a doctor. I was taken to the hospital in an ambulance with suspected perforated appendix. I was operated on almost immediately. On waking the next day, I left nauseous and my belly was hurting. Mother had been called and stood beside my bed, worriedly looking at me. I was in a long white room with several beds. The man next to me, a hunter with a crop of white hair and a ruddy face, had been shot in the buttocks with bird pellets by another hunter in a dispute over a shot pheasant. His fat wife came to see him with his young daughter and brought him a bottle of homemade grappa, which he hid behind his bedside table. The daughter was blond, pretty, wore trousers and entertained us with a hula hoop while chewing gum. She offered me a piece, and later when I fell asleep, I got it stuck in my hair.

On the other side was another middle-aged man. As soon as I recovered from the anaesthetics, he pulled his pyjamas down and showed me his huge testicles. The scrotum was swollen and blue and almost ready to burst. He suffered from hydrocele, an accumulation of liquid in his scrotum, the nurse told me. But he thought that the size of his testicles was due to his great virility. He spent hours telling me of his conquests and sexual adventures all over Tuscany. His wife visited, a grey lady modestly dressed. She brought a delicious apple cake that we all shared.

The young nurse in charge of the ward was very dark with a hint of a moustache but tall and very shapely. She had large brown eyes. I was very fond of her and strained my neck every time she crossed the ward to look at her bottom. On the day they took my stitches out, she stood beside the bed holding a dish. My penis was so shrivelled with the pain that I felt ashamed of myself and kept checking to see if she was laughing.

Another day, having pulled the curtain around my bed, she proceeded to sponge wash me with the help of an older nurse. When the warm soapy sponge rubbed my penis, I got an erection. I did not want it to happen! They giggled. I closed my eyes trying to think of something that would make my penis shrink, but I could not, and it stayed hard even when the older nurse flicked it with the towel laughing.

I had time to talk to the young nurse in the two weeks I spent in the hospital. She was called Gina, the daughter of the guardian of the flower market – a very modern building by the river with a single concrete arch that housed the flower market several days a week. When I left the hospital, I contacted Gina. We met at the market in the evening before dinner, in the dark, under the huge arch. We kissed surrounded by the smell of large quantities of carnations packed in boxes ready for the morning market. I touched her warm, hard nipples. She shivered with my cold hands. She wanted to feel the scar on my belly; I let her, and she said it was healing nicely, and we laughed. She touched my penis, and I put my hands on her round bottom. We lay on a pile of jute sacks. She did not let me make love to her, but she played with me until I came silently. We did not talk much! We met many times in the dark in the evenings. I whistled, and she would come out of the small villa beside the dark canopy. She would not let me make love to her but always gave me pleasure. One evening as I was kissing her, she pulled away and told me that she was getting engaged and could not see me anymore. It was a blow! I had got used to this dark, silent woman. She let me kiss her a bit longer and then she walked away, disappearing in the darkness of the market amongst the carnations. I saw her again in Lucca a few years after, pushing a pram with a red-haired boy inside. She was fatter, happily married and radiant.

*

Nearly every Saturday, I took the tram from Pescia to Lucca, bought chewing gum at the bar by the tram stop, sat on the worn grey leather seats and enjoyed the slow journey, passing small towns, vineyards and musing at how often dogs asleep on the line stopped the tram. I listened to the voices around me, chewing gum to a rhythm in my head, generally jazz. Sometimes lines of poetry would come into my head. I often wrote verses on the back of the chewing gum wrapper.

At home, Granny was getting older, her hair was completely white, and she still wore the dark clothes I remember her wearing when I was a boy. Mother was greying too, her hair in a bun and energetic as ever. When she asked me about my studies, I reassured her all was well, knowing that I had not done any work at all. Auntie Bice had completely renovated her bedroom with new furniture and bed, all very chintzy! She had developed a fixation regarding the toilet. There was a note on the door asking not to throw anything that would block the drains. She asked me every day how many pieces of toilet paper I had used. I picked her up and made her laugh. My sister was growing too, very tall and very pretty. She wore dancing shoes in pastel colours and tapering trousers. She reminded me of a young Audrey Hepburn.

On a weekend in November, I decided to phone Carlo in Garfagnana. "*Vieni, vieni,*" he said in his Florentine accent, "we will have a good time. I know some new girls. You will see!" I walked to the station on Saturday morning, after a breakfast of ham and eggs. There was fog outside the walls and the grass was covered with frost. A dog had left tracks on the grass leading to a big tree in the centre of the field. I had coffee in the steamed up, smoky bar and boarded the train to Castelnuovo. I walked from the station to La Pieve. It was cold and windy with a clear sky, the smell of chestnut wood smoke everywhere. I stopped at the small shop in the main road of La Pieve to buy some chocolate for Auntie Barbara. The shop had a smell I remembered as a child, and Signora Cesira looked exactly the same, rounded, hair in a bun and thick glasses. She did not recognise me at first and when she did, laughed at how tall I was and went in the back to call her sister to look at me. Auntie Barbara had lost some more of her teeth and kept her lips closed self-consciously. I felt chocolate was not the best present, but she liked it and kissed me on the forehead. She still smelled of chestnut flour. She gave me a drink of grappa in a small green cut glass, one of her prized possessions! I went to look at her bedroom where I had slept as a child. The iron bed with the polished brass knobs, the yellow washing basin with a jar full of water! The pink China pig with the small velvet cushion full of pins. All so neat! The room smelled of talcum powder as I remembered. She cried when I left, drying her cheeks with her apron.

I walked up the mule track along the Jara River. There had been some floods, and the bed of the river was full of uprooted trees and branches. I picked a dried-up apple from a tree and chewed it, walking fast. At the bridge, I took the road to the house beside the power station. Carlo had grown too, less tall than me but stockier. We shook hands; he tried to crush mine. We pushed each other, lost balance and hit the shotgun hanging on the wall in the hall. A dog started to bark, and Carlo's father opened the kitchen door. He was fatter and wore a greasy beret and plus-fours. In the kitchen, the smell of small birds on a long skewer roasting by the fire! Juices slowly dripping into a low tray! The dog among the distraction started to lick the tray, and Carlo's father kicked him. We ate sitting on straw chairs by the fire, the dog under the table chewing the birds' bones we threw at him. The birds tasted strong, rich and slightly bitter. Carlo's father cut long slabs of grey bread with an enormous knife against his chest. We toasted the bread and drank red wine that left a stain on the short tumblers. After lunch, we went into Carlo's room. The walls were decorated with pictures of sportsmen and pinups of the time. He had feathers in a spent cannon shell and a bayonet on the wall. He got a worn pinup magazine from under the mattress, some of the girls were naked, one of them was using her hands to open her buttocks! We laughed!

"Shall we go to the cinema in Castelnuovo? There is a war film," he said. Later in the cinema, we entered a dark balcony smelling of sawdust; I could not see anything at first. On the screen, an aerial dog fight in colour was taking place. We approached the padded balustrade and, being suspended in the dark standing at screen level, I almost felt I was flying myself. The noise of the planes and gunfire was almost unbearable. When I tried to move sideways to make room for Carlo, I stepped on a girl's foot. I apologised and smiled at her pale face with large eyes and dark hair. Carlo knew the girl and introduced me to her.

"Maria," she whispered in my ear against the noise, her breath smelled of alcohol. Maria in turn introduced a girl on the other side of Carlo. She was tall, blond and had hair piled up high. I didn't catch her name. My hand reached for Maria's hand on the balustrade and her body got close. I felt the coarse texture of her dark coat, the soft skirt underneath and the warmth and softness of her body. Her curly hair smelled earthy and exciting. She turned around, and we kissed. Her mouth was soft and giving, and the noise of the gunfire seemed to disappear as our bodies got close together. We didn't speak. When the battle finished, I looked at Carlo. He was kissing the blond with the beehive hair. She was taller than him. Around us, nearly everybody was snogging. Maria turned and took off her coat that fell on the floor and placed her hands on the balustrade. I felt her bottom pushing gently against me. My erection accommodated by the cleft of her cheeks. Bliss! The film ended with a wedding ceremony and the bouquet flying in the air with jets in the background. We filed out, holding hands, chatting with the rest of the audience, Carlo's arm around the blonde's waist. We walked, almost silently passed the prison, the frozen fountain with bronze spout in the shape of a bull's head and approached the railway station. We walked into the crowded bar and ordered punch al mandarino. The blonde introduced herself.

"Carla," she said snivelling. Carlo tapped his feet on the sawdust floor. We drank blowing on the hot orange-coloured drinks, standing at the bar. The locals, mainly old men, looked at us critically. We got out into the cold again, warmer now. We opened a rusty gate and entered the goods yard under the moonlight. There, on a rail overgrown with small trees and weeds, stood a wagon with an open sliding door. I jumped up and gave Maria a hand to climb up. I tried to close the door, but it was jammed. Inside, it smelled of rust and damp. We kissed rapidly reaching for each other's body in the dark. She was warm. To my surprise, she took off her coat and put it on the wooden floor. She knew what she wanted! I felt almost scared of her. She gently lowered me onto her. I felt excited but clumsy, my hands cold on her thighs. She took my hands with her slightly coarse hands and moved them around her body where she wanted them. Her soft breasts in her satin bra, her belly shivering with my touch, her crotch wet! I lowered my trousers and pants, my bottom shivering from the cold, my belt buckle clinking on the metal floor. She parted her knickers and helped me to enter her warm body. She kissed me harder, my weight on her and we moved together. I felt excited but strangely detached, as if it was not happening to me and as if I was looking at myself. What I had been dreaming about for years seemed disappointing! Now only the noise of our breathing in the confined space, our mouths searching, breathing heavily! She moaned. Energy welling inside me, I felt like screaming. She quickly pushed me out, and I came on her belly. I heard her fumbling in the dark and then she kissed me, reached for her bag and lit a cigarette. The light from the match briefly on her face. She looked serious and older. We adjusted our clothes, sat on her coat, smoked and talked.

She worked in the local shoe factory and lived with her mother, had a younger brother and she never knew her father. Carlo whistled outside. I stood and looked out of the door, jumped down and offered my arms to take Maria's weight. She was heavy. We laughed, and she landed on my feet. Carlo patted me on the shoulder and giggled sideways, a fag in his mouth. We walked on the gravel path to the road, the blonde's beehive was a bit askew, and she put lipstick on under the streetlamp by the station.

"We will meet by the fountain at 11," said Carlo taking the blonde's arm. The girls kissed, and we parted. We walked across Castelnuovo hugging against the cold. We had a sandwich and a cappuccino at the bar near her house. They all knew her and glanced at me with curiosity. We kissed briefly in the dark hall of her council house, swaying on loose tiles smelling of cats' pee. I said goodbye with a last hand squeeze. I didn't see her again until years later, on a walk with a friend in summer after dinner. I saw her against a tall wall under a light on the outside of Castelnuovo.

"Would you like some business?" she said to us, her voice coarse with smoke. In a mini skirt, her hair was cropped short. I wanted to tell her who I was, but I only managed to say, 'No, thanks, darling,' for both of us and walked on.

I met Carlo, freezing by the fountain. "Did you fuck?" he said punching me softly.

"Yes," I said.

"Great," he said. We skipped up the mule track laughing and pushing each other. Then talked and smoked on the tarmac road towards the bridge white in the moonlight.

*

Back in Pescia, we started going to a working club behind the main road. We met many characters, older people pleased to see younger faces. We drank beer, played billiards and courted the members' daughters. Cristiano, the well-endowed count, and I started to date two girls. The one I was with had a strong body with large hips and breasts and blonde curly hair and always on high heels. She presented me with a hand-knitted pale blue jumper on our second date. I had told her it was my favourite colour. The other girl who lived near the school was slim, dark, delicate and very pretty. She looked like Francoise Hardy. We met in the countryside near Pescia. I petted heavily with mine, but she was very strong and never let me go too far. Once in a cane field bordering a stream, I tried to open her legs. She pushed me off so strongly and I landed in the green slimy stream. Cristiano had fallen in love with his girl and didn't even try to fuck her. One Sunday in early summer, we invited the girls to come to Lucca. We waited for them after lunch at the bus station. The sticky tar on the tarmac had splashed on my white suede moccasins, and I made it worse by rubbing it with a handkerchief. The smell of diesel from the bus was suffocating in the hot air! The girls emerged from the blue dusty bus in pastel summer clothes, looking radiant. We took them to a bar in Piazza Grande and all had Cuba Libre. Cristiano had taken the keys from his father's office and the plan was to take them there. To my surprise, they accepted to come. The office on the ground floor of the huge palace built by Napoleon's sisters was cool and consisted of many vaulted large rooms. My girl and I ended up petting on the narrow bed used to examine new recruits. She pushed me off again after a while, and I smashed against the glass cupboard containing medical equipment. Nothing broke this time! I don't remember the girl's name, and I never saw her again.

II Casino

Cristiano and I had long talked about going to the brothel in Via della Dogana. We were both underaged and decided to change the year on our identity cards and go before the lady, Senator Merlini, closed the brothels for humanitarian reasons in 1958. The brothels were legally run by the Italian Government.

"Ciao Cristiano. How are you?"

"I don't know...not too well," he said.

"Why?" I said grabbing the soft wet sleeve of his green Loden and pointing him towards the neon sign of the Bar Astra across the square. We ran avoiding a car and splashing in a puddle by the footpath. "Why?" I said again as we entered the bar almost empty with its warm smells of coffee and alcohol.

"I don't know," he said, and I found myself looking into dark shiny eyes in a face lean and humorous; I used to call him l'Etrusco. "I don't know if we will be able to go in...if my father finds out, there will be trouble," Cristiano said trying to attract the attention of the barman.

"Due Corretti al Rum," I shouted and grabbed Cristiano's slim wet shoulders. "Listen," I said, "in six months they will be closed...we got to find out what it's like. We can say that we lost our identity cards after and they'll never know. I cannot wait to be eighteen…and then see them closed."

He stared at his brown wet moccasins, shuffling on the sawdust, then looked up and smiled nervously showing his white sharp teeth. "Okay?" I said.

"Yes," he said without much conviction.

"Let me see the identity card," I said, "did you correct it yourself or did you give it to the fixer?"

"I did it," he said taking his wallet out and slowly handing me the card, still shuffling and looking around.

"It looks okay," I said. "It's perfect. Stop worrying. Did you use dissolving fluid?"

"Yes," he said smiling. The coffees arrived, and we drank in silence, smiling at each other and blowing on the hot liquid. I felt it going all the way down to my belly, warming it and making me feel less tense. I paid, and we left. Outside, it was still raining.

"Look, it's four o'clock," I said. "Let's go now; it won't be busy. It will be perfect. Okay?" He nodded, and we walked past the bus ticket office and the cinema showing *Seven Brides for Seven Brothers*.

In the distance, the theatre with its cast iron gas lamps and pink 18th century facade formed a corner, darker than the rest and beside it was Via Della Dogana with its smelly, tarred pissoires with the pierced iron sides. I could smell the damp and the cats' pee coming from the shallow, dusty window grilles at ground level. Nobody was in the narrow alley. We arrived at the worn steps and peeling brown door with the sharp diamond-shaped studs. I took a breath and placed my hand on the clammy iron knob, pushed and entered a dark corridor with a stone floor leading to a hallway. At the desk was Nuccia, our enemy. She had been described by older boys, newcomers to the brothel, as the equivalent of Caron the Demon from Dante's Inferno.

"Come in, come in," she said in her Bolognese dialect. "You look pretty. Have you come for a fuck, or just a look? Show me your documents."

"Hello, Nuccia," I said opening my coat and extracting the carefully placed card. She took both our cards with a fast movement, showing her strong hand and deep red talons. She laughed and her soft full breast almost burst out of her red dress. She lit a cigarette still peering at our cards with semi-closed eyes. She picked an imaginary fleck of tobacco from her thick lips, coughed, looked serious and slowly handed us back the cards.

"Okay. Go in, but don't waste my time. Fifteen minutes to look then either you fuck or you leave. No wanking. Okay?" I quickly winked at Cristiano and he smiled back. I pushed open the leather-padded door, and it felt sticky to my touch. Inside, it smelled of stale smoke, and it was dark. There were a few settees and armchairs in dark leather with girls in revealing clothes perched on them. It looked strangely like a large sitting room of a cheap hotel.

Somebody pulled at my sleeve, and I saw the idiotic smiling face of Elfo. "How are you? You have come, eh? Are you going to fuck? I have already, but I like being here. I like looking." He said all this rapidly shouting in his strange drawling voice, his head with very short hair, bent on one side and his large teeth permanently showing. Elfo, the over-sexed idiot son of the local owner of a large ice cream shop! His father allowed him a daily visit to the brothel to keep him out of trouble. "I like pussies," Elfo said dribbling and rubbing his large head. "I like pussies."

"Come here, boys, come here. Let us look after you," one of the two ladies on a settee to our right called to us. We walked towards them. One took my coat off and showed me a seat.

"My name is Sonia," she said. She was short with long dark hair and a curvy figure, dressed in a black cocktail dress showing her deep cleavage and wide hips. I looked into her face; she had friendly brown eyes and dark make-up with full red lips. "I have never seen you here before," Sonia said picking the slice of lemon from her drink and biting it with pushed back lips, revealing small pearly teeth and sucking the sharp juice.

"No, it's our first time," I found myself saying. Cristiano gave me a dirty look. "I wanted to come before the closure in six months' time," I added with a nervous smile. She smiled and sat back drinking. She placed her red high-heeled shoes on the table. Cristiano was sitting beside a large dark lady wearing black panties and bra under a revealing transparent black negligee. She winked at me, and Cristiano offered her a cigarette, which she took without thanks with a red hand with bitten nails. We sat around in silence smoking.

"Do you want to go upstairs?" said Sonia.

"Yes, sure," I said looking at Cristiano. "Shall we go?" I said to him.

"Okay," he said, "this is Tamara." I shook the red hand across the table, and we stood and moved towards the stairs. Sonia put her arm around my waist.

"You are so tall," she said and stood on the tips of her red shoes looking up and laughing. She still carried her drink. We followed Tamara and Cristiano up a long flight of well-worn stone steps smelling of bleach. We slowly reached the first floor. It was dark, Tamara puffed and laughed and put Cristiano's arms around her large behind to push her up. With Sonia beside me, we climbed, giggling. I had a hard-on, and I felt happy. I was worried about not being able to do it with an adult woman or being teased by Cristiano and the other boys. But now I was definitely hard and very willing.

Almost at the top of the long flight of stairs, Cristiano stopped suddenly, and I bumped my head on his behind. He was grasping at Tamara's breast, kissing her neck and rubbing against her great wobbly behind, smiling and moaning while she laughed and teased him. Then he stopped, slowly turned around and whispered to me, "Shit, I've come. Can you believe it, I just came?" Tamara turned around.

"What happened little boy?" she said and grabbing at Cristiano's red cheeks said, "Did you get too excited? Never mind, come up to my room and maybe we can try again, eh?" We reached the top and Cristiano, looking worried, walked through a well-worn curtain with Tamara behind him, hands on his shoulders.

Sonia opened a brown door, and we entered a white room with a large iron bed and a yellow cover and blue tiles on the floor. The straw chair in the corner looked like the one in the Van Gogh painting. The room smelled of disinfectant, almost like a lavatory. There was a bidet and a basin in the corner. Sonia put her drink on the floor, took her red shoes off and then her stockings showing her strong white legs. "Take off your clothes, don't just look at me," she said laughing. I started to undress and put my clothes on the chair beside the bed. When I turned around, she was naked, beautiful and strong like the marble statue of an Amazon in the history books. I looked at the dark triangle of hair and her firm breasts as she moved across the room. She took my hand and led me to the basin. With her warm hands, she washed my penis with some carbolic liquid as prescribed by the brothel doctors. The girls, she told me, were visited once a week by a doctor who examined them for venereal diseases. I felt reassured. I rested my shoulder on the cold rough textured wall and put my lips on the back of her neck. I could smell the strong scent coming from her dark hair. She dried my then limp penis, slowly, gently and led me to the bed. She pulled the yellow cover off with a swift movement and the draught made me shiver. We lay on the bed looking at the small skylight and the rain gently tapping. We kissed; she didn't open her mouth, and she touched me till I was ready. "I like lying with you," she whispered to me, "but this is a brothel and time is precious."

She pushed me on top of her and with a bit of help, I entered her. I saw her open her mouth and close her eyes. We moved together slowly. I felt almost carried by her body. Here I was making love to this beautiful woman, and I felt nothing. I felt alone, hollow, as if my body was not my body. "What's wrong?" she said. "Let's change position. I'll go on top of you." She straddled on top of me and tossed her hair back. I saw the reflection of our naked bodies on the skylight, and I felt as if I was looking at someone else making love to Sonia. I closed my eyes and took a dark hard nipple in my mouth, greedily, one nipple then the other. I moved with the noise of our breathing on the rickety bed, the rain on the skylight and the movement of our bodies. Then I came, silently, solitarily, pushing my head back. I saw for the first time, a card of the Virgin Mary pinned on the wall above the headboard!

Sonia stopped moving and collapsed her sweating body on mine, our heads near. I turned and smelled stale smoke on the cushion. She got up. "Get dressed," she said and sat on the bidet washing. I dressed in silence then sat on the bed while she dressed. She did not look at me. She sat on the bed to put on her lipstick, and I touched her neck briefly. "You feel cold," she said, stood up and walked towards the door. She opened it and started to walk downstairs without turning. I followed close behind, and at the bottom of the dark stairs, she turned and looked at me with a sad smile and said, "Ciao."

I felt alone, conspicuous and looked for Cristiano. Only Elfo was in the room, sitting knees together, hands in his pockets, rocking and smiling. "Pussy is beautiful," he said. I walked out and a girl ran after me with my coat. I didn't see her face. "Single or double?" said Nuccia.

"Single," I said and fished out 500 Lire. She took the money and winked at me. Outside, it was still raining. I lifted the hood of my duffle coat. The air smelled of the oil refinery and cats' piss. I turned the corner, back into the square and towards the bar. Cristiano was standing at the counter. He looked pale in the neon light. He grinned at me and ordered another Corretto.

"I could not do it again," he said putting his arm on my shoulder. "How did it go for you?" he asked looking into my face. I just gave him a disappointed grimace, twisting my mouth down. "Oh," he said, "let's go and see a film. They're showing *Cat on a Hot Tin Roof* at the Mignon." I looked at the rain on the window, distorting the images of the square outside, and again, I felt as if I was not there and as if I was someone else.

Many years later, I heard from a friend that Cristiano had a form of Alzheimer's. During a visit to my sister in Lucca, I phoned his house and his wife, Donatella, invited me to go and visit but to be prepared for a shock. Donatella opened the door, and we embraced. Much time had passed; she cried briefly and led me upstairs to the sitting room. Cristiano sat on the settee, his back to me. He wore slippers and pyjamas, his legs tightly closed together. His beautiful face had softened, his hair sparse. He seemed to recognise me. I asked him if I could kiss him, and he nodded. I kissed his soft cheek; he was crying. When I spoke to him, he just repeated my words in a whisper. His arms and shoulders were trembling. I reminded him of our friends, our visit to the brothel, but he only repeated names ending in an incomprehensible whisper. I put my arm on his shoulder and his trembling stopped. Donatella told me how the disease had started. Their beautiful, vivacious granddaughter joined us smiling and playing with her Play Station. Just before I left, I knelt in front of Cristiano, his dark eyes met mine, and it was the saddest look I can remember. I left and going down the wide echoing stone steps of the medieval palace, I felt lucky with what I had.

June came and I did fail my exams on one subject – maths. All those long walks by the river with my mother as a kid trying to memorise the timetables and carrying a fishing rod without a hook had not been very useful. I failed with a 5, 6 would have been a pass. I was very surprised with the result as I had helped the maths and physics teacher to keep discipline in the class. I also helped her with the equipment during physics experiments. We had two hours of maths in the morning, and I hated it. Towards the end of the second hour, I could see the teacher, who always wore very tight skirts, shifting from foot to foot and clenching her buttocks. We knew she was desperate to pee. Once before, the boys at the back had started with the hissing sound like when you want a child to pee. She looked at the class with hateful eyes and ran to the loo leaving the classroom door open. Her high heels echoing in the empty corridor! I had stopped the boys hissing and kept discipline. She should have given me a pass!

Mother was very disappointed at my failure to be admitted to my third year at the school in Pescia and having to retake maths in October. She decided it would be good for me to work for a few weeks before starting to study again. Mother's employer, Mr Fortuna, found me a job with the Count Minuzzoli Tegrini in one of his farms by Lake Massaciuccoli specialising in growing rice. A very tall man called Giovanni turned up in Lucca to take me to the farm twelve kilometres away. He rode a Vespa and was very tanned. We must have looked very funny, two tall men on a scooter! He kept telling me one joke after another, and I laughed politely although I could not hear much with the noise of the Vespa and the wind. He also worryingly kept turning around to check my reactions, and I kept breaking with my foot on the hold. We reached the farm in the early evening, the lake full of light from the sun setting in the West. The old farm consisted of many buildings in the pale local stone by the water's edge. I was given a room, white and neat with a huge iron bed and a night table, on the ground floor of one of the buildings. It had a tap over a stone sink and a toilet outside, just a well-polished plank with a hole and a wooden stopper over it. As you lifted the stopper, a suffocating smell of ammonia brought tears to your eyes! Not a place to relax and read my latest book, *Lady Chatterley's Lover*.

We had dinner of bean soup and sausage. Very tasty! Giovanni cracked jokes all through dinner and now I could laugh for good reason – he was good at it. We had coffee brought by a lady in her forties wearing clogs and hair in a tight bun. Under her loose peasant clothes, it looked like she had a good figure. Giovanni told me that my task in the next few weeks would be to weigh the sacks of rice and calculate a 55% weight to go to the count and the rest 45% for the farmer. "You can calculate percentages, can't you?" he said staring at me.

"Yes, of course," I said. "I multiply the weight by the percentage and divide by a hundred." One of the few things I remembered from school. I slept well, but I dreamed of huge farmers, cross at my miscalculations, throwing me in the lake. In the morning, Rosa made us piles of toasted farm bread with fig jam and caffe latte. She had lovely brown eyes with long curved lashes and beautiful teeth.

Giovanni whispered to me when she left the room, "She is very attractive, isn't she? I tried a few times, but she does not want to know. She is a widow, you know. No children. Her husband was a Cavatore who got killed in an accident at the marble quarry in Carrara." She walked back swaying carrying more milk and coffee. I smiled at her, but she shyly turned back to the kitchen. Outside, the lake, covered in a fine mist, seemed to extend forever. What you could see shimmering in the distance was the sea. We walked to a large stone barn open to the lake. There was a large old-fashioned scale near the entrance with piles of iron weights, a table with a notepad and yellow pencils and pigeons cooing on the beams above. The farmers started to arrive, some with carts pulled by donkeys, some with an ape, a small three-wheeled Vespa with a cargo base in the back. One man with a Basque cap arrived pushing a bicycle with two sacks strapped on the saddle and crossbar. I weighed and divided the heavy sacks and felt more and more confident. The farmers treated me with respect and did not seem to mind my young age. At lunchtime, Rosa came with sandwiches and a quarter of sharp white wine. I sat by the lake, my back to a poplar, eating and thinking. The afternoon was less busy, and I found a flat punt, used by duck hunters, tied to a tree hidden by the canes at the water's edge. It was painted a pale lapis colour peeling off and revealing pink and even a yellow colour underneath. A sort of artistic camouflage reflected on the clear waters. Giovanni told me at dinner that his task consisted of making sure that the farmers took all the rice to be weighed by making frequent inspections to the farms on his Vespa. I felt red from the sun and pleasantly tired. We had stew of wild mallard from the lake and rice. Giovanni seemed to be happy with my work, and I went to bed glowing. A yellow rose stood in a glass of water on the marble-topped bedside table! Days passed, my arms ached from lifting the sacks of rice, but I got stronger. At the end, I could make lifting look as easy as some of the farmers.

During my lunch break by the lake, the local priest arrived with a young very animated man. They carried what looked like a small cannon. It was an old long punt gun. It got bolted to the front of the boat, the sombre metal patina of the gun contrasting with the pastel colours of the punt. They left smiling, having taken a swig each from a flask of red wine, almost reclining in the punt rowing with small paddle oars. Later on, before I left for dinner, I heard the boom of the gun on the lake and for a while all was silent in the fading light of the evening. The weeks passed slowly, early rise and early to bed.

During lunch one day by the lake, I saw an enormous pike cruising just below the surface by the shore, green and slow moving. He left the water to take a frog on a lily pad with such force he created a wave! The lily pads moved in the water, droplets rolling on the waxy green surface, joining, separating, catching the light like the mercury we spilled on the museum floor!

On the last night, we had a party in the barn by the lake. A large pile of sacks stood by the side of the barn – the count's share! Giovanni, in his joking way, announced to me that I had made mistakes with the weighing and I would not be paid but, in fact, I owed the count money. I saw his round ruddy face look at me seriously and then slowly break into a laugh that reassured me he was joking! Some of the farmers and their families turned up. There was a bonfire just outside the barn, an accordion player sat on the grass and the table was laid with wine, cheese and salami and huge loaves baked by Rosa. Later on, the young son of the count arrived with friends and a pretty blonde girl on a red Giulietta Alpha Romeo in a cloud of dust. They all wore blue jeans, espadrilles with no socks and peasant shirts of different colours. We ate looking at the young count and the blonde dancing by the bonfire. They tried to sing the latest rock and roll songs, and the accordion player gave a comic rendition of *Rock Around the Clock*. Later, on the way to bed, I met Rosa working in the kitchen. She looked sad; we spoke; she offered me a rolled cigarette, and we sat outside the kitchen on a bench looking at the dying bonfire. We said little, but I felt warmth and a special sort of love from this lady. We never touched, but somehow, she touched my heart! I left in the morning, a roll of crisp notes in my pocket, shook hands with the laughing Giovanni and placed a kiss on the warm cheek of Rosa. I got a lift with the young count and his friends in the open Giullietta. I sat in the back beside the blonde, the warm wind in my hair, listening to the stories of the holiday they had just had together in the Camargue.

*

During that time, I made friends with Mauro, a young and hopeful opera singer studying at the conservatory in Lucca. He was very talented with a magnificent voice, but he was also quite mad. He suffered from a series of manias and compulsions that made his life unbearable. He called everyone Talpone (rat) on a variety of modulations of tone according to what he felt about the person! When you talked to him and changed the subject of the conversation, you had to say 'basta', which means enough, to separate the subjects. If you did not say 'basta', Mauro would get very agitated and shout in his booming baritone voice 'Basta, basta'. When he saw a girl he fancied, he would start to moan and stamp his foot on the floor till the subject of his desire had passed by. He was terrorised by pigeons and birds in general and was afraid they would crap on his head. To purify himself in case of contamination, he would spit in the air and use his hand to fan the spit towards his head, like a priest with incense. During the Passeggiata in Via Fillungo, he would suddenly start to sing an aria from an opera with such a powerful voice and energy that people would jump 'out of their skins'. On occasion, the stomping of feet, spitting for purification and singing would happen at the same time. He also got terribly disturbed if you mentioned the names of any diseases.

Cancer was on top of the list and would send Mauro in a fit of cleansing and spitting. Late one evening, I went back to his house to listen to some records. We walked into his kitchen and ate the remains of an excellent bean soup. We listened to Madam Butterfly in his room and when Callas sang *Un Bel Di Vedremo*, we both cried! Later, Mauro told me of the ritual he had to perform before he fell asleep. First, he had to count all the cracks, spots and stains on the ceiling. They ran into the hundreds, but if the count did not correspond to the previous number, he had to start over again. Sometimes after hours when he was satisfied with the count, he folded the thin mattress with great effort under his body and remained like that trying to sleep under that self-inflicted torture. I left his house walking down the dark steps, smelling of cats' pee, relieved that my few manias were under control. Eventually, his state of mind stopped him from continuing his studies at the conservatory. Later, Mauro told me how he tried to avoid his military service due to his obvious mental illness. He was, nevertheless, drafted into the air force, and when he was guarding a large fuel depot at Pisa Military Airport, he had a strong compulsion to fire his machine gun into the tanks. Sometimes he had to force his finger away from the trigger. Years later, after I left Italy for England, Mauro somehow arrived at my bedsitter in Knightsbridge. His hair was longer and his mad eyes very shiny! I offered him a spare bed and regretted it immediately! Mauro would do special ablutions in the very small sink, splashing water everywhere. He ate the fruit and nuts from my bowl on the table and spat bits of it on the British flag I had bought in Carnaby Street, which was pinned to the wall. All this, the first morning! Later, he did a lot of stamping of feet with the many mini skirted beauties we met in Central London. Eventually, I had to get rid of him and found him a bedsitter somewhere in the East End. I left him in the grey, dusty room opening drawers and spitting to purify the air! I heard later that he had found a job as a singing waiter in an Italian pizzeria. I met him again many years later on one of my visits to Lucca. He was with a rounded, dark lady resembling a Renaissance Madonna. He was calm and normal, and when I reminded him of his previous antics, he said, "I have got Maria to keep me sane now." And he laughed with the booming voice of old!

*

Towards the end of summer, I started to take maths lessons so that I could retake my exam. Mother chose a teacher for me having been advised by a friend. He lived in Piazza San Pietro. I walked up the long flight of stairs to a door, the brass knob and the nameplate highly polished. "Buongiorno," I said to the lady who opened the door. "I have come…" I didn't finish the sentence. I don't know if she recognised me, but I am sure she did. She did not smile. The lady in front of me, greyer and fatter was the French teacher from Mutigliano. She turned around and said, "I will call my husband." She still had a great arse! The husband wore a grey dressing gown and slippers, was very tall and thin and had a very feeble voice that sent me to sleep. I went to lessons once a week. The apartment was dark and smelled of cabbage. I very seldom saw my French teacher; she had lost her smile! I didn't learn much maths and hated the lessons. Once, I rang the bell but did not wait for the door to open and ran downstairs towards the sunshine away from the oppressive apartment and the voice of the teacher! I told Mother I rang the bell, but nobody answered.

During the lessons, often missing the point and trying not to look too stupid, I nodded fighting the desire to close my eyes. At the end of one of the lessons, as I was counting the chimes of the grandfather clock in the hall, the teacher started to write a letter to my mother with long white hairy fingers using an old-fashioned pen and brown ink. He licked the ivory-coloured envelope and wrote my mother's name slowly, deliberately going over the letters twice. Finally, he said to me in a resigned voice, "I cannot teach you anymore; you don't have your heart in it, and I am sorry. I have explained this to your mother." He handed me the letter, and I opened it outside in the bright sunlight of Piazza San Pietro. I read it and tore it to pieces! It was near the time of retaking the exams in October and I knew I would fail. I told Mother all was well, and when Cristiano invited me to go to a small village in Maremma called Porto Santo Stefano where his mother had an apartment, I decided to go. Cristiano was retaking an exam also; we could study together. I told Mother again that all was well with my maths and I could afford to take a few days off.

We went by train from Lucca; Cristiano's mother, Mrs Bardi, was carrying a cat basket with her beloved Siamese inside. She was in her fifties, a dark, slim lady, well dressed and jolly. She brought with her thick soft sandwiches with cheese and prosciutto and wine from her estate in San Miniato. I felt great; I had bought some new summer clothes, gabardine trousers, sandals and striped shirts. The impending exam was not on my mind! Mrs Bardi was asleep and snoring, the cat mewing in his basket, his alarmed amazing blue eyes showing through the bars of the basket. We went outside to smoke in the corridor. Cristiano told me he had fallen in love with one of the girls we had invited to Lucca and took to his father's office. He said he wanted to marry the girl, the fool! They wrote to each other often, but the girl had a very strict father who did not want her to become engaged. In fact, having heard about Cristiano, he did not allow her out of the house unsupervised. Cristiano was very miserable. We arrived at Porto Santo Stefano and went to an old apartment overlooking the sea. It had a large terrace with terracotta tiles and a pergola with a yellow climbing rose. After dinner, we sat under the striped awning billowing in the sea breeze. During the night, I heard the cat mewing, and in the morning, Mrs Bardi, tired looking in her dressing gown, told us the cat was very sick. We all walked to the vet in an old building near the harbour. During the walk, I carried the basket, the cat inside had stopped mewing and made strange sneezing noises as if it could not breathe. The vet, an old gentleman with thick glasses, examined the cat and explained that it was cat flu, and there was no chance of recovery at this late stage. Cristiano's mother remained strangely silent. She gently put the cat back in the basket, paid the fee and we left. On the way back, we stopped for breakfast in a bar by the harbour. We had coffee and brioches, but Cristiano's mother left after she had her coffee, carrying her cat. I had loved animals, but I liked to dominate them; if they did not do what I expected, I had been cruel to them. But I was strangely moved by what had happened to this cat. Later, we collected our swimming gear and towels from the apartment. The cat was on a towel on the floor in the kitchen, hardly breathing. Mrs Bardi was on a chair, her eyes swollen and red. We swam in a cove near the harbour, the water cool and clear. We dived trying to reach large shells, called Nacchere, sticking out of the sandy bottom. We had lunch at the little snack bar on the beach. Later, hot and sunburned, we returned to the cool apartment. The cat had died, and Mrs Bardi was sitting on a chair beside it in the dark kitchen. She had lit a small candle and put a yellow rose from the terrace between his front paws. His beautiful blue eyes closed. We went at sunset to bury the cat on a steep hill behind the apartment. The cat, looking asleep, had been wrapped in a monogrammed pillow case with the rose still between his paws – a strange procession of three people! I dug a hole with a spade borrowed from the grumpy gardener of the flats. The soil was full of rocks. Cristiano made a cross from the branch of an ash tree with his Swiss army knife and secured it with a piece of his tennis shoe laces. We left the pathetic little burial in the fading sunlight and walked silently back to the apartment. I sat with Cristiano on the dark terrace, smoking and drinking wine, listening to the sound of the music from the nightclub by the harbour, coming and going with the cool breeze. He told me of his lovesick pains for the girl from Pescia and his lack of communication with her because of her stern army father. Mrs Bardi had gone to bed with a headache after cooking us spaghetti alle vongole. In the morning, she seemed more cheerful and made us sandwiches for the beach. We swam and discovered a grotto on the rocky side of the beach. Inside, it had a shelf covered with seaweed where we sat in the cool, lapped by the sea, talking, our voices echoing strangely, blue lights reflecting on the grotto wall! That evening, we went to the nightclub. I wore my blue Lacoste shirt and was glowing from the day in the sun. I danced with a tall, dark girl on holiday from Rome. She was a university student of palaeontology and I told her about our bear find, and she was very impressed. We joined Cristiano at the bar. He was talking to another girl, the friend of the one I was with, but he seemed not to have his heart in it. He kept making connecting rings on the shiny surface of the bar counter with his frosty beer glass. We met the girls at the beach the following morning. My girl looked more fleshy in her bikini and the other girl never stopped talking. Cristiano nodded distractedly, smoking and tapping his foot on the sand. I hired a rowing boat from a burly man in a red fez, and the fleshy girl and I rowed out. The wind from behind the promontory cooled us. We swam in the clear water, and later, we climbed into the boat again and lay on the bottom on salty rough planks. Her hot perfumed skin taut under my fingers! We kissed, our lips tasting of the sea, the noise of the water against the boat alarmed me. I raised my head over the side of the boat; we were going too near the rocks! The sea was noisier there. I sat on the seat ready to row, but one of the oars was missing. I rapidly lost my erection! I tried to keep the boat from the rocks by paddling from one side to the other with the heavy oar. I was sweating feeling powerless. The girl tried to paddle with her hand, her heavy brown breasts bouncing in her bra. It took more than an hour to get back to the beach. We got there exhausted. I beached the boat and quickly took an oar from another boat, luckily the boatman was not there. Cristiano was asleep under the umbrella. Many stubs of Peter Stuyvesant in the sand were beside him! His girl had left. My girl went to join her. *Sapore di Sale* was playing somewhere on a transistor radio. I ate my dry sandwich and fell asleep under the umbrella, my legs in the sun. I dreamt of my exams. "Coming for a swim?" Cristiano said. He was looking down on me, brown against the yellow umbrella. He seemed more cheerful. I grabbed his foot and tried to wrestle him to the ground. He ran, and I followed. We got to the surf together. We swam slowly. The golden light of the afternoon illuminating the wooded hills behind the beach! We floated on our backs.

"What does it feel like when you are in love?" I asked. He hesitated and spat some water out of his mouth.

"This girl is always in my thoughts," he said keeping his mouth above the water. He looked sad. He seemed to want to say something more. He took a deep breath and spoke in a different tone. "I am getting cold. Are you coming? I will race you," he said swimming fast towards the beach a few hundred yards away. I swam fast catching up. A shocking searing pain shot up my right arm to my neck and chest, like a burn; I felt sick and weak. I called to Cristiano, but he was swimming fast, his head in the water. I did not seem to be able to breathe properly. I doggy-paddled towards the white line of the sand in the distance. I felt really sick, almost about to faint. The sound of blood rushing in my ears, a burning taste in my mouth! Paddling slowly in pain, I carried on not sure I could reach the shore. I passed beside a child in a small red inflatable, but I felt too proud to grab it. My hand reached the reassuring feeling of sand, but I stayed there unable to pull myself up. Cristiano was towelling himself beside the yellow umbrella. A red mark like a brand was on my arm and my shoulder and chest! I lay in the shallow water looking at the sky through water drops still covering my lashes.

"Are you okay?" the burly man in the fez in charge of the boats knelt beside me. "You got stung by a jellyfish. Let me get some ammonia," he said. He came back and splashed some ammonia and helped me to my feet. I felt guilty about losing the oar! Cristiano approached, and I saw the reflection of my pale face on his mirrored Ray Bans. I felt sick and lay for a while, wrapped in a towel in the fading sunshine, thinking that I had been lucky. I nearly hadn't made it!

In the next few days, the weather changed; it was grey and windy. The colour of everything so bright in the sunshine seemed to have faded now. We sat on the terrace under the striped awning and talked little. I read my book on the North West Passage and tried not to think about my exams. Cristiano kept his daily letters from his love in his now bulging book by Gide. There was a feeling of loss and sadness relieved only by the great food Mrs Bardi cooked silently, a sad smile on her lips. We went back to Lucca in a downpour, got soaked in just a few yards from the waiting room to the train and sat shivering in an empty compartment.

The next few days, I carried on reading, sitting on the bed in my room, maths books beside me in case someone came in. I travelled to Pescia for the exams by tram on a foggy day in the beginning of October. I felt detached climbing the long straight road to the school. We sat at separate desks, and the teacher dictated in a monotonous voice the subject of our exam. She did not acknowledge my presence and looked coldly at us from behind the desk. She wore a dark mauve, tight jumper and had cut her long hair short. I didn't make much sense of the subject she gave us; I seemed to remember less now than a few months before. I wrote the words and formulae on the subjects and looked busy as she walked around the desks, but I knew most of it did not make sense. The hour passed; I listened to the pigeon on the roof outside, the noise of the teachers' high heels scratching on the tiles and the pens of the students busy on the paper. "Time up," she said deliberately. I put my paper on her desk and smiled at the teacher. I knew it looked neat! I had had fun writing nonsense formulae of my making. I tried to imagine what the teacher would make of it! The next day passed slowly; Mother had asked me about the exam, and I reassured her all was good. I acted confidently; she believed me and fed me well and was generous with my pocket money. I walked the streets of Lucca feeling detached. Walking distracted me from thinking about my results. On a bright cool day a week later, I went back to the school for the results. What a joke, I knew what they would be! I shook hands rapidly with a few boys and approached the noticeboard in the hall. Heart thumping, hands sweating, stupidly hoping for a miracle! 'Pieroni 4' written beside it. I had failed with a 5 before, so 4 was an even lower fail, and there was a red cross after the 4 mark. I looked below, and it meant that I had to go and speak to the headmaster. I knocked at the heavy brown door; I was sweating.

"Come in," said the baritone voice of the headmaster. His studio was very disorderly, full of books and notes stuck everywhere. He was a tall ancient man with a big head and a thin body, always reminding me of an old tomcat. He sat at a desk covered with books, behind him was a leaded light window depicting *Leda and the Swan*, which threw multi-coloured light on his desk. He stubbed his cigarette in a bronze ashtray in the shape of a bull, but it remained alight sending a thin spiral of smoke against the leaded window. "Pieroni," he said lifting his bushy eyebrows. "I must say, your teacher and I were surprised by your paper. Are you taking the piss or what?" he said red in the face. "We could not make any sense of it. Are you trying to create new algebra or are you mad? You cannot stay at this school. You will have to find another one. You can try the one in Florence." I kept my eyes on the bull ashtray. He lit another cigarette, the one in the ashtray was still smoking, fire spreading to other butts and rolled papers. I slowly approached the desk. He looked at me exhaling smoke through his nostrils, his eyes squeezed. I picked the surprisingly heavy ashtray and threw it with force towards the leaded window. Cigarette butts and ash spilling on the desk! The 'bull' made a jagged hole in the belly of Leda. A shard of pale glass still attached by a strip of lead now neatly hiding the head of the swan! I ran out of the study, slamming the door, before the headmaster could react. The sound resonated in the empty corridor! I ran all the way to the tram stop for Lucca. I bought some chewing gum and chewed furiously all the way, jaw muscle aching!

"How did it go?" said Mother as soon as I arrived home. She was cooking lunch.

"I failed," I said. She went pale and turned away towards the stove. She was frying rolls of thin meat filled with artichokes, ham and cheese – my favourite! She took it better than I expected, and I spent the next days reading and walking on the walls in the sunshine.

A letter arrived a couple of days after announcing not only my exam failure but, due to the incident with the headmaster, my exclusion from all the agricultural schools in Italy. Mother went into a sulk, not talking to me or allowing me to the dining table when she was there. It was all very depressing! After days of not communicating, I decided to speak to her about a new school I had heard about from Benzo, the old friend I had been catapulting lizards with years before. He was studying to be a hotel manager at a school in Montecatini. I went with Mother to visit the school in an old villa in the centre of town. The lady director liked me and said she was very happy for me to start there the same year. Mother seemed reassured with my choice and stopped sulking. After the interview, we had coffee and pastries in a cafe. I had a few weeks off before starting at Montecatini, and I lazed around town and visited friends. One morning, not in a very happy mood, I sat in Via Roma, the rounded shape of the stone bench felt smooth and cool under my hands. Its surface shiny after generations of people had sat on these benches, set on the outside of the wall of Palazzo Cenami, a perch and a meeting place for young people. The pale, stern lady in the *Marriage of the Arnolfini* by Van Dyke I saw at the National Gallery years later in London, belonged to the Cenami family. I sat alone and felt tense. I had walked slowly the length of Via Fillungo with a lump in my throat; I was still recovering from my expulsion from Pescia! I sat looking at the people passing trying not to think too much about the future. Then I saw her walking towards me with another girl. A strong, sensuous figure with a Renaissance face, the thin summer dress defining her full body! The friend, shorter with a wide face, was pushing her bicycle along. The girl in the summer dress looked my way and seemed to smile before tossing her long dark hair. I looked at her back swaying and followed her, if only I felt less depressed! I kept looking at her head bobbing in the distance in the sunshine of Piazza San Michele. Then I met Cristiano. He had passed his exam and only had this last year before university. I asked him about his girl from Pescia, but he said that he had to forget her; it had been too complicated!

"Good," I said. We talked for a while; he looked handsome, still brown from the holiday. I felt better after talking to him. Then I saw her again, the same subtle smile and darting eyes. "I think she smiled at me," I said to Cristiano, "let's go and meet them." We followed them towards Piazza Bernardini a few paces behind. When we emerged in the sunshine of the Piazza, the shorter girl turned around giggling. We introduced ourselves. The self-assurance of Cristiano had extended to me, and I found myself talking and smiling a lot. We went to the cafe at the corner of the square and stood at the bar and had Cokes. Her name was Isetta and her friend was Adria. They were students at the local technical school. Isetta had blue almost violet eyes and beautiful lips. She lived outside Lucca in Ponte a Moriano – an industrial village with many paper mills by the River Serchio. We met again as a foursome for a picnic by the river. We found a sandy beach concealed by bushes and sat on a blanket, eating sandwiches; the strong smell of the polluted river mixed with the chemicals from the mills. I held Isetta's hand, and we kissed, her lips soft and giving. Cristiano and Adria argued about politics, religion and the bomb. I saw Isetta a lot that autumn; we were falling in love. We often met at the bus stop in Piazza Santa Maria. We climbed the cobbled path to the walls and sat on the grass of the baluard kissing. I bought her a foulard matching the colour of her eyes. The fanfare below in the Luna Park was playing Petit Fleur.

I started at the hotel school in Montecatini. I left the house early, down the stone steps, three at a time. I had stopped counting but tried not to hold too long the iron railings which left a smell on my hand almost as if it was blood. Downstairs, I would pick up my locked bike from the hall and ride through the empty streets with the Bertolli oil refinery smell in the air. I passed San Frediano's church emptying of early morning worshippers, mainly ladies in dark clothes. The wheel of my bike vibrated on the cobble of Via Fillungo. Seeing the same people walking their dogs and the noise of crows on the Torre Delle Ore. Waiting at the only traffic light near the train station then at the station, I waited for the steam train from Ponte a Moriano to approach with hisses of steam and slamming of doors. When I saw Isetta, we ran to each other and kissed. Often, we put a note into each other's hand before I jumped onto the train to Montecatini on the opposite platform. Friends already on the train looking and drawing rude words or signs on the steamed-up windows. I sat alone and read her message, which always made me very happy. On some days, I would come back to Lucca early. After a hurried lunch with the radio playing American records and my sister trying to understand the words, I would ride the bike in the pale sunshine. At the crossroads by the river, I would see Isetta sitting on her bike and waiting. I would speed up to her and we embraced and kissed, our bikes propped against our bodies. We rode on a rough road to a cane field near the river and sat on the grass. We had started to discover each other's body, but we never went all the way. We softly touched each other and took pleasure without actually making love. You did not at the time, not with the girls you loved. That was the way!

Once, we decided not to go to school but took a train to the seaside. On the bus, we held hands and kissed. The hair from the woollen scarf she wore went up my nose and made me sneeze; we laughed. When we arrived, it was sunny but windy, and we walked along the pine avenue to the sea. The beach strewn with tree stumps carried by the river nearby, bleached tree trunks and branches festooned with plastic and paper. The littered sand and sea strangely monochrome! We lay on the sand closely together, touching and kissing with only the noise of the sea and the wind and our breathing. On New Year's Eve, we spent the night together at the home of a friend in the hills near Lucca. I ran all the way to the station. It was cold, and I wore a suit and tie under my camel duffle coat. Isetta joined me on the train with her friend Adria at Ponte a Moriano, and it started to snow. Isetta had snowflakes on her hair and lashes and her face looked older with makeup. When we got to Borgo station, our friend collected us in his VW Beetle and drove uphill laughing and smoking. We drank Vin Santo, ate farm bread and ham and opened bottles of Spumante when the clock struck midnight. We danced slowly till early morning with the lights low, body and faces close together, sliding on the smooth tiled floor. We played the English and American records of the time, straining to understand the words. I remember a slow one we played a lot; it said over and over again 'around the bay of Mexico'.

Winter passed slowly at the hotel school. I listened to the portable transistor a lot and studied little, and I met Isetta almost every day by the river in the afternoon. Spring came and we felt more adventurous and confident on our afternoons by the river. I remember the smell of her skin hot after riding her bicycle and the strong desire to go all the way. In June, at the end of the first year at the school in Montecatini, I heard that I would be sent to do my summer apprenticeship to Greux Les Bains, a village in the Basses Alps region of France. I was excited by the prospect of leaving Italy; I had never been abroad before, but I hated leaving Isetta for three months. A few days before my departure for France, the film *La Dolce Vita* by Fellini was showing at the cinema Astra in Lucca. Isetta and I sat at the bar drinking coffee by the busy bus stop in Piazza Napoleone and discussed whether to go to the cinema or for a walk by the river. We chose the river. We had so very few days left together! I collected my bicycle, and Isetta sat on the crossbar. We rode past the great doors of the walls of Lucca with the marble panthers on their plinths, past the cemetery with its high walls bordered by cypress trees, then the dusty road beside the river. We rode to a cool spot under the poplars near the old rifle range. We lay on the grass and touched each other and kissed. We lay on our backs, close together looking at the blue sky and the swaying tops of the poplars listening to the shrills of the darting swallows in the sky. We talked about my departure. "I will be back. Only three months," I said smiling.

"I know, but what will I do all this time – three months!" Isetta's blue eyes looking into mine started to fill with tears. A twig snapped behind our heads followed by a burst of laughter. I stood up; three men were running towards the river edge. They saw me and made explicit gestures with their arms and bodies.

"Why aren't you fucking her?" they shouted disappearing in the distance. We sat in silence; the afternoon was cooling down. We stood, picked grass from our clothes and I combed my hair, and she put her pale pink lipstick on. We walked in silence on the raised path holding hands on the handlebar of the bicycle. Down by the field near the river, the three men I had seen were loading a cart with hay. Looking up at us, they started to laugh, shouting the same abuse as before. Without thinking, I pushed the bike on the ground and ran down the steep bank towards them. A tall, fair guy with a nasty smile told me to go back to my girl or maybe I needed some help. He tried to push me back with the handle of his pitchfork, which he held with both hands. I grabbed the middle of the smooth handle with my left hand pulling the guy towards me while I punched him hard on his face with my right fist. He went down and stayed down, a look of disbelief on his friends' faces. They ran and tried to grab me. We fought an untidy fight, rolling in the grass, kicking and shouting abuses. I got hit on the head and face with fists and fork handles, but there was no pain. I felt detached, even looked at Isetta on the bank shouting to us to stop. All seemed to happen slowly as if in a dream. Strangely, I even noticed the smell of freshly cut hay and the taste of blood in my mouth. It seemed to last a long time, and we even stopped propped against the trees to catch our breath. I managed to knock down another short guy with a thick moustache. The first guy I had punched stood up touching a bleeding gash like a lip under his eye. The police arrived on a jeep under the trees as we all sat on the grass exhausted. Somebody from the nearby farm had called the police. My hand was swollen and my face felt beaten. Another police car arrived, and we were all taken to the hospital to be patched up and then to the San Giorgio prison in Lucca. Before we left with the police, I asked a pale-faced Isetta to take my bike home and speak to my mother. She did so, met my family, and somehow, I found myself engaged!

We all ended up in prison. The police did not take kindly to affrays and wanted to make an example. I thought that going to prison would be a great experience and felt proud of the way I handled myself. But later, alone in my cell when the light started to fade, the cries of the swallows through the small barred window made me feel very sad. I fell asleep almost immediately curled up on the hard palliasse under a grey blanket. The day after, the lump in my throat stopped me from eating the greasy pasta we were given. I concentrated on the few images and sounds coming from the outside. Later, I was taken to the barber to have a haircut. The barber, an emaciated middle-aged man, was in for murdering his wife. He cut my hair very well, and when I asked him what he did outside, he told me he was a wood carver and gilder for most of the churches in the parish of Lucca. He offered me a newspaper rolled into a cone full of ripe cherries brought to him by his children that morning. The three men I fought were in cells beside mine, and we found we could talk through the barred windows. We exchanged news of the various attempts by our parents and solicitors to get us out. My father came to collect me on the day we were set free, and he made an attempt to reproach me for fighting, but I think he looked proud of what I had done. He drove me in his new grey 600 Fiat to Via Fillungo where I changed my clothes. Mother and Granny were crying hysterically! Later, I went to dinner with Father, and we talked for the first time man to man. We got a bit pissed on several bottles of wine and became less inhibited. "Why did you leave home?" I said suddenly. He twitched his nose, lit another Nazionale, offered me one and lit it for me, his face becoming more pensive.

"I don't know," he said disappointingly. Then, after another sip of wine, he said, "Your mother is a great woman. Did a lot for me when I was still a student, but I realised shortly after we married that we were not meant to be together." He kept drawing strange signs on the tablecloth with his beautiful tapering fingers. "We quarrelled even on our honeymoon," he said smiling. He looked at me in the eyes and almost whispered, "When your mother had her periods, do you know?" I nodded and took a sip of wine. "She became a different person, impossible, capable of rages. I couldn't take it…Then all the three women in the family ganging up on me. It was impossible…But I am guilty too," he said blowing sideways the ash of his Nazionale that had fallen on the tablecloth. "Yes, I should not have married. I am not the marrying type. I love women too much." He smiled a sad smile. "I cannot stay faithful to one woman." He put his warm brown hand on mine, winked at me and said, "I hope you are not the same as me. It is a blessing and a torture at the same time." Then he looked up and gave me a big smile. "*Due corretti al rhum*," he shouted at the barman.

Before leaving for France, I went by train to Ponte a Moriano with Mother to meet Isetta's family. It was strange to enter her home. I had spent hours looking at the windows of her flat by the railway station while waiting for her in nearby lanes. Her mother was still young and attractive but with a sad smile. Her father, a tall, strange, mild man with ginger hair and freckles. I did not take to him from the first moment. We had lunch in the dining room of the modest apartment, and after Isetta and I went for a walk together, holding hands and feeling slightly subdued. We tried to discover why we felt that way, but we could not. Mother and Isetta's parents remained in the small stuffy dining room drinking coffee.

Greux Les Bains

I left for France with a boy my age from the same hotel school, called Olinto. A few days before, his sister had tripped and fallen down the stairs in her house and killed the newly born baby in her arms. Olinto was large and jolly and we talked, sharing experiences and drinking beer in the empty compartment of the train weaving in and out of the many tunnels of the Ligurian coastline passing La Spezia and Genova to the border with France and then Marseille. We arrived in Marseille hot and hungry. Olinto was as tall as me and very broad. We looked good in our dark shades and linen suits, like two Mafia hitmen, but we were just two hotel school students going to work as waiters in a small hotel in Provence.

Olinto had an auntie in Marseille, the sister of his dead mother. We walked the still sunny streets of Marseille asking directions in broken French and getting lost. We got to a grey tenement house near La Canebiere and walked up the dark stairs carrying our cases to an attic apartment. A middle-aged lady with impossibly red hair and a fag in her hand opened the door and kissed and hugged both of us like old friends. She was fat but moved daintily on light feet. We were given tumblers with Pastis and ice. She spoke Italian with a strange accent and asked news of relations in Lucca while shrieking and laughing. When Olinto told her about his sister's baby, she cried. Dinner was a real feast, charcuterie and pate de Foie Gras followed by roast pigeons and Bouillabaisse and fried artichokes. We listened to old French songs on a wind-up gramophone then went to sleep in a huge bed in the attic. In the morning, full of black coffee and croissants, we walked to a bus station followed by Auntie still giggling and laughing. We travelled through the hot midday hour through wooded slopes, green deep gorges with rivers at the bottom to the village called Greux Les Bains. The hotel was near the bus station, like a villa with beautiful gardens all around. We were greeted by the attractive Madame Hermini and her large Corsican husband. We were introduced to their teenage son, Alain, and the chef de cuisine, a small dark man with a large moustache. The washer-up man, le plongeur, was tall and lanky and immediately told us, folding and unfolding his apron, how he had fallen into a bamboo trap in Indochina and showed us large deep sores on his legs, and he said they would never heal. He had to clean and fill his wounds with a special cream daily. The clientele of the Hotel La Residence was mainly Parisian and very chic. Middle-aged men smoking cigars and bejewelled ladies smelling of Chanel! We served lunch and dinner in a cosy chintzy dining room. The chef was very generous giving us extra food and teaching us the different sauces and the subtle way of French cuisine. Once during service, he got into a terrible rage and shouting in Argot threw a knife at the plongeur, missing him by inches.

I had brought with me a special felt pen, called a Flow Master, for drawing with ink and in my free time walked around the town sketching. I was put in charge of the bar in the conservatory open to the garden with chairs and umbrella. I served drinks to very friendly Parisians reading Paris Match or sleepily playing chess. The local priest visited the bar one afternoon. He was small, cheerful and balding, ordered mint tea and seemed to be interested in my life and background in Italy. He invited me to his vicarage in the village. One afternoon, I went to see him. He lived alone in a large house near the church. We sat and drank lemonade in a large and unadorned sitting room and talked about Italy. He asked, to my surprise, if there were brothels in Italy and if I had ever visited one. "And did you ever go with a prostitute?" he asked me in a strange way gritting his teeth. I answered that I had been with prostitutes, and he seemed not to mind.

I finished my lemonade. It had tasted rather bitter and decided it was time to go. I made a move to leave. "Before you go, could you please help me replace a bulb in the kitchen? I can't reach it, and you are so tall." We went to the kitchen, a cool room with a flagstone floor. I climbed on a chair, and having removed the spent bulb, I took the new one from his hand. He was now holding my legs with the excuse that I might fall off. He held my legs tightly, and after I screwed in the new bulb, he buried his face in my crotch and seemed to breathe rather heavily. I jumped off the chair and stared in the leering red face of a very confused priest. Nothing more was said, and I left the vicarage in a hurry.

Outside, I met one of the village boys who delivered groceries to the hotel. He smiled at me and asked, "Did the priest ask you to replace his bulb?"

Olinto and I slept in a shed beside the hotel. I fixed a wooden pole horizontally under the overhang of the roof and did chin-ups to keep in shape. Olinto laughed at me and pointed to his belly looking larger with the delicious food the chef gave us. In the afternoon, I went swimming in the green pools of the Verdon, the nearby river famous for its gorges. I sunbathed on smooth rocks and lifted stones, did chin ups on tree branches and admired Narcissus-like my reflection in the calm pools. The presence of a mother and child on the gravel beach on the other side of the river distracted me from my self-indulgence and found myself looking from behind my dark Ray Bans at the young mother. She had a curvy figure, dark long hair and a polka dot bikini. She played by the water with her young son and occasionally looked at me. When she smiled at me, I picked up courage and swam to the other side to join her. She was friendly and corrected my French. She told me she was staying in a small hotel in the town square. She invited me to sit on the towel, and I found myself aroused by her warm firm body. We kissed and pressed against each other, the child asleep beside us. She asked me to her hotel that evening and I entered, as instructed, her room from a courtyard at the back, through a window at ground level. She wore a nightdress revealing her full breasts. There were wet marks on the material covering her erect nipples. She had just fed her child who was asleep in a cot. We kissed and touched each other; she took my clothes off and kissed my body. I took her nightdress off and saw her dark pubic hair against her bikini pale marks. She took me to the bed and pushed my head to her crotch. I kissed her there and smelled her strong female smell. She took my penis in her warm mouth, and when she sensed I was getting too excited, she put it inside her and started to move slowly under me. It made me feel hard and powerful, and I heard her moan while she dug her nails into my shoulder. I stayed on top of her plunging deeper and faster, then I came arching my back in a burst of pleasure. We slept briefly and then made love again, slower and deliberately. The child called his mother, and she calmed him down in the semi-darkness, then returned to me whispering in my ear how much she liked me. I left the room in the coolness of daybreak and ran back through the empty streets to the hotel. The shed room was warm and smelly, full of Olinto's snoring. I made love to that lady in lavender fields and by shady pools by the river but her husband, a wine merchant from Digne, came to collect her one morning so early that I had to escape from the back window clutching my clothes. We never had time to exchange addresses, and I never saw her again. I only knew she lived in Martigue, a town full of canals, she described to me many times.

Time passed slowly at La Residence. I made friends with Alain, the young son of the owners. We went swimming in the Verdon, and he started to train with me on the chinning bar in the afternoons. I went back to Greux les Bains in 2005 while driving to Italy. Over forty years had passed and the small village had turned into a town. I had difficulty in finding the hotel! I eventually found it and it seemed smaller and grey, the beautiful gardens unkempt. As I entered the main rattling glass door, the smell of stale food assaulted me. I called but nobody was around. A small dog bolted out of a side door and bit my leg tearing my trousers. I managed to shake the little beast off and an old lady in slippers and turban appeared looking sternly at me and scooping the dog off the floor. I enquired after the Hermini family; she knew nothing about them, not even of Alain. An old man shuffled out of another door smoking and coughing – the hotel was now an old peoples' home. I walked to the car park, the shed where I slept with Olinto was still there, the old wood bleached by the sun. I was dazed and saddened and on the way out of the car park; I drove on the left narrowly avoiding a truck full of sheep! I decided to drive on the mountain road to the famous Gorge du Verdon, a winding narrow route with deep drops to the river hundreds of yards below. I stopped at the viewing place and looked at the green river, deep in the shade of the gorge. Apparently, the gorge was only explored in 1930. I stopped at the village called Palud and stayed in a small empty hotel nearby. I visited a museum of shepherding and 'transumance', a place of peace showing simple tools and ways of a lost practice once so common in the area. After a dinner of outstanding lamb chops and watercress salad, I went back to the hotel. I walked in the fields beside it, a surreal place full of abandoned overgrown fruit trees, gnarled, mossy but alive with fruits. I walked over stonewalls collapsing with rusty barbed wire. I sat with my back to an apple tree and smoked a Toscano thinking till darkness came.

But back in 1959, the time came to leave Greux Les Bains, and Olinto and I stopped again in Marseilles for a night with his auntie. Over huge tumblers of Pastis on ice, I asked her what she did for a living. She started to talk in French giggling a lot without giving a real answer. We were again made very welcome and many questions were asked about our time in Greux. This time, we took her out to a little restaurant in the old port. We had a fantastic Bouillabaisse and wine. I smoked too many Gitanes and made eyes at the barmaid, a dark, gypsy-looking girl in a white shirt showing her breasts. When she eventually came out from behind the bar and I was ready to look at the rest of her figure, to my shock she had a wooden leg. A real wooden leg like a pirate! We walked slowly back to the flat saying hello to the many prostitutes on the Canebiere. Auntie seemed to know many of them! They waved at us giggling. We left by train in the morning to go back to Italy.

I heard from a friend years after that Olinto, after finishing at the hotel school, had gone to live with his father in a small farmhouse in the hills near Lucca, helping him with his olive grove. While his father was burning diseased olive wood in a pit near the farm he somehow fell in. Olinto heard the screams, ran to the pit and in trying to help his father, fell in and they both died consumed by the fire!

Hotel school started again in October. Isetta seemed more mature and at times behaved in a manner older than her years. We still met by the river and enjoyed our unconsummated love-making but with less passion – the mood had changed somehow! At the school, I met

Stefano. He had short hair, looked like an American GI and ran in his spare time. He collected jazz records and read the latest books. After dinner, I went to his house and listened to Dizzy Gillespie, Duke Ellington, Chet Baker and Thelonious Monk on a wind-up old gramophone in his sitting room. His mother worked in the local factory making Toscani cigars and his father was the caretaker of the Manzi Palace nearby in Via Galli Tassi. I started to go out a lot with Stefano; I liked his mind; he was a lot of fun. He belonged to an athletic club called C.U.S. Pisa. I joined too and met a lot of athletes like Franco Radman, a decathlete with a record of almost 80 metres in the javelin. He came from Pola as a refugee and looked like a blond god.

Another guy, Marco, was a runner, a very unlikely athlete – he chain smoked, drank a lot and had many girlfriends but still managed to compete. His father owned a successful opticians shop in Lucca and had just opened another branch for Marco to manage. His new shop was a meeting place for us, distracting Marco from his duties. He sat behind the counter snipping and grinding lenses to be fitted into frames but often ended up breaking them distracted by a shop full of friends. His father would come in begging us to leave him alone. We would all clear off only to return later. We piled into Marco's 500 Fiat, four, sometimes five, large men in a small car full of smoke and laughter going to Pisa to train. I was given a nice wool tracksuit, red and blue, by the club. We ran together around the track, and I started to throw the discus and the shot. The discus went well although my technique was very poor. I managed to throw nearly 40 metres, which was quite good for a beginner. One cold foggy Saturday, I went to Florence by train to compete in a shot throwing competition. I changed in a cold concrete dressing room and ran to warm up on the track outside proudly wearing my new tracksuit. Meconi, the Italian champion, was taking part in the competition. He was as tall as me, powerfully built with a bull neck and a face reminiscent of the statue of the boxer sitting and fitting the straps on his wrists. He was fast and threw the eight-kilo shot five or six metres further than me every time. Even another boy, a youngster with a Renaissance face and slender than me, beat me. I travelled back to Lucca feeling low.

I liked to run on the freshly cut grass – the rolling feeling of accelerating from a slow run to an almost full speed! Another friend was Goffredo, a large boy from Rome. He threw the discus and shot like me, and his fridge was always full of great food. In between Isetta and the newly found athletics, I studied little and was behind especially in German.

In early summer, Chet Baker played at La Bussola, a nightclub attracting international stars, and was arrested on drug charges. He was eventually locked up in San Giorgio, where I had spent a few nights myself the previous year. He was allowed to play his trumpet, and we sometimes went to listen outside the walls of the prison. He mainly played marvellous varied sad arrangements of *Summertime*.

Perranporth

The year in Montecatini ended, and somehow, I managed to scrape through. I was told that I would be sent for my summer apprenticeship to England to a hotel called Ponsmere, The Hotel on the Beach in Perranporth, Cornwall. I left Isetta again but this time with less anguish. We went all the way to Calais in sleeping compartments with other students from the hotel school. I loved the many different people entering the small compartment by day when the couchettes were drawn back – the different languages, smells, clothes – it was all very new and exciting. We got to Calais after about one day and transferred to a boat to Dover. The sea was rough and grey, and I expected the White Cliffs to be whiter. When we got to London, we stayed in a hotel in Paddington. We went to Piccadilly by tube, escorted by one of our teachers, rolled around laughing at the speed and how near the walls of the tunnel were. Then went to Soho full of colourful restaurants and coffee bars serving undrinkable coffee and strip clubs. A girl scantily dressed with very blonde hair and a painted mole on her large breast grabbed my sleeve and invited me in. I did not understand her English and after, having tried to explain, coming very close to my face with her mouth smelling of alcohol, she gave me a V sign and patting her large behind told me to fuck off several times. I got a dirty look from my teacher, a pale bald man teaching us practical English. Later, I asked him about the V sign and the F words I understood; he explained to me about Agincourt and the cutting of fingers but seemed confused and failed to explain the meaning of the words.

We had sandwiches in a busy, greasy snack bar in Piccadilly Circus. Later, back at the hotel, I found myself talking to Carla, another student, a dark, pensive girl, not beautiful but interesting. The previous year in Germany, she had been worked so hard that she went through a sort of breakdown. She lost weight and became anorexic. When I saw her again at school, she had become very hairy, her face and arms were covered with dark woolly hair. By now, in London, she had put some weight on but her body hair was, if anything, worse. We went to one of the other girls' room, a small group of students excited by the buzz of London, smoking Gitanes, drinking whisky bought in Soho and laughing a lot. Carla told me more about her tribulations in Germany. She had been working as a chambermaid during her summer apprenticeship and her life had been made miserable by a cruel housekeeper who kept her working very long hours and threatened to give her a bad report. Carla was very stressed, ate little, hurt her back making beds and lost so much weight that she had to be sent back home. A doctor told her that her breakdown has precipitated a glandular disfunction that caused her hypertrichosis. She hoped her stay in England would be more fortuitous. In the morning, after a large English breakfast, I walked to Paddington Station and in my school boy English managed to find my train to Cornwall. A steam train! I walked to the front to look at the locomotive being made ready. A large, dark shiny mass of steel and steam smelling of coal and oil! I sat in a comfortable compartment looking at the English countryside, so different from Italy – so green and neat with brilliant light. At Exeter, a girl got on the train and sat opposite me. Red hair, grey tailleur and amazing blue eyes! We started to talk; she was called Mona, and it made me laugh because in Venetian dialect 'mona' is a rude word, the equivalent of pussy. I asked her where she was going, and to my surprise, she told me that after a brief holiday she was heading back to the same hotel in Perranporth as me. She was working there as a nanny. We had sandwiches in the buffet wagon and drank weak horrible coffee. The train ran close to the sea, rocky coves with green water and lots of bends where it was possible to see the engine, its moving steel parts glinting in the sun ahead. When we got to a small station, the name I cannot recall, and a cab had been sent for us. We travelled on narrow country roads flanked by tall hedges bent by the wind with occasional glimpses of the ocean in the distance.

We got to Perranporth, named after St Perran, an early Christian saint. The main road with houses in pale colours, strong sunlight, wind and the ocean roaring in the distance! The hotel stood on a rocky outcrop surrounded by the beach stretching flat and golden all the way to the surf. The owner of the hotel, Mr Pollard, was an avuncular bald Cornish man with dark shiny eyes. He was clean shaven with very bushy eyebrows and strange tufts of hair on his cheeks. I kept wondering if he had missed them when shaving or cultivated them on purpose. He instructed me on my duties and offered me a large whisky in his office that looked like a cabin on a yacht. A tall narwhal tooth stood in a corner and the whisky glasses came from a box made from tortoise shell. Apparently, I had been assigned to the kitchen. I was taken there later to meet Mr Schmit, the chef, a large German man with a red face and enormous ears. He showed me a little side pantry with various machines and tables and said I was going to learn how to be a pastry chef. I had to start working early in the morning. I was lodging in a small, pebbledash house on the bend of a road leading out to the sand dunes. I carried my heavy case uphill and wondered at my stupidity – I had carried from Italy a set of dumbbells in the case to train with, weighing probably 20 kilos. The owner of the house was in her thirties, tall, slim and tired-looking. She gave me a cup of tea in a dirty cup and showed me to my room. It had twin beds, green wallpaper and the window looked towards the sand dunes covered in marram grass swept by the wind. I unpacked and went back to the hotel to have dinner in the staff room. We had a dark stew with vegetables and sat on benches at a grimy refectory table. I saw Mona, and she asked me if I wanted to go to the pub. The pub was near the hotel, an old pub with a dark interior smelling of ale and smoke. Mona seemed to be a regular and knew a lot of the locals. Three Scottish men, working as builders, joined us and were amused to learn that my father had been born in Glasgow in Govan. One of the guys was from there, a tall bearded fellow with mad eyes. I had difficulty understanding spoken English especially with a Scottish accent and spent the evening drinking strong ale and nodding and laughing at jokes I did not understand. We were joined later by a dark, pretty French lady, also working at the hotel. Her Cornish husband, John Penrose, was a dark, handsome man with a streak of white hair on his forelock. She told me he taught maths at the local school and liked to fish. At closing time, I walked back to the hotel with Mona. We kissed sitting on the lawn outside, the tide had come in and splashed on the dark rocks below. In the distance, you could make out the surf lines rushing in. I walked back to the house and went to bed exhausted. I got up at 5 am. It was cool, and I walked briskly to the hotel. One of the porters poured me strong tea from an enormous brown teapot. The chef was busy making dough in the mixing machine – he showed me how to roll and cut the sticky dough making balls to be baked into rolls for breakfast. I did my best to make rolls of equal size and placed them on metal trays to go into a large electric oven. When the rolls were cooked, I had breakfast of bacon and eggs. It tasted so good with toast and Cornish butter! I sat with the chef, the porter a dark man from Portugal who chained smoked, and the washer – an English man from London with red cracked hands. After eating, I helped to cook breakfast for the guests. I was shown how to make porridge and the rolls came out of the oven golden and puffed! By ten o'clock, breakfast was finished, and I cleaned the mixer and the tables in the pantry and washed the trays. After that, I helped to peel potatoes and cut vegetables for lunch. It was very busy, and I found myself worrying at the many new tasks I had to remember. Mr Schmit shouted in a booming voice at everyone around. His face and ears redder than ever! He stood giving orders, and I noticed he kept squeezing his earlobes, turning and pinching them until they almost bled. The Portuguese man told me to be wary of the chef. Apparently, he drank a lot alone in his room at night and could be violent when stressed. My duties lasted till lunch when I ate another dark stew in pastry with grey vegetables and then walked to the beach. Glad of the wind and fresh air taking the smell of the greasy kitchen out of my clothes. The surf was faraway, white lines in the distance against a blue sky. On the soft sand below the hotel, whole families sunbathed behind colourful screens driven in the sand. Red bodies and the smell of sun lotion! I walked on, and at the point I reached by the surf, the sand became hard, and I walked faster towards the sea. The roaring noise of the surf was continuous! People surfed between flags on bodyboards. Guards in white caps stood on tall step ladders checking the surfers. I learnt that they were Australians, and they were instructing the English in the art of surfing. I walked back to the village and bought a plywood bodyboard, leopard-print swimming trunks and a bottle of mead. I went surfing in the afternoons washing away the smell of the kitchen in the cool water. I loved the feeling of comfort, after the cold ocean, sitting shivering wrapped in a towel, smoking and falling asleep on the warm sand.

In the evenings, I went to the pub and met Mona and the rest of the gang. I instructed everybody to correct my

English and discovered the advantages of asking 'what is the English for that?' pointing to whatever I didn't know the name of and learning at the same time new words and how to pronounce them. The Scottish trio had the reputation for violence and after many drinks would pick fights with the locals. They tried to involve me, but I kept out of it. They often tried to push and punch me in mock fighting, and I was glad for my size and weight so that I could look after myself. One evening, Mona and I decided not to go to the pub. We bought a bottle of mead from the off licence and walked towards the sea. When we got there, it was getting dark. I placed my hands against her slim waist and lifted her up. Her pale summer dress flew over my head. I found my face against her warm belly in the shade of her shirt. I heard her laugh – she wore a bikini of pink towelling material. The soft, padded indentation of her crutch against my chin! I breathed in and smelled her. My lips pulled apart to kiss her there. She was still laughing, her back arching, and I let her slowly slide down against my chest till I found her belly soft against my hard penis. She balanced there, her nails digging into my shoulders. She slowly reached the sand with her feet and found the surging surf. We joined hands and ran shouting, our voices lost in the roar. The sun was rapidly going down in a fine mist. We started to climb the dunes, my feet warming against the dry sand. We climbed in silence stepping on the coarse marram grass. An orange full moon was coming up behind the sand dunes. We sat on a hollow in the sand and slowly, sweetly made love with the noise of the sea, shivering from cold and pleasure. Later, we went back to the sea, took our clothes off and body surfed naked, finding each other for warmth in the semi-darkness. She wanted to climb on my shoulders, her bottom and thighs warm against my neck. I started to run, splashing in the shallow water. She giggled begging to stop then she peed laughing uncontrollably, rivulets of warm liquid over my body. I bent and threw her down in the water. Stars were coming up over the ocean. We ran towards our clothes and drank from the bottle of mead, the sweet liquor warming our shivering bodies.

My day started early in the kitchen, and I took pride in everything I did and tried to do it well as I read in my book of Buddhist practices. The chef drank even more now. Sometimes in the morning, he would greet me with a stupefied look, a red face, nervous fingers twisting his earlobe. I could smell alcohol on his breath even several feet away. One afternoon, after lunch, I found him shouting at the porter who kept his head down while mopping the greasy floor. The chef grabbed the little man by the shoulders and shook him uncontrollably. His mop dropped to the floor. I rushed there and tried to intervene; the chef turned his anger on me. He slapped me hard on the face. I threw a quick punch and got him on the chin. He looked straight into my eyes with a surprised look before he sank to the floor, swearing in German. Mr Pollard arrived out of breath into the kitchen. The porter explained what had happened in broken English. The chef and I were made to shake hands, and later, I was told that from tomorrow I would be transferred to the dining room. The first morning serving breakfast was confusing – all those cereals, porridge, cornflakes, Rice Crispies, Weetabix. I was sent to help the French lady, Mrs Penrose, and we became friends. I went out fishing with her husband. Having bought a toy rod and reel, I caught small trout from the stream going into the sea near the hotel. I surfed nearly every afternoon after lunch in the freezing surf. The worst moment was coming out of the water exposed to the cold wind running to the towel. I lifted my dumbbells after sleeping in the late afternoon before dinner. I went to Truro on my day off, and from a sports shop, I bought a new discus made of shiny steel and wood. In the afternoon, I threw it on the beach counting the paces on the firm sand to measure my throws. I liked the way it flew when I did a good throw and the thud on the sand on landing. I covered miles throwing and pacing. At the end of the beach, there was a café, and I would have cream teas sitting in the sunshine. I found a dead bird on the rocks beside some caves. It was a large herring gull. I picked it up heavy and limp, looking at its formidable beak and padded feet. I left it on a rock, his spread wings lifting in the wind as if alive!

After a couple of days, I noticed a hungry red pimple on my right wrist. It turned into a large boil. I felt feverish, stayed in bed and had hallucinations with high fever. I dreamt of drowning and being so small that a seagull scooped me from the water. The landlady brought me soup and orange juice, and when the fever continued, she called a doctor, an old man with white hair. He told me I had a carbuncle and was lucky I did not get blood poisoning. He asked me if I had been touching a dead animal, and I thought of the herring gull.

The carbuncle had many heads and oozed pus and blood. It healed eventually with the sunshine and the clean salty water but left a crater-like deep hole on my wrist.

There were girls renting rooms in the house by the dunes where I stayed too. One of them a large, tall, white skinned girl with very dark hair kept making me cups of teas and coming to my room to ask for 'fags'. One night, we got intimate, and when I took her dress off, I exposed her white body full of cellulite, angry pink stretch marks and flabby flesh like an old lady. I was turned off, but I felt sorry for the girl, and we slept together anyway. A big mistake! It was like sleeping with a blancmange! She continued bringing me cups of tea, but I could not bring myself to sleep with her again. One evening, we got into an argument and shouted abuse at each other. I managed to get her out of my room but then the door opened again, an irate landlady asking what was all the shouting about in the middle of the night. I tried to explain, but she started to pound me with her arms, and we wrestled. The wrestling turned to hugging, and we had sex. She had a tattoo of a seagull on each cheek of her pert bum. Mona announced she had become engaged to a boy from Exeter. It suited me – the landlady kept me good company at night! She even got up early to make me tea before I walked to work. Her teenage daughter hated me, and I never found out if she was jealous of her mother or wanted to protect her.

At the end of the summer, I went back to London, and on a specified day, I met the rest of the students at a Victorian hotel in Russell Square. Carla looked tanned and less gaunt. She had fallen in love with a Belgian chef, and they were planning to get married. I had saved a fair amount of money and bought myself a brown pair of brogues from Jermyn Street and several tartan shirts from Westway & Westway, a Scottish shop near the British Museum. I have a photo taken on the deck of the channel ferry looking tanned and wearing one of the shirts.

Lucca Again

Back in Lucca, I was not particularly happy to meet Isetta. I had tasted freedom and did not like settling down as she expected. She had got a temporary job working for the council responsible for the census, and I accompanied her on a few of her outings in the countryside near Lucca. On a cool windy day sitting beside a canal full of fast flowing green water, I took her beautiful face in my hands, and staring into her violet eyes, I told her I didn't want to be engaged to her or marry her. I needed freedom, and we had to end it. She sobbed quietly for hours, her eyes and nose red and swollen. We hardly spoke on the crowded steamy bus back to Lucca.

Life without Isetta seemed strange. We had seen each other so much and now I had lots of time on my hands. One of my friends Nello, called Nellino, was a small sensitive boy with oriental looking features and a great body. He could walk upstairs on his hands and although small was very strong. He was also a very good draughtsman. He drew a postage stamp of a penis imitating a stamp of the period and posted the letter to himself. It arrived with the post office mark! He used to come to my house in the afternoon, and we would train, competing on press-ups and parallel dips, pushing and encouraging each other to the limit. After our efforts, we sat and talked in my small cosy sitting room drinking strong coffee. I sat on an old Art Deco armchair feeling the familiar texture of the ribbed design of the velvet cover, listing to Nellino telling me of his domineering, cruel father. He wanted Nellino to become a dentist like himself when he actually preferred to be an artist. I still went to train in Pisa piled up noisily with the same four or five boys in Marco's cinquecento. My last year at the hotel school started again. The school had been transferred to a more modern building on the outskirts of Montecatini. The Germany language teacher, Miss Desideri (Desires), was a dark, not pretty but sensuous lady with dreamy dark eyes. The German language still eluded me, but my teacher liked me and helped me wherever she could. Bless her!

One day on the train to Montecatini, I met Vittorio, my old friend from Pescia. He had got his diploma and was going to Florence for an interview. He looked good, tanned and his skinny body had filled out. "Come with me to Florence. Fai Buco (play truant)," he said. I accepted laughing, and we shook hands and patted each other on the shoulders. At Montecatini, the students got out looking at me in surprise. I winked at them, and they understood. Vittorio and I sat in an empty compartment.

"How is everybody?" I asked.

"The old director died of a massive heart attack," he told me.

"Shit," I said feeling guilty thinking of my outburst with the bull ashtray.

"Mr Pilucco is still the same, getting older," said Vittorio smiling.

"And Leonardo Guidi?" I asked.

"His father died of a heart attack too, and he has enrolled at Pisa University doing agriculture."

"And Giovanni?" I asked.

"He is working with his father in real estate in Livorno." He told me about other boys. Cavallini had started to work in his family's salami factory in Maremma and Angelo had taken over the breeding of the chianina cattle from his father. Fico Nero was working in a shoe factory near Montecatini. Vittorio knew of the drowning of Baffino and talking of him brought tears to my eyes. We arrived at Florence Santa Maria train station, a modern building in the Fascist style, busy, noisy, full of colourful foreign people. Vittorio went to his interview, and we planned to meet again for lunch. There was a cinema near the station, and they showed a film by Fellini I wanted to see, *La Strada*. I sat almost alone through the black and white gripping story of street performers, starring Giulietta Masina and Anthony Quinn. I felt comfortable and secure in the small cosy cinema. I emerged slightly stunned in the sunlight of a clear sunny day and met Vittorio in the buffet of the station. The interview had gone well, and he had been offered a job in a laboratory analysing olive oil and wine. He was ecstatic! We had toasted ham and cheese sandwiches and beer and looked at the many foreign girls passing by. Near our table sat a group of giggling Japanese girls.

Vittorio decided we should go to Via Dell'Amorino to a brothel. When we got to the narrow lane, it had started to drizzle; we found a huge wooden door and entered the dark hall. At the end of the hall to the right, a few stone steps led to a narrow door. I felt nervous and hot. We rang a very loud bell and a tall lady in a black dress let us in. The room was hot; it had an electric fire in the corner. "Documents," said the lady in a hissy voice. She sat behind a desk smoking from a long cigarette holder. She had a beaky nose, orange hair and reminded me of La Goulou in the Toulouse Lautrec painting. After briefly examining our documents, she took the holder out of her mouth and used it to point to a door ahead. Inside were a few girls sitting on settees looking at us with bored faces. One of them invited me with a grand gesture of her hand to sit near her. I took my coat off, but I felt clammy. The girl had a fixed smile on her face; the exaggerated makeup made her face look like a clown. She moved closer to whisper something in my ear; she smelled of talcum powder and sweat. I stood up and made for the door; I needed air! La Goulou hissed something to me, but I rushed out. Outside, I lifted my face to the fine cool rain and the darkening sky. I waited for Vittorio in the cafe at the entrance to Via Dell'Amorino. I sat sipping coffee feeling sad looking at the wet world outside through steamed up windows. The occasional hisses from the coffee machine sounded like the reproaching voice of La Goulou. I saw Vittorio before he saw me, and I went outside. He looked flushed.

"Why did you go?" he said.

"Oh, I felt hot and I had to get out." He gave me a strange look then while we were walking he took my arm and gave me all the details of his brief encounter with a lady from Bologna with the largest breasts he had ever seen and nipples the size of olives, he said. We parted and I took the train back to Lucca. Staring at the dark countryside, I drew the silhouette of a lady with large breasts on the steamed-up window and felt uncomfortable when an old lady entered the compartment.

Before the Christmas holidays, one of our teachers asked for a volunteer to work in a ski resort hotel managed by a well-known hotelier from Montecatini. I volunteered, bought trousers, boots and a ski jacket and left for Foppolo by train just before Christmas. Got to Bergamo many hours later and took a bus to the ski resort. I was tired, and it was bitterly cold, and I was glad for my ski jacket. My job consisted of helping as a waiter at breakfast time and guarding the hall of dependence nearby from 8 pm to midnight. In the afternoon, I rented some skis but spent most of the time on my arse. My fitness saving my skin on many occasions! Later, during my evening hours in the hall, I smiled at ladies coming back drunk but with no luck! I kept fit running up the stairs listening to the jukebox from the nightclub outside playing the twist. Sometimes I took the ski lift to the top of the mountain and sat in the sun thinking of the future. I knew I had to go for my army service, and I really felt like going back to England after that. I made a few friends at the hotel, but I was generally alone. One evening, a red-haired lady in a white and pink ski suit talked to me resting her elbows on the wooden counter and staring into my eyes. She was pissed, about forty and from Milan. When I gave her the key, she held my hand and whispered to come and see her later after I had finished. I locked the outside glass door and walked upstairs, my heavy boots noisy on the wooden floor. I knocked at the door, and I had to wait a while before the door opened slowly and the lady, in a bathrobe and without makeup, let me in. "Do you make a habit of visiting lonely ladies?" she said in a low smoker's voice.

"Only when I am invited," I answered. She laughed.

"Take your boots off. What would you like to drink?"

"Have you got whisky?" I asked.

"Yes," she said.

"Don't think that because I invited you I want your body. I just want company." I smiled in surprise.

"I am okay with that," I said taking a tumbler half full of whisky and ice. We sat on a large settee. We smoked her menthol cigarettes, and she told me she was an interior designer in Milan. Her gold Rolex and square diamond ring told me she was successful.

"I have just divorced my husband," she said removing a fleck of ash that had fallen into her tumbler with her slim finger. She laughed, her head thrown back, tossing her red hair. She played with her glass holding it with two fingers and rattling the ice inside. "Do you want to do some coke?" she said not looking at me.

"I don't know. I have never done it before. I don't mind." She drank the rest of the whisky and put the glass on the floor. She collected a crocodile skin box from a case inside the wardrobe. I looked at her curves inside the bathrobe. She got a jade bottle, removed the red stopper and tapped it on a square vanity mirror making two long parallel lines of white powder. She looked at me with a satisfied look, rolled a large denomination note into a tube, brought the mirror close to her face. I could see her breasts; her dressing gown was slowly parting. She looked at me smiling, inserted the tube into her nostril and inhaled rapidly a line of powder. Then she slowly passed me the tube and with the movement of her brows, invited me to do the same. I did and she tapped some more powder on the mirror. It felt strange, some went to the back of my mouth and throat; it tasted bitter and my mouth and gums started to feel numb. I felt I was not in control and did not know what to do. I rested my head back on the settee. We sat talking for a long time. I cannot remember the conversation. At some stage, I put my hand gently on the lady's breast, her pink nipple was showing. She slapped my hand gently and covered herself. "Naught boy!" she said through her teeth. We talked some more. I felt inhibited not knowing what to do. The village clock outside chimed two o'clock. The lady stood up, offered me a hand and I felt a bit wobbly. She picked the rolled note from the table and put it in my pocket, pointed to my boots by the door, blew me a kiss and let me out. The working holiday passed quickly, and I got a good pay packet. I never had so much money before.

I got a lift to Milan in a sports car with a young client of the hotel. I stayed in a cheap hotel on a foggy tree lined avenue, and after a pizza, I went to see a Western from which I remember the words of a song 'little pretty girl in yellow dress'. In the morning, I window-shopped in the smart centre of Milan and fell in love with a .22 Derringer pistol. It felt heavy in my hand, its chromed barrel shiny, beautiful, but I could not buy it without a licence. I bought instead a beautiful recurved Peterson pipe and some Clan tobacco. I showed off my pipe on the train back to Lucca, blowing great puffs of aromatic smoke in the stuffy compartment.

Back in Lucca, my sister opened the door. She had somehow matured even in the few weeks I had been away. She looked great in a blue jumper like some starlet of the time but classier. She told me a boy from Perugia, Marco, was coming to meet her the day after. She was very excited! The guy turned up in the morning with a friend in a beautiful red Giulietta Alpha Romeo. He was a student of medicine at Pisa University and his older friend, Bedrick, was a trainee surgeon specialising in heart surgery in a hospital in Holland. Mother cooked a fabulous meal. I smoked my pipe, and we drank grappa. We got a bit drunk and the boys invited me to go to Perugia with them in the morning. Marco told me of his love for my sister, but apparently, she had not accepted his offer to become engaged. The boys slept in the spare room near my bedroom, and in the morning, after coffee and toast, we left in the red car. We stopped in Florence and the boys, impressed by my pipe and the irresistible smell of Clan, bought a pipe each and tobacco. We went to the Uffizi and spent the afternoon staring at great works of art. Later, in a long corridor, the afternoon sun from a great window threw a strange light on a painting of a young man by Parmigianino, and when I stood in a certain way, my face reflected on the face in the painting, and it looked as if I was there wearing a Renaissance costume. We all tried the trick and laughed till the guard, sitting on a chair by the door, stood up and walked towards us. Later, we looked at shops, and I bought a pair of brown moccasins from Arfango, at great expense. We had dinner at Sabatini of Fiorentina e Funghi. We stayed at an old hotel near the station sharing a large room. We sat in bed smoking and talking of our dreams. Bedrick spoke of wanting to become a great surgeon, Marco of taking over his father's medical practice in Perugia and I of leaving Italy for England. In the morning, we drove to Perugia, and Bedrick and I stayed in the loft of Marco's house. His parents were charming and very welcoming. That evening, we went to a party. We made a hit by smoking our pipes and everybody was very friendly. I danced with a girl slowly in the semi-darkness. There were candles set on Chianti straw bottles dripping wax slowly, almost in time with the music on a long table set with bread, salami and wine. The girl was a student at Perugia University, wore a short pleated tartan skirt and danced much better than me. Bedrick was smoking his pipe deep in conversation with a girl with a fringe and very thick glasses on the settee by the door. The girl I was dancing with showed me how to combine the twist with the jive. I felt clumsy and hot, but everyone else seemed to be having a good time. Marco was dancing very close with a blonde girl; he must already have forgotten my sister! My girl and I walked through a French window to the terrace. The lights of Perugia in the distance and the smell of the pines in the garden below! I lit my pipe, but she took it out of my mouth, laughing, and we kissed. I lifted her Fairisle short jumper and felt her body. She did not let me touch her below the waist, and when other couples came out, we went back inside. We drank red wine, and she told me that she was not sure she liked boys. She had had an intimate encounter with an older girl while away skiing in Emilia, and she was now confused. Later, we went back to Marco's loft and talked till very late, smoking our pipes. My mouth felt rough from too much smoking.

In the morning, I said goodbye and left for Lucca on a train that stopped at every station. The last of the winter passed slowly training two or three times a week at Pisa, the occasional party, the Passeggiata in Via Filungo, nodding at familiar faces and eating a lot. We were bored, and late in the evening, we went to each other's houses and ate what was left in the fridge or pantry. At home, Mother had retired from her job as an accountant and had more time to nag and reproach me for something or other. In the evening, I met my friends perched on the benches of the Palazzo Cenami, talked about sport and girls and was generally quite bored with life in a small town. Spring came with more trips training in Pisa, long runs on the grassy strips around the track with jokes told while breathing heavily and digs at each other. My discus throwing was improving. Franco, being a national athlete, had been exposed to better techniques, and he was coaching me with good results. We lifted weights on the grass and concentrated on speed and power. Hotel school ended in June. We had a final examination, and to my surprise, I passed. My oral German exam with

Miss Desideri was surreal. She was so determined to pass me; she was so sweet. Every time she noted me getting into difficulties with the language, she would ask me an easy question like 'how old are you' and 'where do you come from', and to my answer, she would say, *'gut gut sehr gut'*. I could have hugged her. So now I had a diploma in hotel management.

I met, again, a boy called Alfredo, alias Pescino, a nickname meaning 'small fish'. Although he really looked like a fish, he was full of confidence and pulled more girls than the more handsome shy boys. Pescino worked with his father as an oil analyst going to various farms and factories and advising them on the quality of their olive oil. Pescino had a small blue cinquecento, his pride and joy! It had various badges and shields screwed to its grille. Most of those badges were acquired with the help of a screwdriver, mostly from foreign cars! Alfredo was dapper and smart and well known in most nightclubs and dance halls near Lucca. On a Sunday after lunch, we went to the Principe di Piemonte, a smart bar with an open pool on the beach in Viareggio. 'Small fish' had no problem talking to any girls and being funny and easy going, was very popular. While we were lying on towels by the pool we noticed a pretty blonde girl nearby applying Ambre Solaire to her freckled arms and legs. The girl looked unmistakably English. "Would you like me to put some oil on your back?" said Alfredo in quite a good accent.

"No, thanks. I am okay," said the girl smiling. Conversation started and I let Alfredo to talk. The girl called Angela came from Kent and was staying at the hotel opposite with her father and mother. She spoke to Pescino but looked smiling at me. I noticed him getting irritated and becoming more pushy and direct. "Would you like to come for a drive? I have a little pied a terre in Viarregio. Or would you like some whisky." Angela became visibly annoyed and turned on her chair to talk to me. I was pleased to have a chance to show off my English, and after a while, Pescino turned to a German girl on a chair nearby. Angela had blue eyes and dimples on her freckled cheeks when she smiled. I put my towel near her chair, the afternoon light reflecting on the pool. She offered me a Kent cigarette all the way from England. We talked easily, and she asked about my experience there. A middle-aged smiling lady approached, and Angela introduced her mother. We talked, and after a while, I was invited to the hotel for tea. I approached Pescino still talking to the German girl, and we made arrangements for him to pick me up by the statue of Viani in Viareggio at midnight to go back to Lucca.

We had tea in the vast dining room of the hotel, and I met Angela's father, a charming Englishman with grey hair and a moustache. There was a strong scent of geraniums from boxes outside the large windows looking towards the sea. We talked easily, and they congratulated me on my English. "We are driving to Pisa to see the leaning tower. Would you like to join us?" said Angela's father.

"Great," I said. Angela smiled at me from the other side of the table, her dimples were irresistible! We travelled in a beautiful open Jaguar with wire spoked wheels and painted racing green. Angela and I sat in the back, the wind in our hair, having to get close to speak to each other. The sun illuminated her face, and I noticed a fine down on her cheeks like a peach. We climbed the marble steps of the leaning tower then we walked on the spiral ascending path with marble columns on the outside flanks of the tower. A weird sensation! Angela felt slight vertigo, and I held her hand. At the top, it was windy, and we looked at the red roofs of Pisa and the silvery Arno River, the pine woods and the sea. The bronze bell at the top rang, and we all covered our ears and felt the sound vibrating in our bodies. On the way back, it was getting dark, and with the excuse of the noise, I kissed Angela's ear. We arranged to meet after dinner, and I had a sandwich and a beer near the pier and walked back to the hotel at nine. Angela looked great in jeans, a blue T-shirt, her face flushed by the day in the sun. We walked holding hands, the evening breeze ruffling her blonde hair. We found a bar on the Passeggiata, sat on the veranda by the beach, drank beer, smoked and held hands under the table. Later, we walked back in the direction of the hotel. I took off my moccasins, rolled my trousers up. She did the same, and we walked on the hard sand, lapped by the surf, arms around each other listening to the music coming out of the jukeboxes of all the bars we passed. Later in the darkness almost opposite the hotel, we sat on a beached boat and kissed. Angela was a good kisser, passionate and strong, but she did not want to go any further, and I took her back to the hotel. We decided to meet again by the pool in the afternoon. I walked to the Viani monument to meet Pescino, but he did not turn up. At about one o'clock, I managed to hitch a lift from a musician from La Busssola nightclub, returning to Florence via Lucca. In the morning, I told Mother of my meeting with Angela, and she asked me to invite her to come to Lucca for lunch. In the morning, I phoned Pescino, and he told me he had a good time with the German girl and returned to Lucca very late. I, in fact, suspected that he had not turned up as he wanted to punish me because of my success with Angela.

I went back to Viareggio by bus and met Angela by the pool. Her skin was pink, and she looked great in a black costume. A beach photographer took some shots of us on the beach. I still have the photos some in silhouette with the setting sun, my body brown against her paler skin, kissing, smiling. After dinner, we met again and went to a luna park. I won a little bear at the shooting gallery. We ate pink candy floss, and we kissed, our cheeks sticky. I took her back to the hotel and arranged to meet her in Lucca for lunch. Her parents, wanting to see Lucca, would drive her there. My whole family, Nonna Armanda, now very old, Auntie Bice, my mother and sister Ughetta met Angela in Piazza San Michele. None of them spoke English so I had to translate a lot. There were plenty of admiring comments even from my sister. "I like her pink lipstick and her skirt and sandals," she said looking at Angela sideways. Auntie Bice touched Angela's hair.

"So fine, so blonde," she said. We ate outside in a restaurant in Piazza Santa Maria. Angela drank a lot of wine and Mother gave her worried looks. "She is so beautiful, but is she going to be all right drinking like that?" I walked a slightly tipsy Angela back to the rendezvous with her parents near the station in Lucca, and she left in the Jaguar, smiling and waving. The next day, I collected the picture from the beach photographer's kiosk and delivered the copies to the hotel. Angela was in her room packing, her parents had gone to Torre Del Lago to see Puccini's villa. We kissed, and she offered me a coke from the fridge but did not want to go any further. We sat on the terrace in the sunshine staring uncomfortably into each other's eyes. She left for England that evening. She sent me a letter thanking me for keeping her company. The pink print of her lips sealing the end of the page. I met her again in Rome the year after. I was there doing my military service. She sent a letter to Lucca, which was forwarded to Rome. We met near the Colosseo; she wore a blue scarf on her head and dark glasses. She told me she was on the way back from Germany where she had visited a boyfriend. She was in a strange mood, remote, distant, gone her easy smile with dimples of the previous summer. We went for lunch to an expensive trattoria in Piazza del Popolo. We had spaghetti alla matriciana, and she ordered some very expensive wine. I did not have enough money to pay the bill, and she gracefully paid. I saw her again in 1966 in London at the Earls Court Motor Show. She was one of the hostesses on the Jaguar stand. I was with another girl and did not speak to her. I still have a photo she gave me of her sitting demurely on the carpet in the sitting room of her house in Kent.

During that summer, I became friends with a guy called Alberto who ran a dentists' laboratory making false teeth, bridges and veneers. I often went to Alberto's place and was fascinated by the various techniques used. Alberto and the boys working in the laboratory made a lot of money. They invited me for drinks and to dinner; they were very generous, especially Alberto. "Do you need any money? Are you hungry?" he would say. At first, I was uncomfortable looking for a motivation, a catch, but there was none. That was his character, very unusual! One afternoon, while I was looking at Alberto working, he said, "Why don't you take my bike and go for a ride?"

"I can't drive it," I said.

"Don't worry, I will show you." He came out of his laboratory wearing his apron. "This is the kick starter. This is the gas handle. That's the clutch. First gear. It's easy." He left me there in the sunshine of the courtyard with this large unfamiliar red Guzzi. I failed to start it several times. Alberto and the guys were looking at me from the window. I managed to put the bike into first gear and left the courtyard. I had difficulties with the other gears but somehow managed to negotiate the narrow streets of Lucca and get out of the Mura onto the avenue outside. I was sweating and was glad of the breeze on my chest with the increasing speed. I decided to go to Cristiano's house and see if he would join me for a ride on the bike. I stopped outside his house; the bike was heavy to lift onto the fork. The colonel, Cristiano's father, opened the door in a blue dressing gown. He was making Karkade in the kitchen, a red tea, he told me, he had started to use it during the war in Ethiopia. He offered me a cup with a spoonful of honey. It tasted quite nice. I showed Cristiano the Guzzi from his kitchen window. "We can go to Viareggio," he said. I hoped he could drive it, but he told me he was not at all confident. Later on the hot road, I opened the throttle and we reached ninety kilometres, Cristiano holding tight onto my waist. I crunched a few gears, but I was getting better. I started to get a searing pain on my liver side either from the wind or the tension created by the new experience. We stopped near Massarosa and had a cool drink in a bar sitting under a pergola. When we got to Viareggio, I felt cocky and tried to reach a hundred kilometres on the promenade. I was starting to enjoy the bike when I saw an old brown dog starting to cross the road ahead. I slowed down, but the dog sat on the hot tarmac licking his droopy balls. I panicked and broke too hard. We skidded but managed to stay on the bike. The dog looked up and just stopped his licking to bark at us. I slowed down after that. I borrowed the bike a few more times and dreamed of having enough money to buy one myself.

Carlo was another assistant at Alberto's laboratory, a large, hairy fat guy always laughing and in charge of carving the waxes for the metal castings. He told me that some friends had found in their cellar an old inflatable left behind by the Americans during the war. We went to the dusty cellar and in a crate was the black inflatable. We staggered to carry the crate to the entrance. Inside were also paddles, ropes and a rudimentary rudder. We got together a crew of four boys I knew and planned a trip to La Spezia from Viareggio. Somebody borrowed a van and the inflatable was carried to Viareggio and made ready. The boys in the crew belonged to a swimming club and trained on the River Serchio, swimming in the current between two pontoons. Carlo collected all of us in the morning of the expedition, and we piled in his large Lancia with food and wine on the way to Viareggio. On the pier stood the black inflatable gleaming in the sun! We managed to put it in the water. I have a photo of us armed with paddles, posing and smiling at the camera. We started to row. We found a rhythm and approached the exit of the harbour. Fitting the rudder had seemed too complicated, and we decided not to use it. Just outside the harbour mouth, we realised how unstable the inflatable was. With every wave, we jumped about and trying to keep a straight course seemed difficult. We managed to turn right and exchanged places trying to balance the strength of the crew. We realised how slow we were and making La Spezia would be rather difficult. Soon Carlo complained of feeling seasick; we teased him, but he was really quite worried and pale in the face. After a while, he started to beg us to take him back. We realised a strong current seemed to run from the north and as we were trying to go in that direction, it made our progress difficult. By now, Carlo was vomiting overboard and offering us money to take him back. We laughed but then realised our predicament, and when we stopped paddling, we started to move south swiftly with the current and soon went past the mouth of the harbour having failed to turn into it. We paddled again, the speed made us a bit more stable, and Carlo thanked us profusely and promised to buy us all dinner. We landed a mile or so south of the harbour, beached the inflatable and started on our provisions of bread, salami and wine sitting on the hot sand. We swam and played catch games while Carlo slept inside the inflatable recovering from his ordeal. We decided to spend the night on the beach and Carlo, having fully recovered, took us to a fish restaurant near the Darsena. We had barbequed mackerel and masses of cold wine. We staggered back to the beach and slept huddled together under a tarpaulin.

When I felt like being alone, I went to fish on the River Serchio. I bought a beautiful cane rod, long and slender and from a shop in Via Fillungo an Alcedo reel, smooth and fast with a retrieving ring made of agate. Using it, I caught barbells and roaches. My catches got fried in a big black iron frying pan by Granny. Coming back from fishing, I met Isetta. She worked in an office in Borgo Giannotti. She looked tanned and more mature. We had coffee, and surprisingly, she invited me to come to see her at her home the next day. It was her day off! Her parents had just left for their house in the mountains in the hope of selling it. I went by pushbike to Ponte a Moriano. Seeing Isetta's old house made me think of how many times I had stared at those windows when secretly meeting her before getting engaged. She welcomed me, made coffee and we kissed. She seemed to be more in command. She took me to her bedroom, and we undressed. I had never seen her completely naked before. She was lovely like a Roman goddess. We got into bed. I felt her body pressing against mine, after all we had never made love properly before. I kissed her everywhere with an enormous erection pushing against her belly. A whistle from the open window brought us back to reality. "Quick it's my father," she whispered. I jumped from the bed and put on my trousers quickly.

"Wait. Go under the bed," she said. I did so, my chest feeling the coolness of the dusty brick tiles. Isetta put back her dress, her bra and panties still on the floor. Using my foot, I pushed them under the bed. I found myself laughing at the situation. The front door opened and closed. I heard her father explaining that he needed some legal papers. I heard him rummage in his bedroom, then he asked his daughter to make him coffee. Muffled talking from the kitchen, then the front door slammed, and he left. Isetta came back, her flustered face smiling at me still under the bed. I jumped back with her under the light linen sheet, and we kissed again but something was amiss. The passion of half an hour before had gone and also my erection. "What's wrong?" she said.

"I don't know," I answered holding my limp penis. She touched and kissed me there, but my penis refused to come to attention. I felt surprised and deflated. This had never happened to me before! Isetta tried again to arouse me, but somehow, she was frustrated, surprised and not terribly sympathetic. Her body language told me she was disappointed with me. She pulled away when I tried to kiss her, shaking her head. We didn't say much, and I left my mind in turmoil. I felt devastated at my impotence; I had heard about such things happening, but I thought I was too young for it to be happening to me.

On the bike back to Lucca, I really suffered. Was it going to be permanent? I wondered. I felt blood flushing in my head and beating in my ears! I remained subdued for the next few days and drank more wine than usual to forget. I compared myself with every man I met and felt inferior imagining their performance to be faultless.

Army Service

One morning, I came back home, having spent the night drinking with friends, and found on my pillow a card from the army ordering me to present myself to a district barracks in Pisa to start my military service the same day. Mother had noticed my change of moods in the last few days and seemed to be glad of my departure. I kissed them all and left for Pisa. At the barracks, I was given a card and tickets to travel to Orvieto, a hill town in Umbria to start my training. I travelled there with other recruits on a slow train. It was still hot. My stomach felt heavy and tense although I had had no food; I fell asleep, and I would have missed Orvieto station but for a tall guy with a broken nose and sad eyes that shook me from my sleep. We walked slowly uphill towards the town; it was getting dark, and I felt awful. My companion told me he was a farmer from the marshes near Pisa and how he had tried to avoid the army in vain, as all the tasks now had fallen on his father. I tried to sound sympathetic, but I could only think of my troubles. At the gate, a stern sergeant from the Grenadiers Corps took our cards and escorted us to a dormitory. It was too late for us to be kitted out so we slept under a blanket. My friend from Pisa on the bunk above me snored all night. In the morning, we woke up with the sound of a bugler, washed our faces but we did not have a towel. We were taken to an enormous room; our names were called, and we got all the clothes and kit we needed for our training period. Most of the clothes looked too large, and we were told they would shrink. The food was bad, someone noticed a date on the side of a bully beef can – 1918! More than forty years old! I became friendly with two boys from Sicily sleeping in the bunks beside mine. One of them, very tall blond blue-eyed guy, a sure sign that, after all, the Normans had occupied Sicily for a few hundred years. The other, also tall but very dark, tough-looking with the whitest teeth. I learned, after we became friends, that the blond boy was the only son of a Palermo Mafia boss that had wanted him to go into the army so that in future no one would accuse him of favouritism. He had used his powers to secure that his only son would be protected by the other boy, his bodyguard and that they would remain together for the whole army service. We went out many times to eat or drink in Orvieto. They were great companions, charming, reliable and generous. Another recruit in the same dormitory was an enormous guy from South Tyrol. He considered himself Austrian and resented being in the Italian Army. He spoke in a strange dialect and could not understand Italian very well. He was a blacksmith by trade and looked like the giant in my childhood fairy tale book. He showed me photos of his work mainly on churches, portals, hinges, gates, crucifixes. He was very religious, gentle and artistic. One day, we were told we were due for inoculations. We lined up in the infirmary room, sweating, bare-chested and worried. A doctor marked with iodine a spot just above our breast and stuck a needle in it. We then walked towards the end of one of the rooms where another doctor inserted into the needle an enormous syringe and injected us with a dose of brown liquid. A nurse collected the needles at the end of the line. Many fainted including the giant from Tyrol. I just managed to reach the dormitory and collapsed on the bed. Some of us had fever and our breasts swelled up. We never found out what was in the syringe! In the toilets, we had to pee in a large metal vat. Our urine was used in the manufacture of salt peter.

A notice stuck on the wall of the dormitory announced that the army was looking for athletes to take part in competitions with other European armies. I volunteered and also recommended the giant. I was sure he could throw the shot or the hammer. There was a small track and field at one corner of the large barracks grounds. I was accepted and was glad of my training in Pisa. The giant, although very strong, proved too slow for the kind of explosive effort required. Now in the morning, instead of boring drills on the main square, I went to train with a select group. My performance improved, and I put on weight. I still felt morose and sad about my impotence with Isetta and when other boys spoke of sex, I felt inadequate and inferior. One evening, I was short of money and didn't feel like going out and lay limply on the bottom bunk. Some other guy was cleaning his boots on the bunk opposite with his transistor on. "Did you hear that?" he shouted. "Marilyn Monroe is dead!" I fell asleep with my eyes filling with tears.

At the end of three months, I was sent to Rome to a newly built barracks with a modern gym and track at the Cecchignola near the Euro. I got to Rome on a rainy day in autumn. Just outside Stazione Termini, I asked a young man the way to the Euro. We spoke, and he told me he had done his army service in Lucca. His name was Enrico. He told me how to get to the barracks and gave me his telephone number. We shook hands, and I took the bus. The barracks were brand new and the sports facilities and food great. The captain in charge of us looked like Mussolini. He had a bald head, was called Basile and was a real pain in the arse. The various dormitories hosted cyclists, athletes, boxers and various other sportsmen including footballers. I trained with other athletes, and in the morning, we were taken by bus to Ostia to run in the surf like racehorses. In the afternoon, we lifted weights and practised our specialities. I still felt saddened at my episode of impotence and when some of the other guys went with prostitutes, I shied away, afraid of trying. One painful initiation ritual inflicted to the recruits consisted of the painting of our private parts with the usual filthy concoction of blue ink, shoe polish, etc. like I had experienced before at school. I don't know how such a ritual was created in the first place, as if young recruits didn't have enough adjusting to the new way of life! I rebelled. I did not want to submit to such a humiliation. I was strong enough to defend myself. I was told that if I refused the initiation, a bidone, a dustbin full of rubbish, would be emptied at night onto my bunk every night until I submitted to the ritual. Nothing happened for a couple of days, and when I started to think they had forgotten about it, a cold foul stinky liquid was emptied on my bunk. I could not sleep again. The dormitory was not centrally heated, and after shivering for a few hours, I went inside the cupboard with the hot water tank by the shower. The next night, it happened again, shocked by the cold liquid I only saw shadowy figures running towards the door. I decided the best thing was to submit to the ritual; I could not operate without sleeping. So I got anointed standing on a stool naked; I let the (older) soldiers brush me amongst taunts and giggles. Pathetic!

When after two years I became an Anziano, due to the fact that I was quite popular, I convinced other 'ancients' to get rid of the stupid and cruel initiation. The only thing the new recruits had to do for us was to sing at every reveille a little song announcing how many days we had left before going home. Teasing was common in the barracks, and there were pranks played by a particular dormitory to another. I made friends with a group of Jewish guys doing athletics. Franco was a small dynamic guy studying to be a vet and practising pole vault. Capra, a tall dark and gaunt, threw the discus like me and studied literature. Roberto from Genoa, wrote poetry and ran the 200 metres. They were all fun and intelligent guys and, although not on their level academically, I found myself accepted and at ease with them. We hated the cyclists who we suspected were the executors of the bidoni.

One day, our group, knowing that the cyclists had got their bikes ready in the hall for an outing and were about to exit the main door, placed a tub of water balancing on the semi-opened door to fall on the first of them. Unfortunately, the first to open the door was Captain Basile. He got soaked and the tub cut his bald head. Red in the face, he shouted that until the culprit was found nobody would be allowed out in the evening. After debating, we all went to the captain's office and confessed. We explained the prank had not been directed at him, but he cut us short and told us that as a punishment we would not be allowed to go on the imminent week-long Christmas leave. So all left for Christmas, only four of us remained in the dormitory apart from a cook and a guard! We played the radio, told each other stories and listened to James Joyce's *Ulysses* read to us by Roberto in his soft Genoese accent. We became so involved with the story that we enacted part of it among ourselves, impersonating various famous characters when we went out in the evening to the amusement and confusion of the local people in the pizzerias and bars. Just before Christmas, we woke up to an amazing snowfall maybe twenty centimetres deep. We could not run or train so we had a snowball fight, and after, we sat by a huge terracotta stove drying our boots, reading Ulysses and smoking. I had spoken, from a pay phone, to Mother and the rest of the family to wish them a happy Christmas, and I was told that a parcel was on its way to me. I got the parcel after Christmas full of chocolates, grappa and salami. For Christmas day, we got a meal of polenta and stew and drank plenty of wine and grappa. Just after Christmas, Franco Muro arrived into our lives, a handsome rascal from Naples looking like a tall North African. He had a great smile and could get away with anything. He was also a good athlete with natural abilities for the decathlon but no desire to train. He helped in the infirmary and soon started to sell various drugs to the rest of the athletes, vitamins, tonics, uppers and downers, anything you wanted for a price. He was extremely successful with the ladies. He had a few girls, and if you needed company, he could introduce you to them for a fee, of course! Eventually, Franco was forced by the captain to take part in a competition, and he did very well beating many other athletes who had been training hard. To the left of my bunk at the bottom slept a small dark soldier from Sardinia with a sad smile and a head too large for his body. He was a marathon runner, shy and silent. His name was Asula.

Above him slept a tall guy from the north, he had a shaved head and a big nose. He was a hammer thrower and a cruel obnoxious character called Pinot. Large men are generally nice and easy, but he was an exception. He teased Asula continuously from farting in his direction getting out of bed in the morning to slapping his large head and throwing rubbish on his bunk below. Asula took it all with patience, quietly muttering in his Sardinian dialect. "Asula, Asula," repeated Pinot imitating his accent and hitting him on the head. One evening just before lights out, Asula sat on his bunk polishing his boots. Pinot started dripping spit from above on Asula's head. I saw a look in his eyes I had never seen before. He stood and looked at Pinot.

"Bastard!" he shouted and kept staring at him. Pinot descended from his bunk and laughingly placed his hands on the small man's shoulders. Asula grabbed

Pinot's neck, and for a moment, I smiled thinking they were going to embrace but with a fast unexpected movement, he pushed Pinot's head down and smashed it against his forehead. There was a cracking noise, and Pinot slowly sank to the floor. Asula sat on his bunk and continued polishing his boots. Pinot's mandible was broken and some of his teeth were missing. He was taken to the hospital and came back weeks later, his jaw wired having to eat mashed food. Poor Asula was court-martialled and sent to the military prison at Gaeta. We tried to explain that the poor guy's life had been made impossible by Pinot but in vain. We never saw Asula again!

Every spring, there was a training camp on the hills east of Rome. I didn't take part because I had a competition in L'Aquila for the Italian Military Championships. Many athletes left under the leadership of Captain Basile in various army lorries carrying food, tents and weapons. I was told later, that during a shooting exercise with a machine gun in a valley beside a stream, Captain Basile, ignoring the most important rule never to point a weapon to anything unless you wanted to shoot it, had engaged a magazine from a crate where spent magazines had been thrown whilst trying to demonstrate the correct way of loading. The magazine was only half empty. A burst of fire killed two footballers and seriously injured a cyclist. A sad ridiculous demonstration of the type of professional men in the Italian Army! Captain Basile disappeared soon after that. A sombre, sad feeling seemed to invade all of us though

I did well in my competition coming second in Italian Army in the discus.

I phoned Enrico, the guy I met at the station, and visited him in Rome. I went by bus to an area of Rome called Aqua Pullulante, a poor depressed area of newly built houses. He lived in a small shanty town on a dirt road in a house built of corrugated iron, plastic and plywood. He received me smiling. He was busy polishing his red 500 Fiat to the sound of his transistor playing 'Telstar'. He was well dressed. His father and mother were hospitable and friendly and did not seem to feel self-conscious of their house. They made coffee, and we sat on armchairs still covered in plastic. I admired their resilience and dignity. Inside, they had everything as in a modest house of the time, only the fabric of the house was missing. So Italian, appearance was everything *'bisogna far bella figura'!* I changed into civilian clothes, and Enrico and I went to the centre of Rome. He drove skilfully and fast in his little red car. We met his girlfriend, and he showed me the bar where he worked, and we had a pizza in Piazza Navona.

Cesare also became a good friend of mine. He was from the north, Cremona, tall, blond, blue eyed and a good 100 metre runner. He kept a small, fast opened topped Fiat outside the walls of the barracks. We had, on a few occasions, jumped the walls at night, changed into civilian clothes and stayed out till the small hours. Cesare had plenty of money. His father was a big landowner. They lived in a huge 17th century fortified house, and they grew mainly melons in vast fields by the River Po. There were huge attics in the farmhouse, full of antiques and junk they had accumulated through the centuries. Cesare had found a dusty small painting on a wood panel that looked important. He took it to Milan and after showing it to various antique dealers, learned it was an old master and sold it to the one that paid the most. He got a small fortune in cash, and he told me that he kept it in a hole in the pigeonaire covered with a brick. Cesare was very generous and during every leave replenished the cash in his wallet from the money under the brick. On a summer day on leave in a bar near the Appia Antica, we started to talk to two girls at a table near us. I had choked while drinking a beer too fast, and while Cesare was pounding my back the girls started to laugh. I tried to laugh with them, foam streaming from my nose, and in the convulsions of my coughing, they laughed even more. When my coughing finished, they introduced themselves. They were from Holland. One of them, tall and blonde, called Atinka the other, her cousin, dark and very pretty seemed to be happy talking to Cesare. We drank some more beer then the girls invited us to go for a picnic in the pine woods with them. They had ripe tomatoes, bread and ham, and we sat under a pine tree. To my surprise, they ate the large tomato without condiment as if they were fruits. We walked, and it was getting dark. Atinka was very natural. She took my hand and smiled at me. We spoke in English, and I loved the Dutch accent. We sat on a Roman monument built of bricks. Cesare disappeared in the distance with the other girl. We kissed, hugged and I felt a stirring in my groin. I was excited; I was sure I could do it! We had to go back before lights out; we had been in trouble before and could not risk a punishment. The new captain, a man from Milan, was fair but very strict. We drove the girls to Trastevere to their hotel, and we arranged to meet later. Cesare just got us back to the barracks in time, and we changed back into our uniforms and left our civilian clothes in the boot of the car. We got counted, went to bed and after a while got up, exited from the toilet window, scaled the wall, changed and drove back to Trastevere. The girls were waiting for us in the bar near the hotel. We had pasta washed down with chilled Frascati and went back to the hotel. We had to bribe the night porter that wanted us to take a double room and joined the Dutch girls in their shared room. We smoked duty free Marlboro, switched off the light and joined the girls in their single beds.

I kissed Atinka and touched her hot body. Finally, I got an erection! She helped me inside her, and we made love slowly, almost silently. It was great. I felt healed. We smoked, whispered and made love again. I had to catch up with lost time! Early in the morning, we left the girls in bed, had coffee in the bar at the end of the road and red-eyed and tired drove back to the barracks. I felt exhilarated; I had been able to make love again! We didn't train too hard that day, and Cesare and I grinned at each other when we met running slowly around the track. The girls left the day after for Florence, but we had time to meet them again for a pizza. I exchanged addresses with Atinka, and we promised to write to one another. A few weeks later, I received a letter with a photo of Atinka standing on the steps at Trinita'dei Monti. She said she missed me and invited me to visit her in Amsterdam. My time in the army was coming to an end. In the morning, the recruits sang their song telling us how many days till our return home. On one of my last days in Rome, I went to Via Condotti and bought a pair of black moccasins and jeans. Cesare said that as he was going via Lucca on his way back to Cremona; he would give me a lift. The day we left was very emotional. I had made so many good friends. Franco Muro gave me a big hug and told me he had now four girls working for him, and he was going to stay in Rome looking after them. The Jewish trio gave me a book, *Catcher in the Rye* by Salinger and a lot of hugs. Even the new captain shook hands and winked telling me that he knew about our nocturnal escapes. It was a sunny, warm September when we arrived in Lucca in the early evening. Cesare was bowled over by my sister. She had become a real beauty. We had a meal to remember. Mother surpassed herself and cooked my favourite tortelli of spinach and ricotta with sage butter followed by involtini di carne ripieni. We sat around the big table full of smiling faces. They seemed glad that I was home again. After dinner, Cesare and I decided to drive to La Bussola. At the entrance, to my surprise, was Piero my friend from Lucca. A very unlikely bouncer! A small wiry guy with hair like a Marine, dressed in a black linen suit and white shirt. Although he didn't look it, he was a tough guy, expert in martial arts and ran a karate club in Lucca. Cesare and I queued patiently. There was some shouting in the front. A large guy with a Florentine accent was arguing with Piero. The guy from Florence, red from the sun wore a blue vest and my friend was calmly pointing out that the dress code demanded a shirt. Piero was trying to make the shouting Florentine to step aside to let other people in. The large guy seemed to turn around but then turned back and pushed Piero hard against the wooden door. My friend composed himself, stood beside the guy only reaching his chin and told him in a quiet voice 'to leave now' before he took him down.

With a look of incredulity in his eyes, the tall guy looked for support from his friends then turned around and threw a slow punch. Piero stood easily aside. Another punch followed, but this time, my friend in the elegant linen suit pivoted, almost in slow motion and kicked the side of the Florentine's knee. A sudden, fast kick, a cracking noise! The tall man collapsed on the floor with torn knee ligaments screaming in pain. Cesare and I looked at one another in amazement. Somebody phoned for an ambulance while a few friends tried to help the injured man groaning on his back. Piero appeared unmoved, shook cool hands with me as I introduced him to Cesare. Inside, we found space by the bar, drank beer and smoked, talking about our lives and our futures. Cesare was going to run the large farm with his father, and I told him that I was planning to write to one of my friends, Valerio, from the hotel school that worked as an assistant manager at a hotel in Stratford on Avon, to try and see if he could find me a job in England. We talked with a few girls and danced a bit. I missed the old way of dancing, now everyone danced a few feet away, no more contact feeling a girl close to you, whispering, squeezing, smelling. The new generation did not know what they were missing! We sat again on the tall stools at the bar and looked around at people dancing, faces sweating, smiling in a fog of smoke. We stayed till late but somehow did not feel like trying to pick up girls. When we drove back to Lucca in the early hours of the morning, it felt cold in the little open car, and we stopped to put up the roof and for a cappuccino at the bar Nelli outside the walls, already noisy and full with early customers. Cesare left his car in the street by the entrance to the Guinigi Palace beside my house. In the morning, after breakfast, Cesare said goodbye to my family. I carried his bag downstairs; we hugged and said goodbye. "Why don't you come to Cremona with me?" he said smiling, his eyes excited. I thought for a moment. Just over the head of Cesare on the wall stood a marble relief and in it the devil's evil smile seemed to encourage me.

"Why not?" I said, and we hugged again. I ran upstairs. Mother was washing the breakfast dishes. When I told her about Cremona, she just raised her eyebrows. I kissed her and picked her up, her wet apron left a wet mark on my shirt. I put a few clothes in a bag and ran downstairs. Cesare had borrowed some newspapers from Milani, the barber, and was scraping the back seat of the red car. A cat had somehow entered the car through a flap of the soft top and crapped there. Milani stood by with hot water and a towel. He shook hands with me and told me how much I had grown. Later, he came back with a bottle and sprayed Patchouli on the wet seat. We left with the roof down, the aroma of cat poo and Patchouli mingling with smell of the Bertolli oil refinery outside the walls. We took the newly built Autostrada del Sole. It was still warm, and we stopped for fuel and lunch at one of the motorway cafes. We got to Cremona by teatime. The farm was just outside the town. Cesare's father, a widower, a large man with a thin white moustache fed us with homegrown melon and Parma ham; it tasted great. I met Cesare's sister Anna. She had long brown hair, and I thought she was very beautiful. That night, we went for pizza in Cremona and met a lot of Cesare's friends, rich, loud, spoiled young people. I talked to Anna and sat close to her warm thighs on the narrow bench of the pizzeria. She was about to start her first year doing psychology at Milan University. The next day, we met the same group of friends at a smart establishment by the river. Rolexes, Ray Bans, Gucci and boredom! A generation of young people in a small town with the same bored faces I had seen in Lucca. We swam in the river; we talked lying on towels in the sun till the evening came. I stayed a few days at the farm in a large room with vast windows and a brick floor. It had a four-poster bed and linen sheets. Cesare showed me the farmhouse; the enormous square building had a courtyard full of tractors and machinery. One side of the square was occupied by the farm workers. We explored the dusty attics where the old master was found. We saw swords, furniture, carpets, a grand piano and even a set of armour rusting in the dust. Cesare gave me a dagger with a square pointed blade and an ivory handle as a souvenir. The next day, Cesare and his father had to go to Milan to sign some legal documents. Anna cooked pasta for lunch, and we talked easily, laughing like old friends. I told her of my plans to move to England and a sad look came over her eyes for a second. After lunch, we went into a cool sitting room with rugs on the floor, a fireplace and a divan. We sat closely smoking and looking at each other. I took her hand, and we kissed, lying on the divan, our bodies touching, legs entwined, but she stopped me from going any further. She told me she liked me a lot, but we lived so far from each other and then my plan to move to England! I lay near to her caressing her soft brown hair until we heard a car arriving crunching the gravel in the courtyard. Cesare and his father had bought truffles and a crate of Barolo wine in Milan. We sat at a large pine refectory table in the kitchen. We opened a bottle of Barolo. Anna was making dough at one end of the table. Having made a mound of flour, she broke eggs into it and started to mix, her brown arms busy kneading, her beautiful breast bouncing inside her T-shirt with the Ban the Bomb sign. She tried to push back her long hair from her face and got flour on her nose. We had tagliatelle al tartufo for dinner. The next day, Cesare drove me to the station. I had the last glance of Anna waving, standing by the front door, the wind pressing her red dress against the shape of her body and tossing her brown hair. The train travelling on the plain beside the river reminded me of the landscape of the River Serio many years before when leaving the seminary. In Lucca, they all seemed happy to see me. I had two letters from Atinka. In one, she told me how much she missed me and told me to come to see her in Amsterdam. In the other was a postcard of a Picasso nude from a museum in Amsterdam. I decided to go; I had saved a bit of money from the accumulation of my army pay and Mother told me she would pay for my ticket. I was very excited and almost ran to the railway station and bought a return train ticket. I wrote to Atinka and told her I would arrive before Christmas.

Amsterdam

Time was now passing slowly. Once, I saw a parked Mercedes car in Piazza Napoleone with a Dutch number plate. I sat in a bar drinking coffee and kept an eye on the car. When an elderly couple came back to the car, on an impulse I rushed to meet them. I was very excited, and they looked a bit alarmed. I introduced myself and told them in English of Atinka and my imminent visit to Amsterdam. They were taken aback, but my enthusiasm and excitement seemed to transfer to them, and they looked at each other smiling. I invited them for a drink at the bar, and they answered my many questions about Holland, Amsterdam and the Dutch in general. The gentleman, a tall guy with enormous hands, told me he was a diamond cutter and not to forget to visit the Rijks Museum. By now, I was counting the days. It was a mild winter. I had started to go to a film club with Stefano and other friends. I saw the *Last Year in Marienbad*. I was terribly bored. *Nacht und Neben* an amazing documentary on the liberation of a German concentration camp, skeletal bodies buried with bulldozers, rooms filled with shoes, glasses, hair, gas ovens – we never knew of such atrocities before! I loved Bergman, *The Seventh Seal*, *Wild Strawberry* – magical! Such films took me to another world away from the boredom of Lucca. Mother paid for a grey tweed coat made to measure for me by a tailor in Lucca. It was double breasted with a high collar and a lining of red wool. It looked splendid, and I was very warm. The day finally came. I walked to the station full of excitement carrying a small case. The train came from Florence, and it looked imposing with its notices in foreign languages and wagon lits. It even smelled foreign. I sat in a compartment with couchettes. People came in and out, and I looked out of the window, slept and smoked my pipe. At night, the couchettes came down, and I shared the compartment with a couple and an old lady who snored sounding like a small engine. In the morning, the couple from the south of Italy offered me food – farmhouse bread and ham. Later, I had coffee in the buffet restaurant. I spent the rest of the day looking out of the window at the ever-changing German landscape. New people came in; the old lady left. Our passports got stamped by surly officials. Then Holland and Amsterdam!

Atinka was waiting for me at the end of the platform – a tall blonde smiling girl. She looked pale having lost her Italian tan. We kissed. I kept looking at her face, smiling in disbelief. I was finally there! It was cold, and Atinka admired my grey coat especially the red lining. We walked through cobbled streets to a small hotel near the station. It was called the Boom Hotel. It had creaky floors and noisy plumbing. Our room overlooked a small square with spindly trees. We undressed and got into bed shivering. We made love greedily wanting each other so much. Then we slept and started again, never satisfied. I had bought Atkina, with the advice from Auntie Bice, a bottle of Chanel No.5, and she used it copiously before going out. We had dinner in a small Indonesian restaurant, and I ate Nasi Goreng, but all I could smell of the exotic dish was Chanel No.5. We had breakfast at the hotel's dining room in the basement, served by a plump waitress with tresses and very red cheeks. We walked holding hands; we kissed on bridges, benches, in bars, and we drank a lot of beer in the evenings. The streets with the ladies in the windows were near the hotel. We passed them often, but we decided it made us feel sad. The ladies had the look of animals in the zoo. The Rijks Museum was wonderful. We sat kissing in the Van Gogh room; we felt so free. At night after dinner, we started to go to a bar at the top of a skyscraper near the station. We sat by the long windows looking at the lights of Amsterdam drinking tall glasses of Amstel beer, smoking and feeling happy in each other's company. We travelled by bus to the seaside, ate roll mop herrings staring at the calm sea, the colour of lead. Atinka invited me to visit her mother, a widow, and her younger brother at the weekend. We travelled by train to Friesland where they lived. On the way, the train passed the Clan factory in Leeowarden. We could smell the aromatic tobacco even with the window closed. When we arrived at the small station, it was cold; the water in the canal outside was frozen. Atinka's mother, a tall thin lady, opened the door of an old wooden grey house. She did not speak English and looked at me sideways smiling. Her face was very lined. She made tea, and we sat in a room smelling of wood polish, the armchairs covered in white dusters. Later, Atinka's brother arrived home from work. A tall and large blond boy who spoke good English and worked in a boatyard nearby. To my surprise, Atinka and I were put in the same bedroom. I couldn't see a bed in the small wooden room till Atinka opened a double door on a wall and there in the cavity was a double bed with a fluffy feather duvet. We got into bed and closed the door and in the dark under the duvet made love, talking into each other's ear, giggling trying not to make noise. In the morning after the rich Dutch breakfast, Atinka's brother brought in a dusty crate containing old fashioned skates – a simple wooden base with leather straps and a metal blade below. "We are going skating," he said smiling.

"I cannot skate," I said looking worryingly at the crate. Atinka laughed; she had started to put out a pair of skates.

"These will fit you," she said. "Don't worry we will help you. It will be okay." Outside sitting on the crunching frozen grass by the side of the canal, I fastened the leather straps of the skates to my boots. I stood on the ice on unsteady feet wearing my grey coat with the collar up. Atinka and her brother stood either side of me with their arms around my waist. We moved forward in the cool air, first slowly then faster. They propelled me forward. The cold had made my eyes water. The willows by the side of the canal were a blur! The noise of our breath and the hiss of the skates in the frozen landscape. It was great! We stopped later under a lifting wooden bridge looking like the one by Van Gogh and drank fiery Aquavit from a hip flask. Invigorated by the drink, I took a few steps myself and ended flat on the ice. They laughed and gave me a hand up. Then we skated back. Just before the house, swans flew low above our heads against the grey sky. The noise of their beating wings louder than our skates! At the house, a group of geese scattered before us skidding on the ice. The morning after, we went back to Amsterdam. The last night, we visited various bars and got drunk. It was a magical night. We seemed to be able to talk to anyone. We felt loved and loved the people around us. It was an ecstatic experience. I wish I felt like that all the time. And all of that only on beer! We staggered back to the hotel but were too excited to sleep. We made love and held each other till the grey morning. We had our last breakfast together, and later at the station, we sat on a bench waiting for the train to arrive, held hands and kissed feeling sad. The train arrived, and I got on, opened the window and held Atinka's hand till we departed. She let the train pull my hand out of hers then she turned and walked away.

I sat in an empty cold compartment; a local couple looking like the potato eaters from a Van Gogh drawing got on later and offered me a slice of cheese. They did not speak English. I picked the red wax skin of the cheese and rolled it in my fingers, softened it and I made it into a perfect ball. I played with it for a long time, and when I got bored, I stuck on the corner of the window. Just before night, a girl in a bright yellow coat got on and sat opposite me. We smiled at each other. She had very beautiful teeth and red lipstick. We spoke. She was German and was going to Milan to join her Italian husband. We had a snack in the buffet, and I ordered a double coffee; I felt sleepy. When we went back, the lights were out, and we did not want to disturb the couple asleep. We found an empty compartment and sat in the dark smoking, the occasional light from outside flashing across our faces. I was attracted to this girl, but I felt guilty.

Only a few hours before, I had made love to Atinka, a very special girl. The German girl asked why I looked so pensive, lifted her legs up and put her head on my lap. Why was it not possible to love many women? I had loved Atinka, but I also fancied this girl; she was beautiful. I loved her body; why did I have to feel guilty about wanting to make love to her? The pressure from this beautiful blonde head on my lap brought me out of my philosophising. I felt aroused, and I bent down, and we kissed. I still felt guilty but also excited. I locked the door, pulled the blinds down and we undressed each other quickly. We made love, her on top of me, the texture of the corduroy seat rough against my back, the rolling of the wagon accentuating our movements. After we were surprisingly tender for two strangers, and we lay in each other's arms. We did not sleep and at dawn got dressed and went to look for coffee. It was my second night without sleeping, but I felt full of energy, almost high. The boy in charge of the small pantry looked almost as sleepy as us but made a good cup of coffee. Back in the compartment, the 'potato eaters' had gone, and we sat looking out of the window and laughing self-consciously when we caught each other's eyes. I picked the red waxy ball, rolled it in my fingers. We knew so little about each other. She was married to a man she did not love, the owner of a pizza restaurant outside Milan, and she was desperately bored with her life. She asked me to stay in Milan for a few days; she could see me every day. I thanked her but said I wanted to go home. We did not exchange addresses. I saw her disappear along the foggy platform, her yellow coat brightening with every light she passed. I now started to feel the lack of sleep. I kept my forehead against the cool, wet window, but I found myself sliding into dreams, a thought would turn into a dream without actually sleeping. It was uncomfortable, and the few times I closed my eyes, I jumped out of my skin at every loud noise. When I got to Lucca, I struggled to carry my case home. I kissed everyone, refused any food and went straight to bed only to find that I was very agitated and could not sleep till the early hours of the morning.

Eventually, I wrote a letter to my friend Valerio asking him if he could find me a job in England. I gave him all my details, and after a few weeks, I received a letter back with my work permit. He had found me a job in Stratford on Avon working at the White Swan Hotel as a waiter starting in March. I was so happy, I walked the streets of Lucca smoking my pipe, talking to myself and laughing like a madman. Christmas came. Auntie Barbara joined our family, and we had a few days together eating a lot, staring at television and looking at old photographs. A week or so before leaving, I went to Garfagnana to see Uncle Beppe, my father's younger brother. He had left a cushy job in Florence to go back to an old house in Castelnuovo where he worked part-time as a designer. He spent most of his time shooting and fishing. His wife, a beautiful dark cuddly lady called Amina, adored him and agreed with everything he did. I found an old clockwork spit looking like a clock complete with tray and skewers. I took it to be overhauled and repainted and brought it to Uncle Beppe as a present. I spent two or three days in Castelnuovo. They had a son, Maurizio, a pensive bright boy of maybe fourteen or fifteen with whom I felt great affinity regardless of our age gap. Beppe took me to the mountains to shoot wild birds. He gave me his beautiful side-by-side Beretta shotgun. He took his father-in-law's old percussion gun with outside hammers. We left in Uncle Beppe's blue 500 Fiat, which he drove like a madman up dirt roads and mule tracks. We walked for hours in the cold windy mountains. It started to snow, and we didn't shoot anything. In the end, out of frustration, we shot a rusty bucket left on a pole on a haystack. We left it peppered with holes. Later, we stopped at the trattoria near Castelnuovo and had mushroom stew and a lot of grappa. We talked freely helped by the grappa, and he told me my father had now three children, including a girl. "Why don't you go and see him? He is proud of you, and I am sure he would like to see you," said Beppe squeezing his eyes and inhaling deeply his unfiltered Nazionale. I thought a bit trying to decide if I should go and see Father before leaving. "It is your father, you know," Beppe insisted.

"Okay. I will go," I said still unconvinced. He smiled and slapped me lightly on the face from across the table.

A few days before I left, I went to see my father at his office. I had not seen him for a long time. He was greyer, older, but he had kept a slim body and walked like a young man. We had lunch at La Casina Rossa by the River Serchio, and he was happy that I was leaving for England. He was now working in a high position as a civil servant and making good money, but I felt he envied what would be my new way of life. He did not speak of his other family in Bagni di Lucca. I didn't ask him about his children. He told me again that he should never have got married and that his dream as a young man was to become a painter. He looked sad, his eyes shining. We hugged and kissed when I left, and I felt closer to this strange old man I hardly knew.

The night before I left for England, my friends booked a restaurant on the hills in Vicopelago. I felt so close to so many of these young men. I sat at the head of the long table holding court. We had many courses and a lot of wine. At the end of the meal, we toasted with brandy and grappa, and I came to realise how many of my friends envied me for leaving Italy. Many of them had more secure jobs, but they still wished they had the courage to leave Lucca. Later on, we went to a bar. I did arm wrestling with the owner, a mature gentleman who had been a boxer and who I had admired as a child. We bet that if I lost, I would have to pay for a round for everyone in the bar, if I won, the drinks for us would be free. I won, and we all got very drunk. My friend Stefano put a fat Havana cigar in my pocket and with an intense look in his eyes told me to smoke it at the border leaving Italy. I felt drunk but full of energy. In Piazza San Michele, somebody offered me a drink from a bottle of grappa. I was barely standing when I decided to ride a bicycle. Some were propped against the wall opposite the church. I rode fast towards the marble wall of the church and smashed the front wheel against it. It didn't hurt. I liked the noise of the wheel smashing against the wall; I had to do it again. I staggered back to the bicycles and rode a few more into the church wall. I felt invincible and stopped only when I heard a police siren approaching. Most of my friends had gone, and I ran towards Piazza della Pupporona (the square with the statue of the lady with large tits!). I winked at the marble lady on top of the fountain declaring my love for her. I also told her that her tits were not that large! I cupped my hands and drank the freezing water; I was sweating, my shirt stuck to my chest. I put my jacket back on, found the cigar and walked back home. I fell asleep immediately.

In the morning, Mother made me coffee, told me I stunk of alcohol and helped me with my suitcase. She had the habit of writing a list of my clothes and pasting it inside its cover. This time, she would not have to check it on my return! I felt distant. I kissed everyone goodbye, but somehow, something was missing. The alcohol of the night before had put a buffer between me and reality. Someone drove me to the station. I took my jacket off and stood waiting for the train. My skin was burning with the alcohol still in my body. The train lulled me soothingly all the way to the border with France. I took the fat cigar out of its wrapper, smelled it, removed the gilt label and lit it. I was out of Italy!